THE GLOBAL LEARNING ORGANIZATION

Michael Marquardt

Angus Reynolds

IRWIN
Professional Publishing
Burr Ridge, Illinois
New York, New York

This publication is designed to provide accurate and
authoritative information in regard to the subject matter
covered. It is sold with the understanding that neither the
author nor the publisher is engaged in rendering legal, accounting,
or other professional service. If legal advice or other expert
assistance is required, the services of a competent professional
person should be sought.

*From a Declaration of Principles jointly adopted by a Committee
of the American Bar Association and a Committee of Publishers.*

Sponsoring editor: Cynthia A. Zigmund
Project editor: Rita McMullen
Production manager: Laurie Kersch
Designer: Jeanne M. Rivera
Art coordinator: Heather Burbridge
Compositor: Precision Typographers
Typeface: 10.5/12 Palatino
Printer: Book Press, Inc.

Library of Congress Cataloging-in-Publication Data

Marquardt, Michael J.
      The global learning organization / Michael J. Marquardt & Angus
   Reynolds.
         p.   cm.
      Includes bibliographical references and index.
      ISBN 1-55623-839-8
      1. Organizational effectiveness.   2. International business
   enterprises—Management. I. Reynolds, Angus, 1936-   . II. Title.
      HD58.9.M377   1994
      658.4'012—dc20   93-2391

Printed in the United States of America
   2   3   4   5   6   7   8   9   0   BP   0   9   8   7   6   5   4

Foreword

Corporations are doomed to failure in today's world unless they are able to learn on an organizationwide basis and to effectively globalize all operations. That is the essential message of *The Global Learning Organization.*

Individual learning is no longer adequate; we must also better understand how teams learn and how to create infrastructures and networks to share learning experiences between teams within organizations and across organizations. Business leaders must become change agents who facilitate adaptation in an era of rapidly changing markets and technology and of exploding quantities and sources of new information.

We are moving from the age of producing to an age of thinking organizations, from manufacturing to mento-facturing, where the results come more from the mind (mento) than from the hands (manu). The future will be dominated by "know-how" organizations—ones that require knowledge workers. At the same time, employees are moving from an era where repetitive, mechanical skills were sufficient to an era where continuous learning and quality improvement will be the norm. Many American business leaders, some of them quoted in this book, have already observed that total quality will be an absolutely necessary but not sufficient condition for survival.

Also, economist Lester Thurow has noted that "Wealth is created by the capitalization of innovation"—by linking new discoveries to customer wants and needs. Accelerating the rate of individual and organizational learning is key to discovering new and better solutions and linking them to customer satisfaction. Only those organizations with highly skilled workers that continuously hone their knowledge and capabilities will succeed in a dynamically competitive global market.

As organizations change from high volume to high-value businesses, they must reach across the globe for new discoveries and for new markets and customers. Few companies will thrive on a domestic scale alone. And few companies will be self-sufficient in their ability to compete. Virtual corporations and global alliances that fuse the technologies and competencies of their partners into imaginative new solutions will be tied together by giant networks of computers, facsimile machines and video conferencing stations. This possibility is real today. Its realization is limited only by our imagination and vision.

In today's business environment, global learning organizations hold significant competitive advantages over other organizations. They are learning how to harness the power of globalization while accelerating the rate of learning at all levels—individual, teams, organization, and societal. This creates a powerful combination where the whole is truly much greater than the sum of its parts. These are the organizations that, as the authors put it, will ''blow the competition away.''

Ray Stata
Chairman of the Board
Chief Executive Officer
Analog Devices

Preface

The world of business has now entered the knowledge era, where knowledge is power, and learning rapidly and competently is seen as the preeminent strategy for global success. We have also entered the global age, where technology, travel, and trade have generated the global village.

"How can we learn faster and smarter in the rapidly changing global environment?" is the question on the lips of more and more people, especially corporate leaders attempting to survive and thrive in a highly competitive global marketplace. Ever more often, their answer to that question is what this book is all about: "Become a global learning organization!"

Read what global leaders are now saying about learning organizations and global learning:

• Walter Wriston, former CEO of Citibank, remarks that the organization that figures out how to harness the collective genius of its people is "going to blow the competition away."

• Harrison Owen, author of *Riding the Tiger*, writes that "there was a time when the prime business of business was to make a profit and a product. There is now *a prior, prime business*, which is to become an effective learning organization. Not that profit and product are not longer important, but without continual learning, they will no longer be possible. Hence the strange thought: the business of business is learning—and all else will follow" (p. 1).

• George Por declares that the "synergistic impact of global economic, technological, social, and environmental trends is creating an ever-changing business environment, in which the survival of the fittest is becoming the survival of the *fittest-to-learn*" (p. 1).

The critical need of organizationwide learning is even more urgent in global corporations. Kevin Barham and Marion Devine predict success only for those organizations that have developed the ability to "learn across borders. The future is not just about global competition, but about global learning" (p. 37).

The overwhelming impact of globalization and almost limitless potential of learning organizations must be viewed in tandem, and their powerful forces must be brought together by corporations seeking to survive the tremendous social and economic forces of the new era. This book carefully considers the concepts of both globalization and learning organizations and identifies how their potentials can be synergized. We wrote it to be useful to those involved with any aspect of the global business: a practical instead of academically oriented or theoretical book. Part of the problem is that people who are, or want to be, intimately involved with global business are often unaware of the complexity therein. Our challenge was to provide enough background to help you understand the problem. Although we report what others have written and said, this is surely not a collection of warmed-over research reports or, worse yet, other-worldly concepts that bear no relationship to the real world of work.

GLOBALIZATION

Globalization has become a reality within the past few years. The "global village" is an old idea that received only lip service for many years. Today, the world has truly become a global village. We watch CNN; we speak English; we wear denims; we dance the same dances; we eat pizzas and tacos; and we travel over 2 billion miles a year visiting each other's village.

The 1992 U.S. presidential election focused attention on the importance of globalization. Bill Clinton spoke out early. He told Bill Moyers, "The lesson of the global economy is that we have to change" ("48 Hours," July 8, 1992). Independent candidate Ross Perot was even more specific about the importance of global business competition. Today, even politicians recognize that the importance of business competitiveness is not a domestic issue. U.S. presidential candidates rarely "surprise" the population with unfamiliar notions. Nor do they force ideas against the general will of the people. More often they reflect to the best of their ability to read polls, what most people believe to be true. On the other hand, when politicians make statements, they sometimes awaken notions that might not have been in the forefront of everyone's mind. Today, Americans clearly value a global perspective.

In the business community, corporations are also becoming more globally integrated and linked. Corporations operate throughout the world, as though it is their local village. Coca-Cola and Xerox are now being joined by Canon, Pepsi, and thousands of other corporations with a global presence and recognition in their corporate strategic goals and planning. Medium-sized organizations are beginning to recognize that the global marketplace is worthy of their attention. They know that it is important for their survival. Small firms are quickly becoming global competitors through alliances and networks. Technology, trade, financial accessibility, education, and a host of other resources have made globalization the single most powerful force of the past 20 years.

LEARNING ORGANIZATIONS

Simultaneously, the concept of the learning organization has emerged. Peter Senge popularized the term in his best-seller *The Fifth Discipline*. Now it is in widespread use in management and training development circles. The "organization that learns" idea has sparked a burst of interest and energy around which individuals and organizations are beginning to solidify. Already a trend, learning organizations will be one of the hottest topics of the 1990s for managers and executives. Jumbo organizations such as GE and Motorola are striving to remold themselves in the learning organization paradigm. The giants are not alone. Much smaller organizations such as AutoMind and Caterair have also joined in the effort.

Essentially, learning organizations struggle to improve continuously. Senge notes, "Work must become a continual process of learning how to create our future rather than react to our past."

There is a direct link between quality management (with its commitment to improve continuously), employee empowerment, and learning organizations. Ford, for example, has established an impressive program to empower middle managers as a part of planned cultural change involving cross-functional learning. 3M has merged its corporate human resource departments and renamed the group the "organization learning services group."

A Marysville, Ohio, middle management employee of Honda exemplified the spirit that characterizes learning organizations. He said, "The Honda philosophy is a way of life. It's characterized by closeness, communication, and frankness at all levels. Honda employs thinking people, creative people. We want people to sound off."

Proof of the burgeoning interest includes many articles and conferences focusing on the topic. An infrastructure to support corporate efforts is also emerging. The American Society for Training and Development formed a Learning Organizations Network. George Washington University created its Academy for Applied Research in Organizational Learning, and Vanderbilt University is also considering a learning organization–focused center. There is no question whether the learning organizations concept has caught hold in the United States.

GLOBAL LEARNING ORGANIZATIONS

Tapping into the forces of both globalization and learning organizations is a process and strategy that has barely begun. Few organizations fully understand either of these forces, but even fewer can effectively implement and activate both of them in a synergistic, holistic way. The complexity of building a learning organization that can be effective in the global environment calls for capabilities in many disciplines, such as organizational dynamics, cultural sensitivities, technologies competence, interpersonal skills, communication excellence, and global economic intelligence.

Overseas failures have been plentiful. Although there is no direct measurement of the cost of global business failure, we have a related figure. The direct costs to return a mid-level executive from a foreign assignment failure can be high. Robert Kohls estimates that the total cost of returning a mid- to upper-level American executive and his or her family home early as anywhere from $150,000 to $250,000.

Managing across borders calls for the organization to learn across borders. Some companies have already begun their transformation to the global learning organization, leaving the cocoon of the past to become a butterfly of the future. They are beginning to learn across oceans, across cultures, across the organization, and across the hall.

The stories of their struggles and their successes are told in this book.

GLOBAL LEARNING ORGANIZATION
ENABLERS NEEDED

As companies prepare to compete globally, the smart individuals and organizations expand their activities to provide support by looking for pertinent information on the global learning organizations. They would like to benchmark their efforts against other successful global learning organizations. Unfortunately, there are too few stories to be told of successful global learning organizations. Too few know how to transform themselves into global learning successes. It is with this urgency and focus in mind that we have written this book. It is for anyone who wants his or her organization to survive in the 21st century and who cares about the people with whom he or she works and serves.

This book can help executives and managers who have responsibility for any aspect of global activity. It will provide valuable information on how to transform your organization into a global learning organization with real-world guidelines and best practices of leading global corporations.

Consultants and HRD practitioners within organizations will find that the book provides a beneficial model and guidelines for aiding organizations to become global learning organizations.

Students studying international business or HRD will be able to gain a perspective on what will be the most critical organizational dynamic employed by corporations of the 21st century.

OVERVIEW

The book is divided into four parts. Together they provide a comprehensive look at the important issues facing organizations that want to become global learning organizations. The part titles are as follows:

- Overview of the Global Learning Organization
- Becoming a Global Learning Organization
- Exemplary Global Learning Organizations
- The Learning Horizon

Part I—Overview of the Global Learning Organization

Part I describes the nine forces compelling organizations to change their existing ways of thinking and operating. We also examine the need for becoming a global learning organization and the key principles of learning, training, and knowledge. Chapters 4 and 5 present the 11 organizational and six global components of the Global Learning Organization Model. In addition, specific best practices of various global corporations are highlighted under each component of the model.

Part II—Becoming a Global Learning Organization

Part II identifies the major obstacles to and challenges of becoming a global learning organization. It describes the stages of development for globalization and learning organizations, provides specific strategies for building a global learning organization, and explores the particular skills and attributes of leaders and learners in global learning organizations.

Part III—Exemplary Global Learning Organizations

Part III examines 16 of the top global learning organizations from around the world that actively and successfully plan and execute learning organization strategies. They are presented with particular regard to their strengths relative to the Global Learning Organization Model. The global corporations included in this part are Analog Devices, ABB, AutoMind, Caterair International, Carvajal, Corning, GE, Honda, Medtronic, Motorola, PPG, Royal Bank of Canada, Samsung, Singapore Airlines, Tatung, and Xerox.

Part IV—The Learning Horizon

Part IV is based on the insights gained from companies on the leading edge of global learning organization practice today. We examine some possibilities for future structuring and operations of global learning organizations. This provides a vision of the transfigurative and interactive learning organization of the future. It identifies challenges and the effort needed to continue the evolution of the global learning organization.

LET'S GET STARTED

The subject of the global learning organization is a challenging, but also complex, still-evolving concept and practice. Our interactions with people and organizations new to the concepts of learning organizations and globalization show that the subject can be overwhelming. We have done our best here to demystify the topic, and to make it as interesting and as powerful as it has proven to be for the successful global corporations.

Global learning organizations are the key not only to organizational transformation and success but also to human development and fulfillment. We hope that you will enjoy the exciting ride toward the corporation of the future—the global learning organization.

In the learning organizations of today and tomorrow, global thinking and global competencies dominate as critical survival techniques. Now we invite you to move to the new way of doing and supporting international business. The first step is to come up to speed on the concept and practice. Chapter 1, The Need for Learning Organizations in the Global Workplace, is the ticket. Let's get started!

Michael Marquardt   Angus Reynolds
Reston, Virginia   Albuquerque, New Mexico

We Thank Our Many Worldwide Colleagues

This book is the product of the help and encouragement of many people. Naturally, we are indebted to the staff and management of Business One Irwin. It is a fortunate occasion for authors to have such patient yet powerful support in the development and dissemination of an idea that we deem so important for organizational and individual success. We are especially grateful to Cindy Zigmund, our editor, who quickly convinced the decision-makers at Irwin Professional Publishing that our book could be the global *Search for Excellence* of the 1990s.

We are grateful for the cooperation and help of many individuals. Some helped specifically with this book. Others gave us the light to see important ideas along the way. People's willingness to share information and make valuable specific suggestions enabled us to reach a coherent picture of the global learning organization.

We are also grateful for the many, many people, from corporate CEOs to leading researchers to workers on the factory floor practicing what we are preaching, who gave us their time, their insights, their ideas, their suggestions, their hopes, and their expectations. These people have come from every part of the globe, from organizations ranging in size from 20 to 200,000, from service, manufacturing, and information industries. This book would never have been possible without their generous assistance, and therefore we dedicate this book to them. With the hope that we will not fail to name our collaborators in this endeavor, we would like to thank Paul Allaire, Roberto Araya, Gary Aslin, James Baughman, Gordon Bennett, Jackie Bohn, Chris Brecia, Bruce Bunch, Anthony Carnevale, Hui-Chuan Cheng, John Cleghorn, Art Collins, Nancy Dempsey, Mindy Denny, Manfried Fiedler, Carla Fischer, Jim Fishbeck, Jim Gannon, Bill George, Alan Honeycutt, David Kearns, Debbie King, Greta Kotler, Robert Levitt, Wei-Shan Lin, Anne Lockie, Justin Lombardo, Dave Luther, Victoria Marsick, Jim May, Steve McIntosh, Janet McLaughlin, Diego Naranjo Meza, R. S. Moorthy, Linda Morris, Pamela Morton, Prush Nadaison, Margie Neff, Glen D. Nelson, Thomas Newman, Sylvia Odenwald, Harrison Owen, Frank Parisi, Tom Peters, Dick Reid, Fred Ricci, Phil

Rittenhouse, Joyce Rogers, John Rollwagen, David Schwandt, Gary Sellers, William Shea, Jeremy Spoor, Ray Stata, Amanda Stroud, Bob Stuff, Bernadete Suwanarat, Nancy Tan, Allan Taylor, Arlan Tietal, Dale Truax, Gordon Wan, C. Y. Wang, Clive Watkins, David Waugh, Jack Welch, Katharine C. Weldon, Bill Whitmore, Bill Wiggenhorn, David Workman, and Art Zuckerman.

Contents

I

OVERVIEW OF THE GLOBAL LEARNING ORGANIZATION

Chapter One

The Need for Learning Organizations in the Global Workplace

Learning is the new form of labor.
                        Shosanna Zuboff
                        In the Age of the Smart Machine:
                        The Future of Work and Power

The future is not just about global competition, but also about global learning.
                        Kevin Barham and Marion Devine
                        The Quest for the International Manager:
                        Survey of Global Human Resource Strategies

B usiness is like riding a bicycle—either you keep moving or you will fall down! Corporations operating in today's fast moving and interdependent global markets face never-before-experienced challenges. They must not only compete against fellow national companies, but against the best from around the world. They must not only survive, but thrive, in a world of rapid, continual change, where chaos is common and surprises are expected. Tom Peters calls it the *nanosecond nineties.*

Today the management of change is no longer the major problem for organizations. It is the management of suprise. Harrison Owen notes further that besides the new business environment, the time available for adaptation is diminishing on the same exponential curve as technology. "Under these circumstances, lifelong learning is no longer a pleasant fringe benefit to be enjoyed by the few. It is the *critical difference between success and failure.*"

GLOBALIZATION

Economically, today more companies—Canon, Electrolux, Honda, Motorola, Samsung—are manufacturing and selling chiefly outside their country of origin. This is so common that we hardly know whether a company is French, Japanese, Swedish, or American. Coca-Cola earns more money in Japan than it does in the United States. Over 70 percent of profits for the U.S. $20 billion music indistry comes from outside the United States. More than 70 percent of the employees of Canon work outside Japan. Over 100,000 U.S. firms are engaged in global ventures valued at over $1 trillion. Ten percent of U.S. manufacturing is foreign-owned, and it employs over 3 million Americans.

Globalization represents the converging of economic and social forces generated by an increased sharing of social and economic values and opportunities. Many pundits have called globalization the "root cause" for change in the 1990s and beyond.

Travel, trade, and television have laid the groundwork for a more common experience of employees everywhere. More and more workers around the world share common tastes in foods (hamburgers, pizza, tacos), fashion (denim jeans), and fun (Disney, rock music, television). People are watching the same movies, reading the same magazines, and dancing the same dances from Boston to Bangkok to Buenos Aires. Ever more of us speak a common language. English is now spoken by more than 1 billion people in over 100 countries where it is either the first or second language. The English language, which, like all languages, carries cultural and social values is the global language of media, computers, and business.

Economically, a single marketplace has been created by five factors:

1. Abundant energy sources.
2. Competitiveness of global corporations.
3. Global telecommunications (enhanced by fiber optics, satellites, and computer technology).
4. Growing free trade among nations.
5. Financial services that are accessible worldwide.

Other incentives that encourage organizations to globalize include the following:

- Ability to earn additional income on existing technology.
- Access to foreign technology, skills, knowledge, capital, and human and natural resources.
- Increased global customer base.
- Increased potential to offset lack of demand for seasonal products.

- Increased product service life cycle.
- Lowered transportation costs and time.
- Opportunities for larger profits owing to economies of scale in production, logistics, and marketing.
- Opportunities to gain an edge in reputation and credibility.

These forces will surely all continue to grow and increase the rapidity with which companies are forced to globalize. Organizations can now shop the world for human resources, technology, markets, and business partners.

Certain industries globalized earlier than others; these include telecommunication, electronics and computers, finance and banking, transportation, automotive, pharmaceutical, petroleum, and biotechnology. Still, success depends upon the ability of the organization to compete globally for every industry and sector throughout the world. Even the largest companies in the biggest markets will not be able to survive based on their domestic markets alone. Thinking and operating globally will be critical to organizational survival and growth in the 21st century.

CHANGES IN THE GLOBAL WORKPLACE

Many changes are happening in the workplace that critically affect the way work is done. In addition, the skills and ability needed to do that work are being drastically altered. Let's consider nine of the most significant forces that give rise to change, if not chaos, in the global workplace.

- Economic and marketing forces.
- Environmental and ecological pressures.
- Information technology.
- Knowledge era.
- New job skills and employee expectations.
- Organization structure and size.
- Societal turbulence.
- Total quality management movement.
- Workforce diversity and mobility.

Economic and Marketing Forces

Globalization, with its huge economic and marketing consequences, has created tremendous competitive pressures on all corporations.

Twenty-five percent of the Fortune 500 companies disappear every 10 years. Markets are rapidly changing. Consumers are pushing for new performance standards in quality, variety, customization, convenience, time, and innovation. These new demands for quality, the constant change of taste, the existence of global fads, and short product life cycles are forcing new global partnerships and alliances.

Regional trade agreements are beginning to emerge. In 1992, with the creation of the European Common Market, Western Europe became the world's largest market with more than 350 million people and a GNP of over $10 trillion, 43 percent of the world's total. A single currency may be introduced, and the free movement of labor, goods, services, and capital has begun. The North American Free Trade Agreement (NAFTA) brings together the economic might of the United States, Canada, and Mexico. Other regional trade agreements are being pursued or are already in place in Asia, Latin America, Africa, and the Middle East.

Environmental and Ecological Pressures

Industrial and population growth has created tremendous environmental problems throughout the world. The city of Karachi provides only 30 percent of the water its populace requires, forcing the poor to drink from untreated water, leading to epidemics and deaths. The pollution in industrial countries will cause as many as 50 percent of their citizens to suffer from a rash or some other skin disease each year. This is compared to 2 percent in the 1950s. At the present discard rate, Tokyo will run out of dump sites by 1995. Tokyo's dumps are already threatening the fishing and shipping industries (*Time*, January 11, 1993, p. 36)

Fortune magazine declared that environmental and ecological concerns were "not only the biggest business issue of the 1990s, but a mainstream movement of massive worldwide force. Companies must and are moving toward eco-responsibility" (February 12, 1992)

Today, people believe that if corporations do not move quickly, we may not be able to avert environmental damage so severe that future generations will be unable to meet basic requirements for food, energy, and clean, healthy air. A recent survey of global executives by Booz, Allen, & Hamilton revealed the increased awareness of the responsibility of corporations in maintaining, instead of destroying, the environment. Managers and employees are being encouraged to find ways for their organization to be ever mindful of energy efficiency in production and services. Corporations are being forced to search for "environmentally advantaged technologies."

Information Technology

Alvin Toffler writes how the advanced global economy cannot run for 30 seconds without the information technology of computers and other new and rapidly improving complexities of production. Yet today's best computers and CAD/CAM systems will be stone-age primitive within a few years.

Michael Morton, in summarizing *The Corporation of the 1990s*, identifies six major imprints of information technology on the workplace:

- Fundamental changes in the way work is done.
- The integration of business functions at all levels within and between organizations.
- Shifts in the competitive climate of many industries.
- New strategic opportunities for organizations to reassess their missions and operations.
- Requirement for basic changes in management and organization structure.
- Necessity for managers to transform their organizations.

Information technology changes the way work is done. Basic changes result, whether they are related to production, coordination, or management work.

Production work and methods are affected by physical supports such as robotics, process control instrumentation, and intelligent sensors; by information production such as data processing; and by knowledge resources such as CAD/CAM tools.

Coordination work means that distance and time (time zones) can be shrunk to zero. The organization's memory (command database) can be maintained over time, contributed to from all parts of the organization, and made available to a wide variety of authorized users.

Management work is more flexible because information technology can better sense changes in the external environment and stay in close touch with the organization members' ideas and reactions to the environment. Relevant, timely information can be a crucial input for the organization's direction-setting process. Information technology also allows more control in two key aspects:

- Measurement: measuring the organization's performance along whatever set of critical success factors has been defined as relevant.
- Interpretation: interpreting such measures against the plan and determining what actions to take.

Information technology enables integration of business functions. Integration of business functions is enabled at every level within the organization and between organizations. This can be done in four forms:

1. Within the value chain. For example, Xerox connects design, engineering, and manufacturing personnel within its system of local area networks and creates a team focusing on one product. Such teams can finish tasks in a shorter time and with greater creativity and higher morale. With information technology, no part of an organization, in principle, needs to be excluded from the team concept.

2. End-to-end links of value chains. These are links between organizations through just-in-time and electronic data interchange.

3. Value chain substitution. These are substitutions via subcontract or alliance.

4. Electronic markets. Electronic markets are the most highly developed form of electronic integration, so that travel agents, for example, can electronically reserve seats from all the major carriers and can look around for the best price at which to complete the transaction.

These four forms of electronic integration have, to various degrees, the net effect of removing buffers. They also leverage organizational and individual expertise.

Information technology causes shifts in the competitive climate. These climate shifts are caused in many industries. Information technology adds considerable importance to the functions of scanning and environmental monitoring. This effective scanning of the business environment, to understand what is changing, is critical. It is needed for an organization to proactively manage its way through an environment made so turbulent because of technological changes.

Information technology presents new strategic opportunities. New strategic opportunities emerge for organizations to reassess their missions and operations. Technology enables organizations to automate (which lessens the cost of production), to informate (which provides information that can be used to get a job done, generates new information as a by-product, and develops new information), and to transform itself. Morton calls this a stage characterized "by leadership, vision, and a sustained process of organization empowerment" (p.17)

Information technology demands basic changes. Successfully applied, the technology calls for changes in management and organization structure. Morton sees information technology as a critical enabler in the re-creation and redefinition of the organizations as we know them. The technology permits the redistribution of power, function, and control to wherever they are most effective; this redistribution also depends on the mission, objectives, and culture of the organization. This enables an organization such as Digital Equipment Corporation to have all its engineers on the same network. An engineer can share information, ask for help, or work on a project with anyone else in the network. In this way, information technology increases the rate at which information moves and decisions are made.

Information technology forces transformation. Information technology forces managers to lead their organizations through a complete transformation process if they hope to prosper in a globally competitive environment.

The Knowledge Era

According to leading futurists and business leaders, we have clearly entered the *knowledge era*; the new economy is a *knowledge economy*. Knowledge provides the key raw material for wealth creation and is the fountain of organizational and personal power.

Information is created continuously in every corner of the globe, and doubles every 3 to 4 years. Ikujiro Nonaka confidently predicts that the creation and dissemination of knowledge are what will differentiate the companies that survive from those that don't. Such knowledge is crucial for staying ahead of the competition in quality, speed, innovation, and price.

Brainpower is becoming a company's most valuable asset and is what conveys a competitive edge in the marketplace. Thomas Stewart challenges us to find and use it. In *Fortune* magazine, he asserts that "Brainpower . . . has never before been so important for business. Every company depends increasingly on knowledge—patents, process, management skills, technologies, information about customers and suppliers, and old-fashioned experience. . . . This knowledge that exists in an organization can be used to create differential advantage. In other words, it's the sum of everything everybody in your company knows that gives you a competitive edge in the market-place'' (p. 44).

In most companies the management of intellectual capital is still uncharted territory. Few executives understand how to navigate it. Managing know-how is not like managing cash or buildings, yet intellectual investments need to be treated with every bit as much care.

The first step in getting more from your intellectual assets, according to Stewart, is to find them. Often, companies are startled to learn how much intellectual capital they have. Step two is matching the company's intellectual needs with its strategic plan. Once it has a handle on its intellectual assets, the company must learn how to best package them.

The greatest challenge for the manager of intellectual capital is to create an organization that can redistribute its knowledge. Intellectual capital is useless unless it moves. By finding ways to make knowledge move, an organization can create a value network—not just a value chain.

Simply put, knowledge has become more important for organizations than financial resources, market position, technology, or any other company asset. Knowledge is seen as the main resource used in performing work in an organization. The organization's traditions, culture, technology, operations, systems, and procedures are all based on knowledge and expertise. Knowledge is needed to increase employees' abilities to improve products and services, thereby providing quality service to clients and consumers. Knowledge is necessary to update products and services, change systems and structures, and communicate solutions to problems. In the new knowledge economy, individuals at every level and in all kinds of companies will be challenged to develop new knowledge, to take responsibility for their new ideas, and to pursue their ideas as far as they can go. The job of the manager will be to create an environment that allows workers to increase knowledge.

Walter Wriston, in *The Twilight of Sovereignty: How the Information Revolution is Transforming the World*, writes that, in the end, the location of the new economy is not in technology, whether its a microchip or a global communications network, but in *the human mind*.

Peter Drucker sees organizations composed more and more of *knowledge workers*. Not only senior executives, but also workers at all levels, must be highly educated, highly skilled knowledge workers. In the new ''post-capitalist society,'' knowledge is not just another resource alongside the traditional factors of production, land, labor and capital. It is the only meaningful resource in today's workforce.

In an economy based on knowledge, the knowledge worker is the single greatest asset.

Robert Reich, U.S. Secretary of Labor and author of *The Work of Nations*, points out that "corporations no longer focus on products as such; their business strategies increasingly center upon specialized knowledge"(p.8).

In the successful organizations of the future (those offering high value), only one asset grows more valuable as it is used—the knowledge skills of people. Unlike machinery that gradually wears out, materials that become depleted, patents and copyrights that grow obsolete, and trademarks that lose their ability to comfort, the knowledge and insights that come from the learning of employees actually increase in value when used and practiced.

New Job Skills and Employee Expectations

As society moves from the industrial era to the knowledge era, job requirements are changing. We are moving from the age of manufacturing to an era of mentofacturing—that is, where the production is more with the mind *(mento)* than with the hands *(manu)*. Employees are moving from needing repetitive skills to knowing how to deal with surprises and exceptions, from depending on memory and facts to being spontaneous and creative, from avoiding risk to taking risk, from focusing on policies and procedures to building collaboration with people.

A U.S. Department of Labor report, *Economic Change and the American Workforce,* notes, "The competitive workplace today—regardless of the product or service—is a high-skill environment designed around technology and people who are technically competent. Assembly line workers must now understand their work as part of a much larger whole." In an unusually candid warning, the study goes on to say that the increased need for education at all levels of the workplace has created an *income polarization* that threatens the basic standard of living for millions of workers. As mid-level jobs disappear, U.S. society is dividing between high earners, "empowered" in the workforce because of their high level of skills, and those in survival wage jobs, consigned to unskilled employment.

Workers will thrive who have the three skills that Reich deems essential in driving high businesses:

- Problem identifier skills (required to help customers understand their needs and how those needs can best be met by customized products.)

- Problem-solving skills (required to put things together in unique ways).
- Strategic broker skills (needed to link problem solvers and problem identifiers).

According to Reich, in enterprises requiring high knowledge skills, profits derive not from scale and volume, but from the following four aspects:

- Continuous discovery of new links between solutions and needs
- Specialized research, engineering, and design services necessary to solve problems.
- Specialized sales, marketing, and consulting services necessary to identify problems.
- Specialized strategic, financial, and management services for brokering the first two aspects.

The key assets of high-value enterprises are not tangible things. They are the skills involved in linking solutions to particular needs, and the reputations that come from being successful in the past. Webber notes that the expected distinction between manufacturing and services is becoming less real. The most significant effect of the information economy is to create increasing similarity in the world of work.

A fascinating aspect about knowledge workers is that they do in fact own the means of production, and they can take it out the door with them at any moment. Therefore, managers have to attract and motivate; reward, recognize, and retain; train, educate, and improve; and, in the most remarkable reversal of all, serve and satisfy knowledge workers. Organizations must provide a structure in which knowledge workers can apply their knowledge. Specifically, organizations must provide contact with other knowledge workers, because it is through dialogue and interaction with other knowledge workers that they can refine and improve their ideas.

Organization Structure and Size

As more companies realize that the key resource of business is not capital, personnel, or plant, but rather knowledge, information and ideas, many new ways of viewing the organization emerge. Everywhere companies are restructuring, creating integrated organizations, global networks, and "leaner, meaner" corporate centers. Organizations are becoming more fluid, ever shifting in size, shape, and arrangements. Tom Peters sees organizations becoming "unglued," and moving "beyond hierarchy." Many of these changes, in one form or another, lead, according to Charles Handy, to the path of "federalism" as the way to manage increasingly complex organizations in the increasingly rapidly changing environment. Handy sees the popularity and success of this way of structuring and sizing organizations happening because federalism is an effective way of dealing with six paradoxes:

- Power and control.
- Being both big and small at the same time.
- Being autonomous within bounds.
- Encouraging variety with a shared purpose.
- Individuality within a partnership.
- Global yet local.

Asea Brown Boveri in Switzerland, General Electric in the United States, Accor in France, British Petroleum in the UK, and Honda in Japan are among the many businesses moving in the direction of federalism. Federalism is becoming a popular form of restructuring for several reasons:

- Its autonomy releases energy.
- It allows people to be well informed.
- Its units are bound together by trust and common goal and not forced control.
- Power is delegated to the lowest possible point in the organization (a good example of this is Motorola employees, who were told by the former chairman Robert Galvin that they have all the authority of the chairman when they are with customers).
- The decentralized structure and interdependence spreads power around and thereby avoids the risks of a central bureaucracy.
- It is very flexible; it can never be static.
- Authority must be earned from those over whom it is exercised.
- People have the right and duty to be responsible and recognized for their work.
- Organizations are much flatter (little hierarchy) without losing efficiency.

FIGURE 1–1
Organizational Shifts

Dimension	Bureaucratic Organization	Network Organization
Critical tasks	Physical	Mental
Relationships	Hierarchical	Peer-to-peer
Levels	Many	Few
Structures	Functional	Multi-disciplinary teams
Boundaries	Fixed	Permeable
Competitive thrust	Vertical integration	Outsourcing and alliances
Management style	Autocratic	Participative
Culture	Compliance and tradition	Commitment and results
People	Homogeneous	Diverse
Strategic focus	Efficiency	Innovation

Another form of restructuring rapidly gaining popularity is that of *virtual organizations*. A virtual organization is a temporary network of independent companies, suppliers, customers, even rivals who are linked by information technology to share skills, costs, and access to one another's markets.

In the purest form of a virtual organization, a company decides to focus on the thing it does best. Then it links with other companies, each bringing to the combination its own special ability. It will mix and match what it does best with the best of the other companies. For example, a manufacturer will manufacture while relying on a product design partner to sell the output.

Such a "best of everything" organization could be a world-class competitor, with the speed, the muscle, and the leading-edge technology to pounce on the briefest of opportunities. *BusinessWeek* stated that the virtual model "could become the most important organizational innovation since the 1920s" (p. 100) when Pierre du Pont and Alfred Sloan developed the principle of decentralization to organize giant complex corporations.

The virtual corporation will have neither central office nor organization chart, and no hierarchy or vertical integration. Teams of people in different companies will routinely work together. After the business is done, the virtual organization disbands.

Charles Savage of Digital sees the emergence of *"network organizations"* replacing the more traditional bureaucratic structure, with the shifts shown in Figure 1–1.

Three other emerging management theories affecting organizational structure and gaining popularity in the marketplace are as follows:

- **Reengineering**. Reengineering is a fundamental rethinking and redesign of business systems that urges an overhaul of job designs, organization structures, and management systems. Work should be organized around outcomes, not tasks or functions.

- **Core competencies**. Companies organize around what they do best. Therefore, they structure according to competencies instead of according to product or market.

- **Organizational architecture**. This is a structural form that evolves around autonomous work teams and strategic alliances.

Societal Turbulence

Massive societal changes are taking place throughout the globe. Eastern Europe has thrown off the yoke of Communism and is now in the midst of further divisions with ethnic warfare. Japan, an economic powerhouse, is experiencing profound economic challenges. China, India, and much of Africa are moving from planned state-run economies to a more capitalistic, free enterprise status. Massive migrations continue in every continent. The specter of AIDS is affecting the availability of an educated, professional work force in central Africa. It also affects the health costs and even relationships and social interactions around the world. In the United States, the highly explosive issues of abortion and gay rights are dividing people of every religious and political persuasion. Society becomes more urban. By the year 2000, more than 50 percent of all people will live in cities, including 21 megacities of more than 10 million inhabitants each. In most of these cities poverty, chaos, and danger will be the daily staples of life.

Total Quality Management Movement

The ability to attract and retain customers by meeting their needs with quality products and quality service has become the survival issue for global business. In a global economy, quality standards are not set in the boardroom, but in the worldwide marketplace. Customers now have many choices, and quality is of high importance. Almost every organization has established a total quality management (TQM) program. Every year more U.S. companies zealously seek the Malcolm Baldridge National Quality Award than the year before. Annual quality conferences are attended by thousands of business leaders. Corporations have begun seeking continuous improvement in manufacturing and service.

Workforce Diversity and Mobility

The global workforce is becoming ever more diverse and mobile. Hispanics and Asians will represent over 25 percent of the total U.S. workforce by the year 2000. Already, in California, Texas, and Florida, nearly half the workforce is Black, Hispanic or Asian. Physicists at Bell Laboratories, for example, are as likely to come from universities in England or India as from Princeton or MIT. At research labs around the world, the first language of the biochemists is equally likely to be Hindi, Japanese, German, English, or French. It is routine for U.S. hospitals to advertise in Dublin and Manila for nurses.

Corporations are increasingly reaching across borders to find the skills they need. These movements of workers are driven by the growing gap between the world's supplies and demands for it. Much of the world's skilled and unskilled human resources are being produced in the developing world. Yet most of the well-paid, high-skilled jobs are being generated in the cities of the industrialized world.

William Johnston, who recently completed an exhaustive study of global work patterns, identified four major implications of the mobile, culturally diverse workforce on global corporations:

- **Relocation**. A massive relocation of people, especially young and better educated, will flock to urban areas around the world.

- **Competition for labor**. More industrialized nations will come to rely on, and even compete for, foreign-born workers.

- **Improved productivity**. Labor-short, immigrant-poor countries such as Japan and Sweden will be compelled to improve labor productivity dramatically to avoid slow economic growth. The need for increased outsourcing of jobs to other countries is escalating.

- **Standardization**. There is a gradual standardization of labor practices around the world in areas of vacation time, workplace safety, and employee rights.

Johnston adds that nations that have slow-growing workforces but rapid growth in service sector jobs (Japan, United States, Germany) will become magnets for immigrants. Nations whose educational systems produce prospective workers faster than their economies can absorb them (Argentina, Egypt, Philippines, Poland, Russia) will export people.

The combination of a globalized workforce and massive mobility forces organizations to work with growing numbers of people with differing cultures, customs, values, beliefs, and practices.

ORGANIZATIONS' RESPONSE

These nine motivating factors for change have forced organizations to reconfigure their ways of thinking, managing, and operating with employees, consumers, and competitors in local and international settings.

A growing number of organizations now have an increased awareness that individual learning and traditional training programs and procedures are not an adequate response to their learning needs in the 1990s. Organizations have to increase their organizational capacity to learn if they are to function successfully in an environment that includes continual mergers, rapid technological changes, massive societal change, and increasing competition. To compete and survive, organizations now have to demonstrably increase their capacity to do the following:

- Accelerate the development of product and process innovation.
- Anticipate and adapt more readily to environmental effects.
- Become more proficient at learning from competitors and collaborators.
- Expedite the transfer of knowledge from one part of the organization to another.
- Learn more effectively from their mistakes.
- Make greater organizational use of employees at all levels of the organization.
- Shorten the time required to implement strategic changes.
- Stimulate continuous improvement in all areas of the organization.

Organizations that achieve these increases would gain a significant competitive advantage. A number of benefits would also accrue for their employees. For example, many workers recognize that they cannot learn all that they need to for their jobs, because the knowledge demands are growing exponentially. An organizational learning culture helps ease those feelings. In addition, if the organization supports continuous growth and learning, the possibility of becoming more self-actualized and fulfilled in one's work increases. With all these challenges and potential benefits to the organization, it was just a matter of time before the idea of learning organizations would emerge.

EMERGENCE OF LEARNING ORGANIZATIONS

The origin of learning organizations can be traced in the research literature as far back as the 1920s. However, it was not until the 1980s that a few companies began realizing the potential effect of the factors identified earlier in this chapter. They also saw the potential power available in linking organizational learning with corporate performance, competitiveness, and success. The changes caused by these nine factors produced, for many organizations, chaos. The same changes proved a boon to those organizations seriously exploring and succeeding in becoming better learners.

In the late 1980s Shell started to consider organizational learning in relation to strategic planning. Teamwork and more extensive communications were seen as crucial factors in creating a more responsive, successful corporation. Shell spent 12 months experimenting with work groups and researching the implications of the learning organization concept. Shell concluded that learning as an organization was essential for strategic planning and corporate success, and that if ways were found to speed up this learning process, it could gain a year or two on its competitors.

In 1990 the Rover Car Group, aware that "as a minnow among whales, it would soon be swallowed up if it stood still," launched the Rover Learning Business. The new group is a $60 million business-within-a-business to make Rover a learning organization. At the launch conference, the managing director observed, "As a company we desperately need to learn."

Over the past few years, the number of organizations committing themselves to becoming learning organizations has increased. Organizations such as Granite Rock, Johnsonville Foods, Quad Graphics, and Pacific Bell in the United States; Sheerness Steel, Sun Alliance, and TMI in the UK; and Honda in Japan were among the early pioneers. The widespread attention directed to Peter Senge's *The Fifth Discipline* and feature articles on learning organizations in business publications, such as *Harvard Business Review, The Economist, BusinessWeek, Fortune,* and *Asiaweek* has led many other companies to introduce the process of transforming themselves into learning organizations.

GLOBAL CORPORATIONS NEED TO BE LEARNING ORGANIZATIONS

Domestic companies seem to have the message. Companies that operate globally must execute the same maneuver in an added dimension. Obviously, with the pressures of globalization, cultural diversity, and the rapid emergence of many competing global corporations, these organizations needed to be more than learning companies; they needed to be *global* learning organizations. What are the differences? New challenges? Ways of achieving such capacities quickly?

The application of the learning organization concept to the global corporation is still emerging. How factors such as culture, borders, language, the globalization process, and global competition affect structures, strategies, communications, and so forth are just beginning to be explored. Yet many global corporate leaders are intensely aware of the critical need to become a global learning organization. They realize, as George Yip stated, in his classic *Total Global Strategy*, that being better able to transfer knowledge from country to country and throughout the global organization would provide a key advantage for global companies, even more than it does for domestic companies. For global corporations to possess the ability to even manage in the global marketplace, with its tremendous uncertainties and challenges, they, by definition, need to be learning organizations.

We believe that the writing is on the wall. In order for any business organization to compete globally, it *must* foster constant learning. International businesses *must* become global learning organizations!

Chapter Two

Learning, Learning Organizations, and the Global Learning Organization Model

D onald Michael observed in his book *On Learning to Plan—and Planning to Learn* that one of the most difficult problems of our age is that people have too much information and limited cognitive abilities to think in systemic terms. In other words, we don't know well enough how to learn.

We know we must learn better how to learn, but we are afraid to acknowledge it. Yet the circumstances around us tell us that learning is no longer a choice but a necessity. The most urgent priority, therefore, is learning how to learn and learning faster. That people in be able to systematically select and store knowledge is not enough the global business environment. They must create knowledge and share it.

WHAT ARE LEARNING ORGANIZATIONS?

Learning organizations, in which learning is accomplished by the organization system as a whole rather than by individual members of the system, have been defined in several ways. Representative definitions come from Beck, Melander, Morris, Schwandt, Senge, and Watkins and Marsick.

Peter Senge, whose ideas have attracted the widest attention, sees them as organizations where people "continually expand their capacity to create the results they truly desire, where new and expansive patterns of thinking are nurtured, where collective aspiration is set free, and where people are continually learning how to learn together"(p.3).

Michael Beck defines a learning organization as one that "facilitates learning and personal development for all of its employees, while continually transforming itself"(p.22).

David Schwandt defines it a "a system of actions, actors, symbols, and processes that enables an organization to transform information into valued knowledge, which in turn increases its long-run adaptive capacity"(p.13).

Karen Watkins and Victoria Marsick see a key strength of a learning organization as its enhanced organizational capacity to change or transform. The learning organization "empowers its people, integrates quality initiatives with quality of work life, creates free space for learning, encourages collaboration and sharing the gains, promotes inquiry, and creates continuous learning opportunities. In learning organizations, learning is a continuous, strategically used process—integrated with, and running parallel to, work. Learning in learning organizations changes perceptions, behaviors, beliefs, mental models, strategies, policies, and procedures in people and organizations. Organizational learning is a metaphor for adaptive responses within the system as a whole to triggers in the environment" (p.1).

Linda Morris was early among U.S. corporate people to recognize the value of the learning organization concept and has been proactive in bringing it to the attention of others. She sees the following attributes as present in learning organizations:

- Individual learning and development is linked with organizational learning and development in an explicit and structured way.
- There is a focus on creativity and adaptability.
- Teams of all types are a part of the learning and working process.
- Networking—personal and aided by technology—is important to learning and to accomplishing work.
- Systems thinking is fundamental.
- Learning organizations have a powerful, clear vision of where they are and where they are going.
- Learning organizations are continually transforming themselves and growing.

Klas Melander describes some companies that appear to be dumb because their people have different knowledge or conception of what the game rules are, or different ideas of what has to be done, of what's important, of what the company's goals are. He uses the term *anergy* for this. Anergy means that the whole is less than the sum of its parts—the opposite of synergy, where the whole is greater than the sum of its parts. In synergy, $2+2=5$; in anergy, $2+2=3$. Melander describes a "learning company" as "primarily a matter of how well the company succeeds in creating conditions in which all of its people can take joint responsibility for the whole—the business" (p. 187). He gives the following prescription for a learning company:

- First, everyone must have a concordant view of the company's activities and goals, and of the direction of future trends—popularly called *vision*.

- Second, each individual must have continuous access to information (data) on all advances that are important to the company's success.

- Third, people in the company must have a chance to learn from each other and to draw joint conclusions on what needs to be done.

We believe that a learning organization is one that has a climate that accelerates individual and group learning. Learning organizations teach their employees the critical thinking process for understanding what it does and why it does it. These individuals help the organization itself to learn from mistakes as well as successes. As a result, they recognize changes in their environment and adapt effectively. Learning organizations can be seen as a group of empowered employees who generate new knowledge, products, and services; network in an innovative community inside and outside the organization; and work toward a higher purpose of service and enlightenment to the larger world. The learning organizations (without regard to global or domestic setting) that we have observed share the features listed in Figure 2–1.

Businesses don't have exclusive rights to the learning organization concept. Normally, one doesn't think of a football team as a learning organization, but the San Francisco 49ers might have qualified. Bill Walsh was one of the most successful college and professional football coaches in the history of the game. He attributed much of the success of the 49ers to the team's ability to learn and function together as a learning team. He saw his *essential* skill as his ability to have all the coaches and players learn as an organization. Only then could they be a winning team. He said:

> Winning starts with the expectations the head coach sets. It is part of the head coach's job to expect everyone in the organization to be an expert in

FIGURE 2–1
Learning Organization's Features

- Capitalizes on uncertainty as an occasion for growth.
- Creates new knowledge with objective information, subjective insights, symbols, and hunches.
- Embraces change.
- Encourages accountability at the lowest levels.
- Encourages managers to be coaches, mentors, and facilitators of learning.
- Has a culture of feedback and disclosure.
- Has a holistic, systematic view of the organization and its systems, processes, and relationships.
- Has shared organizationwide vision, purpose, and values.
- Has decentralized decision making and employee empowerment.
- Has leaders who model calculated risk taking and experimentation.
- Has systems for sharing learning and using it in the business.
- Is customer driven.
- Is involved in its community.
- Links employees' self development to the development of the organization as a whole.
- Networks technologically within company.
- Networks within the larger business community.
- Provides frequent opportunities to learn from experience.
- Resists bureaucracy and turf wars.
- Rewards employee initiative and provides structure for it.
- Spreads trust throughout the organization.
- Strives for continuous improvement.
- Structures, fosters, and rewards all types of teams.
- Uses cross-functional work teams.
- Uses skill inventories and assessments of leaning capacity.
- Views the organization as a living, growing organism.
- Views the unexpected as an opportunity to learn.

his particular area of responsibility, to refine their skills continually and to be physically and intellectually committed to the team. The head coach has to make it clear that he expects everyone to participate and volunteer his or her thoughts, impressions, and ideas. The goal is to create a communication channel that allows important information to get from the bottom to the top (p. 114).

To make Walsh's words work in the corporate setting, it is only necessary to substitute *executive* or *business leader* for *head coach.* We think that he is right on target.

FIGURE 2-2
Learning Organization Action Imperatives

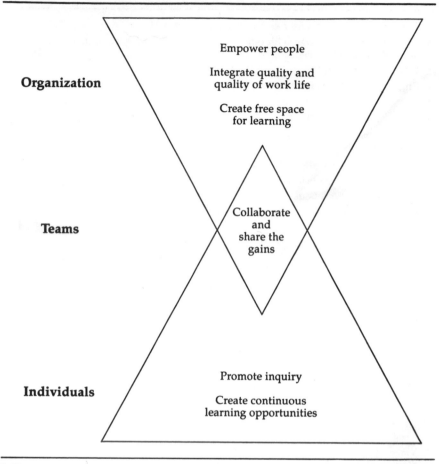

Organization

    Empower people

    Integrate quality and
    quality of work life

    Create free space
    for learning

Teams

    Collaborate
    and
    share the
    gains

Individuals

    Promote inquiry

    Create continuous
    learning opportunities

MODELS FOR LEARNING ORGANIZATIONS

Because of the relative newness, complexity, and evolving under-standing of the learning organization idea, very few models of learning organizations have been attempted.

We have developed a (domestic) learning organization model. It is shown later as Figure 2-7 because it is related to the Global Learning Organization Model that we want to introduce at that point.

Watkins and Marsick's model, represented here in Figure 2-2, cap-tures the relationship and learning among individuals, teams, and the organization. This model illustrates teams' nature and the learning organization as the union of individuals (the lower triangle) and organizations (the upper triangle). The key to this model is the overlap. This overlap is where teams function, and it brings the benefits of learning organizations. The utilization of the combined resources and energies of the individuals, teams, and the organization is what creates the learning organization.

Michael Pedler, J. Burgoyne, and Tom Boydell developed a learning organization model that contains five clusters—strategy, looking in, learning opportunities, looking out, and enabling structures. These five comprise 11 features.

To capture the energetic, evolving, living aspect of learning organizations, they present the same 11 dimensions in several formats. These formats include fishbone, fountain, and fir tree configurations. Their complete model concept is represented here, in graphically simplified form, in Figure 2–3. It illustrates the factors that combine to create the learning organization. The linear flow emphasized by arrows in Figure 2-3 gives rise to the fountain concept, in which flow continues up and out the top. The fountain idea also suggests feedback—as the fountain's spray is returned to its basin for recycling.

David Schwandt of the Center for Organizational Learning at George Washington University has developed a model that integrates the multiple concepts of learning and change. His systems integration model, represented here in Figure 2–4, shows how the interrelationships of the four learning subsystems (environmental interface, action-reflection, memory and meaning, and dissemination and diffusion) enable the organization to understand its changing internal and external environments, and thereby adapt and survive.

The environmental interface subsystem serves as the information portal for organizational learning and provides the adaptational function. This function is seen in organizational actions that scan or test the environment. It also selects which inputs are to enter the organization.

The action-reflection subsystem defines the relationship between the organization's actions and the examination of those actions, thus creating valued knowledge from this new information and helping to satisfy the learning goals of the organization. Schwandt sees this function as manifested in organizational actions such as experimentation, research, evaluations, critical thinking, and problem solving.

The meaning and memory subsystem helps the learning organization make sense of its environment and experiences by creating criteria for judgment, selection, focus, and control. This subsystem sustains and creates the cultural beliefs, values, assumptions, and artifacts of

FIGURE 2–3
The Learning Company Model

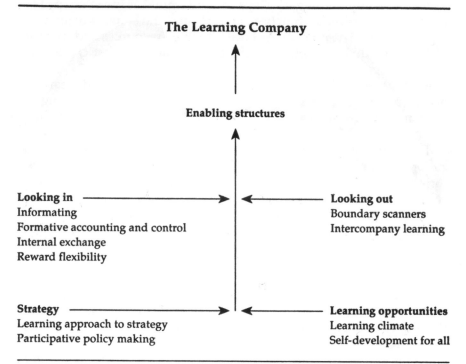

The Learning Company

Enabling structures

Looking in ——————→ ←——— **Looking out**
Informating   Boundary scanners
Formative accounting and control   Intercompany learning
Internal exchange
Reward flexibility

Strategy ——————→ ←——— **Learning opportunities**
Learning approach to strategy   Learning climate
Participative policy making   Self-development for all

Simplified from illustrations in Mike Pedler, John Burgoyne, and Tom Boydell, *The Learning Company: A Strategy for Sustainable Development*. London: McGraw-Hill, 1991.

the organization. It stores and makes available organizational knowledge and is illustrated in organizational actions such as reasoning processes, comparisons, making policy and procedures making, and the creation of symbols reflecting organizational values.

The dissemination and diffusion subsystem coordinates and structures the elements of the learning system. It includes the acts of communication networking, technical processes of electronic data transfer, and determination of leadership roles.

GLOBAL LEARNING ORGANIZATION MODEL

The global learning organization takes the learning organization definitions and models to another magnitude. The relationships and interac-

FIGURE 2–4
Organizational Learning System

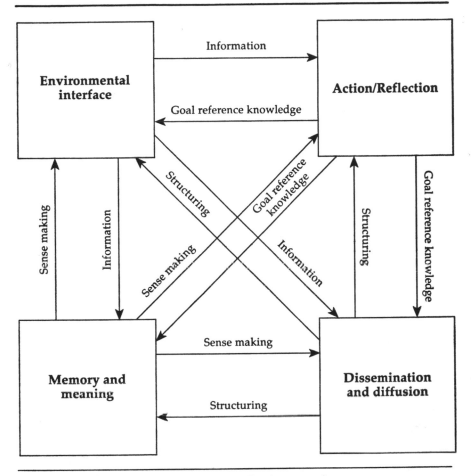

tions in global learning organizations are even more complex, and certainly not intuitive.

To develop a global learning organization model that would contain and portray the important elements, we surveyed over 50 global corporations deemed as learning organizations in the professional literature and by leaders in the field. Based on this extensive investigation, we created the Global Learning Organization Model. In the model there are 3 spheres (learning, organization, and global) as illustrated in the cross-section shown in Figure 2–5.

FIGURE 2-5
Simplified Global Learning Organization Model

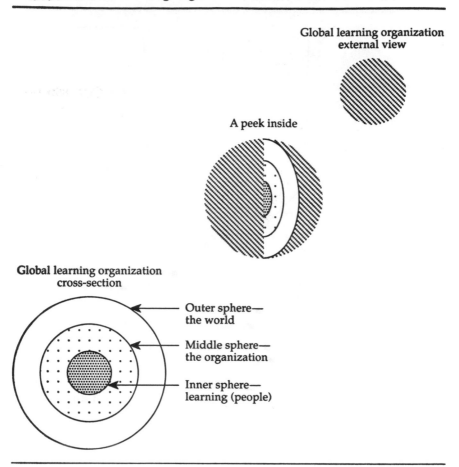

Global learning organization
external view

A peek inside

Global learning organization
cross-section

Outer sphere—
the world

Middle sphere—
the organization

Inner sphere—
learning (people)

© Michael Marquardt and Angus Reynolds, 1992

The three spheres and labels represent the more complex full Global Learning Organization Model shown in Figure 2-6. The spheres hold a total of 19 elements relevant to global learning organizations. We will briefly define each of the spheres and elements here. We provide more explanation and real-life organizational examples in Chapter 3 (learning), Chapter 4 (organization), and Chapter 5 (global).

As mentioned earlier in this chapter, we also have developed a Learning Organization Model. We had to—in order to develop the *Global* Learning Organization Model. Our (domestic) Learning Organization Model is simply the two innermost spheres of the global one.

FIGURE 2–6
Global Learning Organization Model

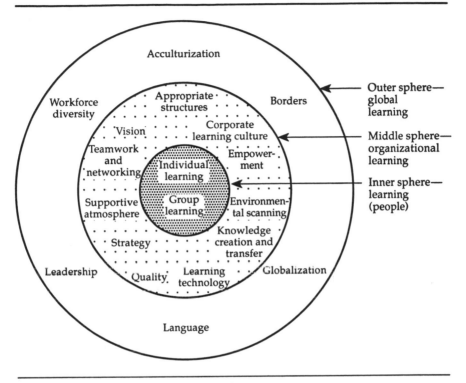

© Michael Marquardt and Angus Reynolds, 1992

Our observations revealed many excellent companies. These were many that are clearly learning organizations but that do not have business abroad. Every company that we found to be a successful global learning organization certainly qualifies as a successful learning organization domestically. Our (domestic) Learning Organization Model is shown in Figure 2–7.

Now, without further ado, let's look at the working parts of the Global Learning Organization Model.

Learning

The inner sphere, learning, includes individual and group learning, both of which are necessary components in building the organizational learning of the middle sphere.

FIGURE 2–7
Model—The Compleat Learning Organization

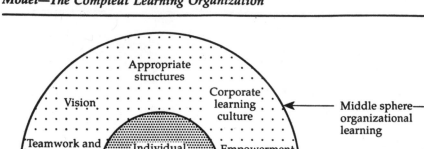

© Michael Marquardt and Angus Reynolds, 1992

Individual learning. Individual learning is any learning acquired by an individual through the organization's human resource development system or by any other means. Examples include self-study, computer-based instruction, observation, or even insight.

Group learning. Group learning is any learning by groups, teams, units, or other organizational subunits. Group learning is most often fulfilled through shared experiences.

Organization

The middle sphere, organizational learning, includes the 11 elements needed in the organization itself:

- Appropriate structures
- Corporate learning culture
- Empowerment
- Environmental scanning

- Knowledge creation and transfer
- Learning technology
- Quality
- Strategy
- Supportive atmosphere
- Teamwork and networking
- Vision

These are the elements needed to support maximum learning in learning organizations. We discovered that successful global learning organizations are not clones of one another. The differences are especially detectable in the emphasis placed on any of the various elements. We believe that newfound emphasis on one of these elements can foster important business improvement. A clear example is quality. Improving quality will drive many other improvements throughout the organization.

Appropriate structures.   This element includes a flat, streamlined, holistic structure. Such a structure maximizes contact, information flow, local responsibility, and collaboration within and outside the organization. In addition, the appropriate structures element helps to adjust the organization's structure to match the local conditions in any given business locale.

Corporate learning culture.   This element represents a corporate culture where learning is highly valued, where risks are encouraged and rewarded, and all have responsibility for their own learning and the learning of others. This is the organizational validation of efforts in the inner sphere of global learning organization.

Empowerment.   This element includes capacity and power. Empowerment is given as close as possible to the point of interaction with the customer or client. Empowerment permits learning to happen through responsibility.

Environmental scanning.   This is a description of comprehensive and considered scanning of the environment. Environmental scanning is done both within and outside the organization. Industry-related, economic, political, and social data that will benefit the organization are the product of this effort.

Knowledge creation and transfer. This element includes the continual creation of knowledge and the ongoing circulation process. In organizations that transfer information best, knowledge is gathered, coded, stored, and disseminated quickly and seamlessly across functions, levels, borders, and cultures.

Learning technology. Learning technology includes all information technology. It specifically includes informating technology, which increases information collection, analysis and distribution, and knowledge and skill development.

Quality. This is the commitment to continuous improvement. It also includes the continuous learning needed to attain total quality. Another dimension of quality in successful global learning organizations is the commitment of all employees to have personal mastery in areas beneficial to the organization.

Strategy. This element comprises conscious and deliberate planning from leadership and key structures within organization to make learning, in its broadest sense, a "prime business" of the organization in which learning is seen as a principal driver.

Supportive atmosphere. Successful global learning organizations do not neglect the development, growth, needs, and concerns—as well as dreams—of their individual employees. Employees are viewed as an important component of organizational strategy and operations. They are valued and nurtured.

Teamwork and networking. Learning organizations are committed to teamwork and team learning. Employees seek ways to work collaboratively with units of the organization and to network whenever possible with the resources outside the organization through global alliances, informal relationships, and so forth.

Vision. Vision is organizationwide consensus and support for the future directions. It includes the mission, values, and beliefs of the organization. The common vision must be shared by and challenging to everyone in the organization.

Global

The outer sphere, the global learning environment, includes six elements:

- Acculturization
- Borders
- Globalization
- Language
- Leadership
- Workforce diversity

The global sphere represents expanded challenges to the would-be global learning organization. Each is a hurdle that must be surmounted to achieve success. Each may be compared to conditions that exist for domestic organizations, but each is qualitatively more difficult. For example, some U.S. companies must follow differing regulatory procedures among 50 states. One international venture is not equivalent to the effort that would be needed for business in a 51st state. The first 50 generally share more similarities than differences. The common economic, legal, and language components alone make the domestic effort easier.

Acculturization. This element represents the ability of a global organization to synergize the various cultures within and outside the organization, and to work with the values and practices of people. Culture for global learning organizations may be interactions between two or more cultures, or it may involve many cultures. In any case, the would-be global learning organization must be culture aware, and it must ensure that its policies, programs, and opportunities are open to people of all cultures. To use a computer term, global learning organizations are user friendly to all cultures.

Borders. This element represents global crossing of the political and geographical boundaries that separate people by distance, economics, and political persuasion. Dealing with that distance and with economics and politics is inherent in this element; this is a crucial step in becoming a globalized corporation.

Globalization. The globalization element of the outer sphere represents the converging of the economic and social forces encountered in the global environment. Economic and social conditions tend to increase the need for sharing and complying with local values and practices. Globalization enables an organization to have a global mindset and to operate throughout the world as a single entity.

Language. Language refers to the verbal and nonverbal communications of people. It is both the carrier and conditioner of culture.

Not being able to speak the language of the customer, employee, or vendor limits the ability of the organization to understand, motivate, and be effective with those individuals. Staff with multilingual skills are essential for global learning organizations.

Leadership.   The roles and skills required of the leaders in would-be global learning organizations include every element in domestic situations. The international dimension, however, adds complexity—namely, global facilitation, coaching, stewarding, learning, language abilities, and cross-cultural skills. These are compounded by the other elements included in the outer sphere.

Workforce diversity.   The global work force is composed of people not only with most of the same basic concerns as the domestic one, but overlaid with a veneer of racial, ethnic, religious, educational, social, and country-of-origin diversity.

WORLD CLASS?

Some organizations call themselves "world class." The organizations we have seen with the best sustained success do not merely address all these elements. Their success in conquering many or most of them at a high level leads others to call them world class. In Chapter 3 we will examine learning, the inner sphere, in detail and begin to link excellence in elements with specific corporate examples.

Chapter Three

Principles of Learning in Learning Organizations

I n this chapter we will look at the inner sphere of the Global Learning Organization Model. Figure 3-1 serves to refresh your recollection of that part of the model.

The center of the Global Learning Organization Model is learning, whether it be individual or group. In order to appreciate and understand the dynamics of learning organizations, it is important to know what learning is, understand the various types of learning, understand the similarities and differences between individual and organizational learning, and distinguish the differences between learning and training. Then we can confidently review and analyze the key elements and principles of learning organizations.

WHAT IS LEARNING?

Learning is generally defined as a process by which individuals gain new knowledge and insights to change their behavior and actions. It is traditionally divided into the cognitive (intellectual), affective (emotional), and psychomotor (physical) domains.

Edgar Schein points out that for individuals (or organizations) to learn faster, they should first understand that "learning is not a unitary concept; that there are distinctly different kinds of learning that have very different time horizons associated with them, and that may be applicable at different stages of a learning or change process" (pp.2–3).

Knowledge acquisition and insight. Most learning theories focus on knowledge aquisition and insight, also known as cognitive learning, and imply that the essence of learning is the acquiring of information and knowledge through various kinds of cognitive activities. This point of view, according to Schein, ignores two things:

FIGURE 3–1
Global Learning Organization Model—Learning

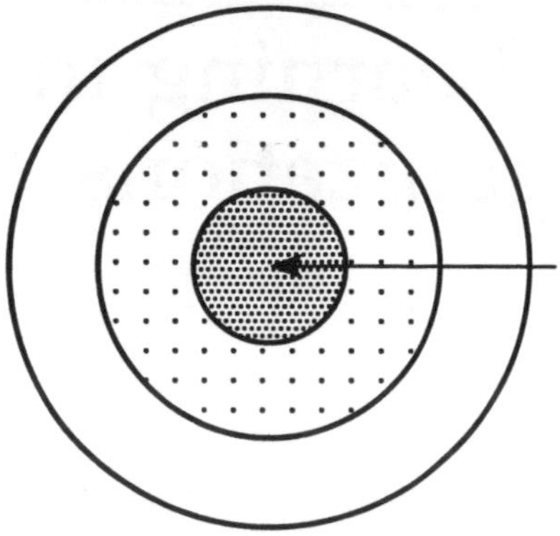

Inner sphere—
learning
(people)

Individual learning
Group learning

- Learning can happen only if the learner recognizes a problem and is motivated to learn.
- Even with insight, the learner often cannot produce the right type of behavior or skill consistently to solve the problem.

Insight does not automatically change behavior, and until behavior has changed and new results have been observed, we do not know whether our cognitively acquired knowledge is valid.

Habit and skill learning. This kind of learning is slow because it calls for practice and the willingness of the learner to be temporarily incompetent. For this type of learning to take hold, we need opportunities to practice, opportunities to make errors, and consistent rewards for correct responses.

Emotional conditioning and learned anxiety. This kind of learning is the most potent. As in the conditioning of Pavlov's dog, once this type of learning has occurred, it will continue long after original causes have been discontinued.

Other learning classifications. Another way of classifying learning is to distinguish between adaptive learning, which is how the individual or organization learns from experience and reflection, and anticipatory learning, which is how the individual or organization learns from expecting the future (a vision—reflection—action approach).

INDIVIDUAL AND ORGANIZATIONAL LEARNING

Individual learning is needed for organizational learning because only individuals can think and act. Peter Senge notes, "Organizations learn only through individuals who learn. Individual learning does not guarantee organizational learning, but without it no organizational learning occurs" (p. 236). Chris Argyris and Donald Schon agree, stating that "individual learning is a necessary but insufficient condition for organizational learning" (p.20).

Ray Stata, president of Analog Devices, asserts that organizational learning differs from individual learning in two basic respects. First, organizational learning occurs through the "shared insights, knowledge and mental models" of members of the organization. Second, organizational learning is built on past knowledge and experience of the entire organization—that is, on organizational memory, which depends on institutional mechanisms (such as policies, strategies, and explicit models) used to retain knowledge.

Although individual learning and organizational learning are interrelated, organizational learning is seen as more than a sum of individual learning. Individuals are the agents through which the organizational learning must take place, but the process of learning is influenced by a much broader set of social, political, and structural variables. It involves the sharing of knowledge, beliefs, or assumptions among individuals.

One way to show the difference between individual and organizational learning is to consider a performing organization, such as an orchestra or a basketball team. A symphony's performance or the winning of a basketball game cannot be attributed to individuals alone or even to the sum of individuals' knowledge and skills. It is the result of the know-how embedded in the whole group working in unison.

LEARNING AND TRAINING

Organization and human resource development leaders have created a remarkable paradigm shift in the past few years. It was a movement from a focus on training to a focus on learning in the workplace. Although some people see only a distinction without a difference, profes-

FIGURE 3–2
Training and Learning Contrasts

Training	Learning
Outside in, done by others	Inside out, seek to do for self
Assumes relative stability	Assumes continuous change
Focuses on knowledge, skills, ability, and job performance	Focuses on values, attitudes innovation and outcome accomplishment
Appropriate for developing basic competencies	Helps organizations and individuals learn how to learn and create own solutions
Emphasizes improvement	Emphasizes breakthrough (metanoia)
Not necessarily linked to organization's mission and strategies	Directly aligned with organization's vision and requirements for success
Structured learning experiences with short-term focus	Formal and informal, long-term future oriented, learner-initiated

sionals lead the growing recognition that there are real and critical differences. Some of the contrasts enumerated between training and learning are shown in Figure 3–2.

Walter Kiechel sees learning and training as being the difference between putting the information out there for the employees to pick up (training) and encouraging them to puzzle, wonder, and figure things out on their own (learning). Learning includes letting them try the new—and occasionally make big mistakes—and learn from those mistakes.

KNOW-HOW WORKERS

Corporations can no longer focus only on products as such; their business increasingly depends on the specialized knowledge, the know-how, of their employees.

These know-how employees are rapidly becoming the most valuable asset of global corporations; and unlike most other assets of the company, which lose value over time, the know-how of employees actually increases in value when used and practiced.

The know-how worker is not necessarily the same as the better-known knowledge worker described in Chapter 1. Know-how employees (also called gold-collar workers) working in know-how companies (consultancies, engineering firms, hi-tech companies, and so on) are primarily involved in activities such as problem solving, problem identifying, and strategic brokering for outside customers. They are the critical core of the company, the essence of the business from which all revenues flow.

HOW ORGANIZATIONS LEARN

How do organizations learn? Although organizational learning is complex, the research does offer some clues. There are a several complementary elements that enable an organization to learn most effectively:

- Systems thinking
- Anticipatory and loop learning
- Action learning
- Information systems
- Learning space

Systems thinking. Systems thinking, particularly systems dynamics, can be a very powerful tool to facilitate organizational learning. Systems dynamics recognizes that organizations are like giant networks of interconnected nodes. Changes, planned or unplanned, in one part of the organization can affect other parts of the organization with surprising, often negative, consequences.

Senge describes systems thinking as a "discipline for seeing wholes, a framework for seeing interrelationships rather than linear cause-effect chains, for seeing patterns of change rather than snapshots" (p. 68).

The critical value and advantage of systems thinking is leverage—where strategic small actions and changes can lead to significant, enduring improvements and advancement.

Anticipatory and loop learning. Related to and based on systems thinking is learning that is anticipatory and deeply reflective—learning that involves a circular or looping process. There are three types of learning that can effectively enhance organizational learning:

- Anticipatory learning
- Single loop learning
- Double loop learning

Anticipatory learning.   Anticipatory learning is an organization's process of acquiring knowledge from expecting the future. It is a vision-reflection-action approach to learning that seeks to avoid negative results and experiences and instead identify the best future opportunities and the knowledge needed to take advantage of these opportunities. This "planning as learning" approach is credited by Royal Dutch Shell as a highly valuable strategy for global learning and success. It enabled the company to prepare its organizational capability to handle a sharp drop in the price of oil. When that scenario occurred, it was the only oil company equipped with the necessary organizational skills and resources.

Single loop learning.   Adaptive learning, or single loop learning, is focused on gaining information to stabilize and maintain existing systems. The focus is error detection and correction. Single loop learning is by far the most common in organizations today.

Double loop learning.   Double loop learning is more in-depth and involves questioning the system itself and the reasons why the errors happened in the first place. Double loop learning looks at deeper organizational norms and structures. It raises questions about their validity in terms of organization, action, and results. We must note here that most organizations and individuals are unwilling to engage in double loop learning because it involves disclosure of errors and mistakes.

Deutero learning.   Another somewhat related type of organizational learning is deutero learning. This occurs when the organization learns from critically reflecting upon its taken-for-granted assumptions. Argyris and Schon call this phenonemon "learning about learning." When an organization engages in deutero learning, its members learn about previous contexts for learning. They discover what they did that eased or inhibited learning, they invent new strategies for learning, and they evaluate and generalize on what they have produced. The results become encoded and reflected in organizational learning practice. Adaptive learning can be classified as a coping form of learning. Anticipatory, double loop, and deutero learning are generative or creative types of organizational learning.

In using these organizational types of learning, the learning is enhanced when people are proactive, reflective, and creative in their learning. Organizational learning may start as a reaction to events, but the proactive individual or organization soon takes charge of the learning.

Action learning.   A powerful method of learning for organizations is action learning. Action learning is the brainchild of Reginald Revans, one of the earliest architects of the concept of learning organizations. It involves small groups of people who take a difficult task or problem in the organization, and act to change it, bringing back the results to the organization for review and learning. As Revans has said, "There is no learning without action and no action without learning" (p. 131).

Corporate exemplar—General Electric.   General Electric has used action learning as the organizational learning strategy to transform itself into a global-thinking, culturally sensitive organization. Learning is built around GE problems that are real and relevant and that require decisions. Formats may vary, but typically two teams of 5 to 7 people each who come from diverse businesses and functions within GE, work together on the project. GE has built into the action-learning projects opportunities for feedback to the participants on strategies and on issues regarding their leadership and teamwork skills. The participants also have the opportunity to reflect on the total learning experience.

Besides team building, action learning has supplied participants with a context for dealing with multicultural and global issues. Global projects usually focus on potential GE markets. An example is the executive development course for global business leaders. In 1991 the program was held in Heidelberg, Germany, a site chosen because it is a market in which GE does not have a strong presence, but it is the home of several key global competitors of GE. The first week was spent receiving feedback on leadership effectiveness and meeting with key European business leaders, opinion makers, and government officials from France, Germany, and Sweden. During the second week, the focus shifted to projects from GE's plastic, lighting, and electrical distribution and control businesses.

One project, for example, looked at the lighting strategy for Europe, reflecting the sharp rise—from 2 to 18 percent in only 18 months—in GE's share of the western European consumer lighting market, mostly resulting from the acquisition of Tungsram in Hungary and Thorn Lighting in the UK. The teams were encouraged to be creative and think of serious ways in which GE could change the market and excite retailers and customers by finding new ways to add value. The participants traveled across Europe to conduct interviews and experience firsthand the effects of local culture, language, currency, legislation, and tax laws—and consumer preferences for national brands. Between interviews, the participants debriefed each other and prepared their final reports to present to GE leadership, including GE's CEO Jack Welch.

James Noel, manager of executive education at GE and a GE consultant, sees action learning as immensely valuable in building GE into a learning organization. Action learning has made "participants active partners in the learning process. Because the team projects provide value to GE's businesses, it has an immediate return on investment. Action learning also provides a viable vehicle for dealing with issues of leadership and teamwork" (p.33). He adds that, when action learning happens in a global setting, it has these added advantages:

- It provides participants with hands-on, cross-cultural experiences.

- It engenders the self-confidence that uniquely comes from international work.

Information systems. Information, of course, is essential to the organizational learning process. Nancy Dixon notes that in organizations, information can be acquired, distributed, given meaning, stored, and retrieved. For organizations to learn effectively and efficiently, these elements should be continuous and interact with each other. The distribution of information should occur through multiple channels, each having different time frames. Likewise, information within the organization is continually subjected to perceptual filters. The knowledge and information elements of organizational learning should be seen as ongoing and interactive instead of sequential and independent.

Successful learning organizations realize how information can become knowledge and know-how for the company. They systematically guide information through all five of these steps.

Learning space and time. Finally, but of great importance, organizational learning calls for time and space for individuals and organizations. This simply means that organizational learning cannot be pushed too fast. For example, despite a person's general creativity, there are times when a needed creative idea doesn't emerge immediately. Pushing harder for the needed creativity may create stress that inhibits, rather than helps, the necessary breakthrough. Although a committed group will want to move quickly to reach the desired state, it is important to remember that there may be a speed limit. People need time to plan and reflect. Individuals need the physical, social, and mental space to be creative and innovative; to listen; to slow things down, and establish linkages; and to build on what's happening.

THE NECESSARY ARCHITECTURE

To build global learning organizations, George Por stresses the need for new social, knowledge, and technological architectures.

Social architecture.   Social architecture is a rich, adaptable culture that supports integrated relationships and enhances learning by encouraging teams, self-management, empowerment, and sharing. A social architecture is the opposite of a closed, rigid, bureaucratic architecture.

Knowledge architecture.   Knowledge architecture is the repository for shared knowledge and collective intelligence that is organized for easy access by any staff member at any time from anywhere. An example is a database that collects the key learning of individuals (such as McKinsey's, as detailed in Chapter 4). Another example is an on-line newsletter that systematically gathers, organizes, and disseminates the collective knowledge of the organization's members.

Technological architecture.   Technological architecture comprises the supporting, integrated technological networks and information tools that allow access to and exchange of information and learning. It includes technical processes, systems, and structure for collaboration, coaching, coordination, and other knowledge skills. It may include electronic tools and advanced methods for learning, such as computer conferencing, simulation, or computer supported collaboration. These work to create *knowledge freeways*.

KNOWLEDGE CREATION

Ikujiro Nonaka, professor of management at Hitotsubashi University in Tokyo, writes that "successful companies are those that *consistently create new knowledge, disseminate it widely throughout the organization, and quickly embody it in new technologies and products*" (p.96).

Nonaka sees organizational learning as a pattern that starts and ends with the knowledge of the individual. The sharing of that knowledge throughout the organization is the nutriment that feeds the organizational learning loop. He identifies four patterns that cause organizations to learn.

- Tacit to tacit
- Explicit to explicit
- Tacit to explicit
- Explicit to tacit

These are patterns based on tacit and explicit knowledge and their interaction. Tacit knowledge is knowledge we hold inside but have difficulty expressing. Explicit knowledge is formal, systematic, and easily shared, as in product specifications, a scientific formula, or a computer program.

Tacit to tacit.   This is a personalized form of learning in which one person passes on personal knowledge to another person, for example, a master-apprentice relationship. By working closely together, the apprentice can learn what is known tacitly by the master. This form of learning is a very limited form of knowledge creation because the knowledge of the two never becomes explicit and therefore cannot be easily leveraged by the organization as a whole.

Explicit to explicit.   This knowledge is gained by combining and synthesizing existing explicit knowledge. For example, the company controller gathers and synthesizes company information. This pattern of knowledge creation is a limited form of creating new knowledge because it focuses only on what already exists.

Tacit to explicit.   This knowledge creation happens when someone takes existing knowledge, adds his or her tacit knowledge, and creates something new that can be shared throughout the organization. For example, the company controller using tacit knowledge comes up with a new system of budget control for the organization. Nonaka notes that the Japanese are especially good at developing this type of knowledge.

Explicit to tacit.   This knowledge creation occurs when new explicit knowledge is internalized within the members of the organization to create new tacit knowledge. For example, the controller's new budgeting process eventually becomes the new way business is done in the company.

In the knowledge-creating company, all four of these patterns exist in a dynamic interaction, a kind of knowledge spiral. These patterns

FIGURE 3–3
Rover Corporate Learning Process Model

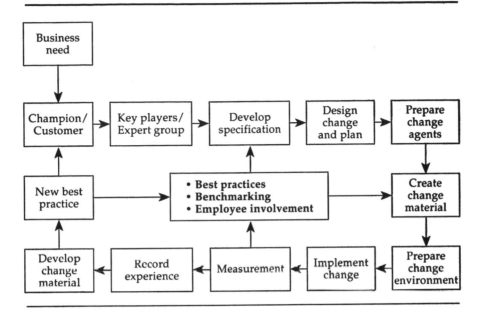

can become very powerful in creating new knowledge because the various interactions can generate much personal commitment and energy.

A CORPORATE LEARNING MODEL

Barrie Oxtoby has developed a 13-step model that Rover has used successfully in its efforts to learn as an organization. This model, internally called the corporate learning process, is illustrated in Figure 3–3.

Business opportunity.   All learning undertaken should contribute directly to bottom line performance. Without this there is no justification for doing it.

Champion.   The person who identifies with the project's goals, opens doors, sets standards, maintains and coordinates the key players and expert group.

Key players and expert group.   This group includes the subject experts, experienced operators, motivators, networkers, and learning experts and outside experts.

Develop specification.   This step includes aims, objectives, learning process and methods, venues, timing, and measurement for success.

Design the process and plan.   This step lists all the major steps that will absorb time, the leader of each step, any milestones, and the resource for delivering the end objective.

Prepare coaches and learners.   Describe the project to employees and subject specialists and motivate them.

Create the learning material.   Develop high-quality materials produced to agreed timing and contribute to complete success of project; this can range from a new model to audiotapes, handouts, and so on.

Prepare learning environment.   The learning should be as close to the workplace as possible.

Implement learning.   This step involves a combination of off- and on-the-job activity to capture the learning.

Measurement.   This step requires measuring the effect of the learning and change process against the original objectives. The bottom-line benefits achieved by a well-specified process will strengthen the value of systematic learning to the organization.

Record experience.   The learning is recorded in a computer system for the organization and in the individuals' personal development files.

Develop learning material.   Develop any lessons for future organizational use.

New best practice.   Revise the best practice standard to share the experience throughout the organization.
Throughout the corporate learning process, the key players and learners can draw on the established best practice and benchmarking,

and can involve company employees. These are the three elements in the internal box.

THE CONTINUOUS WORKPLACE LEARNING MODEL

Katie Weldon, Ernst & Young's director of education methods, working with Jill Harper, a program designer, developed a model to describe the process of workplace learning. Two years ago during some focus group sessions, Weldon and her colleagues learned that Ernst & Young professionals believe that 90 percent of their learning takes place on the job. Struck by this information, they decided to study workplace learning. They conducted a literature search, held discussions with other organizations, and called in university consultants.

Their product (after much distilling and reworking) was the identification of eight learning skills. Then they incorporated the skills in an industry education needs assessment. The survey, including the eight learning skills, was sent to managers, senior managers, and partners in the practice. Approximately 500 responded and rated *all* of the learning skills as important now—and more important in the next 3 to 5 years. The survey also asked for self-rating of current skill level and optimal skill level for the current job. The results showed that, for each skill, there was a significant gap between current and optimal.

Reinforced by their own data, Ernst & Young believes that its professional development group can make a difference to its practitioners if it can help them do their workplace learning. To do that, it developed the model and placed the skills around the model, emphasizing that a user can enter the model at any place and that the user must consciously and intentionally use assignments and job experiences as learning opportunities.

The Ernst & Young model is called the Continuous Workplace Learning Model. It is illustrated in Figure 3–4.

Directions for the use of the model are distributed to Ernst & Young employees along with the graphic and directions:

> The reasons for developing and improving our learning skills are compelling—the world is smaller and yet more complex, there is too much to be learned, information is easily accessed, and the business environment is constantly changing. Since the majority of our learning takes place on the job, we need to get consistently better at this kind of learning.
>
> The continuous workplace learning model provides a process for turn-

FIGURE 3–4

Ernst & Young Continuous Workplace Learning Model—Managing Self as a Learner

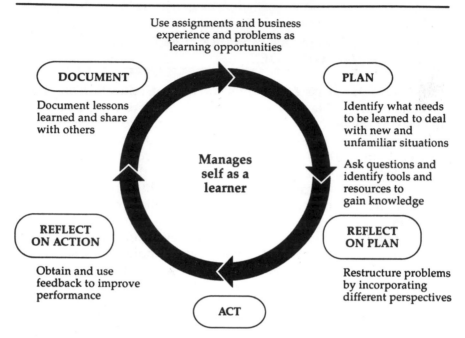

Use assignments and business experience and problems as learning opportunities

DOCUMENT

Document lessons learned and share with others

PLAN

Identify what needs to be learned to deal with new and unfamiliar situations

Ask questions and identify tools and resources to gain knowledge

Manages self as a learner

REFLECT ON ACTION

Obtain and use feedback to improve performance

REFLECT ON PLAN

Restructure problems by incorporating different perspectives

ACT

- Use business experiences and problems as learning opportunities. These are the "triggers" for learning.
- Identify what needs to be learned to deal with new and unfamiliar situations. This refers to figuring out what you don't know and what you need to find out about the situation.
- Ask appropriate questions to obtain knowledge related to business problems. Here you identify the resources needed to gain the knowledge.
- Restructure problems by incorporating different perspectives. This means you change your lens—frame and reframe the problem to look at it from a variety of ways.
- Obtain and use feedback as tasks are executed and completed to improve performance. Reflect on how it went, assess how you did vis-a-vis your plan, and seek input from others so that you can extract the lessons learned from the experience. Identify the learning you didn't anticipate.
- Document the learning so that it becomes part of your business experience database and share it with others so that others can build on your experience.

ing work assignments and business problems/opportunities into learning experiences. And what could be a better metaphor for this than the kaleidoscope—a lens for viewing a series of patterns through the reflection of an image produced by mirrors. Through planning, reflection, and feedback,

FIGURE 3–5
Ernst & Young Continuous Workplace Learning Model—Helping Others

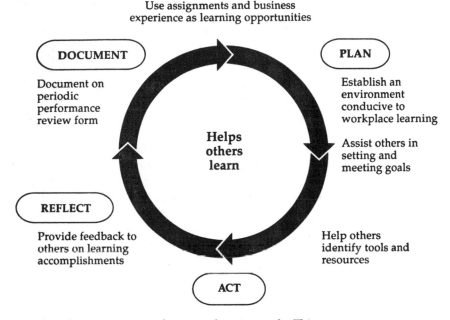

Use assignments and business
experience as learning opportunities

DOCUMENT

Document on
periodic
performance
review form

PLAN

Establish an
environment
conducive to
workplace learning

**Helps
others
learn**

Assist others in
setting and
meeting goals

REFLECT

Provide feedback to
others on learning
accomplishments

Help others
identify tools and
resources

ACT

- Assist others in setting and meeting learning goals. This can occur as assignments are made or during a performance review when developmental needs are identified and goals are set.
- Provide feedback to others on their learning accomplishments so they improve on their performance and capitalize on their successes. Timely feedback enhances the learning and lets people use the feedback on the next assignment.

we can develop a series of different "pictures" of how to deal with new, unexpected, and complex challenges facing us.

The continuous learning skills can help us respond to our clients' needs with better, quicker solutions if we consciously and intentionally learn from past experiences and new opportunities. By asking questions, looking at problems with a different lens, developing plans of action and reflecting on them, acting and then seeking feedback and reflecting again, and documenting what we learned, we can develop a systematic way of using the workplace as a laboratory for learning.

You can enter the model at any place to start the process. To simplify how it works, let's assume you have a new work assignment or a unique client business problem. Here's how the learning skills fit around the model to help you turn that opportunity into a learning experience.

Assist others in setting and meeting learning goals. This can occur as assignments are made or during a performance review when developmental needs are identified and goals are set.

Provide feedback to others on their learning accomplishments so that they improve on their performance and capitalize on their successes. Timely feedback enhances the learning and lets people use the feedback on the next assignment.

The model also has a second component for helping others to learn, illustrated in Figure 3–5. You might suppose that this part of the model is for supervisors only. That isn't how it's used at Ernst & Young. It describes any employee's helping any other employee, particularly a co-worker, to learn.

The Continuous Workplace Learning Model is very new at Ernst & Young, and the firm is working at implementating the model and analyzing its findings. Currently it is using the model as the framework for a video on learning to learn. Ernst & Young is also trying to *live* the model. That is, it goes through the process when it has new assignments or is challenged by a business problem. It is also looking into ways to incorporate the model in the way the firm designs learning activities. And in the future Weldon plans to develop a desktop application to let practitioners rate themselves, compare those ratings to the ones already collected, identify their learning style, and practice using some of the skills.

CRITICAL ELEMENTS

Now that we have a more comprehensive understanding of the key aspects of learning, organizational learning, and ways in which organizational learning can happen, let's move to the middle sphere. In Chapter 4 we will examine the 11 critical organizational elements needed for being a dynamic and potent global corporation.

Chapter Four

Eleven Essential Organizational Elements for Global Learning

T he second sphere of the Global Learning Organization Model contains the 11 organizational characteristics identified as being essential by a majority of the global learning companies we contacted in our worldwide research. Figure 4-1 serves to refresh your recollection of that part of the model.

We will describe and explain the purpose and importance of each characteristic. Following the descriptions, we will provide exemplary practices from different corporate global learning organizations.

APPROPRIATE STRUCTURES

For many organizational learning specialists, structure is the determining factor in helping or hindering learning in organizations. The best structure is small and streamlined. The learning company structure does away with restrictive job descriptions, overcontrolled hierarchies, and red-tape procedures. It also sweeps away the rigid mindsets that continue unproductive practices indefinitely. Giant corporations, such as Tatung and Honda, may be large, but they seek to act with the dynamism and hunger of a small company. As GE's CEO Jack Welch puts it, we want to "pull out the dandelions of bureaucracy and the tentacles of rituals. Territoriality has to give way to a growing sense of unity and common purpose." They do have appropriate structure. GE's business units are not all organized in the same way. They are organized differently to reflect the environment in which they compete.

FIGURE 4-1
Global Learning Organization Model—Organizational Learning

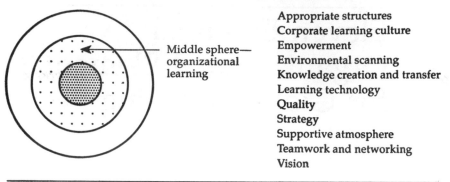

Middle sphere—
organizational
learning

Appropriate structures
Corporate learning culture
Empowerment
Environmental scanning
Knowledge creation and transfer
Learning technology
Quality
Strategy
Supportive atmosphere
Teamwork and networking
Vision

© Michael Marquardt and Angus Reynolds, 1992

Holistic structures. Linda Morris sees successful learning organizations as having a holistic structure—like an organism, not committed to any particular structure. A holistic structure can evolve and transform as needed to meet the collective sense of the organization's identity and purpose. A hologram is a good analogy to illustrate another point. Holograms are created with a laser. The resulting photographlike material is three dimensional. If you cut a hologram into pieces, each piece amazingly will be a smaller original. Therefore, any part of the hologram contains the seeds of the whole. A holistic company structure does represent the company.

Teamwork. The global structure should encourage collaboration and integration. It should stimulate energy flow between ideas, action, operations, and policy. It should enhance the ability to think and work with others, with an emphasis on team learning and action. Integrative processes should involve personnel in multiple locations, especially those beyond the boundaries of a single organization. Cross-functional work teams are often used. Such integration can accomplish the following goals:

- Capture team learning.
- Develop new approaches to accountability.
- Learn to focus and coordinate multiple-task-focused teams.
- Overcome organizational fragmentation.

Corporate exemplars. *Hewlett-Packard.* As Hewlett-Packard prepared to celebrate 50 years in business in 1989, the company was in a downspin. According to *Business Week,* "the one-time innovator had become a lumbering dinosaur." Three dozen committees oversaw every decision, delaying new products and crushing new learning, speed, and innovativeness.

Since then HP has looked more like a gazelle, with speed a top priority, and employees urged to rethink every process from product development to distribution. The keys to breaking loose the new learning in HP were undoing the bureaucracy and creating a new enabling structure. HP found that small teams can develop products faster than the company's formal organization (a point reinforced by Roberto Araya in Chapter 12). The old procedures followed at HP included the following steps: (1) product designers came up with a plan, (2) engineers refined it, (3) manufacturing studied it, (4) finally, marketing executives reviewed it. HP now has a team of people from all the company's disciplines working together from the start. Such teamworking has resulted in enormous timesaving and improved learning on several products, including the Kittyhawk disk drive.

Saudia Airlines. Another global company that has restructured to improve organizational learning is Saudia Airlines. Saudia is recognized as one of the top companies in the Middle East in learning and quality. Zain Ameen, chairman of the main stations reorganization committee, notes, however, that even greater learning will be necessary to be able to operate in the rapidly changing world. Saudia's hierarchy was flattened. The results include a reduced number of layers to improve communication, enhanced effectiveness of training, utilization of new electronic mail technology, and dynamic rostering. We must expand our horizon beyond today . . . beyond tomorrow to the next century." Ameen adds, "If we focus on employee development rather than on employee efficiency, we will be much more ready for the next century."

CORPORATE LEARNING CULTURE

Learning organizations provide a facilitative climate where learning is highly encouraged. Beyond that, mistakes are not only allowed, but valued, because they can be the source of new ideas and can help discover new ways of doing things. There is no such thing as a failed experiment—as long as the organization learns from it.

August Jacacci sees a learning culture as one where there is "collaborative creativity in all contexts, relationships and experiences" and the measure of success is the combined wisdom and synergy of the organization as a whole. The whole culture learns in a self-aware, self-reflective, and creative way. "The groups become cells in the body of an organization, which itself become a new learning individual in the emergent global culture" (p.50).

Incentive for innovation. Learning organizations take brave, bold steps to encourage as many people as possible to take risks, innovate, and get out of the habit of asking for permission and waiting for instructions. In learning organizations employee initiative is rewarded, and inquiry and innovation are promoted. Even pay-for-knowledge incentive schemes are established to reward employees for their learning.

We think that 3M provides an interesting example of corporate support for creativity. 3M has undertaken many actions to create an innovative climate and encourage creativity in its organization. For example, 3M allows workers up to 15 percent of their paid work time to work on their own projects. In like manner, Honda instituted a competition for inventions among employees.

Learning from experience. The corporate culture of learning organizations strikes a balance so that both an individual's and the organization's developmental needs are addressed. There is participatory policy-making in which all diverse groups have a right to take part.

Learning organizations also foster a culture of feedback and disclosure. There are daily opportunities to learn from experience. Managers see their prime task as facilitating members' experimentation and learning from experience. The managers make time to seek feedback on how well they are easing learning.

There are self-development opportunities for all. People have resources including courses, workshops, seminars, self-learning materials, development groups, coaching, mentoring, and data banks. Employees are expected to learn not only skills related to their own jobs, but also the skills of others in their unit.

Employees have responsibility for their own learning—as well as the learning of others. They must also understand how their responsibilities relate to the goals of the organization as a whole. Finally, employees are expected to teach, as well as to learn from, their coworkers. The entire workplace culture is geared to organizational learning.

The learning habit. The "learning habit" is an automatic part of production, marketing, problem solving, and customer service, Because of its origins, it yields a harvest of reflections, insights, and new ideas for action.

It is important for the learning culture to recognize and appreciate that different people learn in different ways. No single style is necessarily best. An organization needs all styles, each of which can complement the deficiencies of the others.

Corporate support. Global learning companies make a strong moral and financial commitment to learning. This is reinforced by J. Y. Pillay, chairman of Singapore Airlines. He says, "Our self-respect will be eroded, if we do not pay attention to the training needs of all our employees." And SIA commits over 12 percent of total payroll costs to learning.

AutoMind spends 6 percent of payroll divided as follows: 3 percent formal training, 2 percent internal seminars and workshops (with internal and external instructors), and 1 percent on external seminars and conferences.

Saturn spent significant amounts of money to conduct a comprehensive training program for workers even before production began. Workers received from 300 to 700 hours of training before entering the assembly line. The training continues afterward in both technical and self-development areas. Saturn's 1993 goal is for workers to spend at least 5 percent of their work time, or 92 hours, in formal training.

Many other companies—such as Anderson, Medtronic, and Motorola—have targets of five percent of total payroll devoted to training. Dave Luther, Corning's vice president of corporate quality, told us, "Our training is broadly based. Corning's 5 percent goes from the chairman to forklift operator. The consequences of our training efforts prove that training is a good investment for the corporation."

Corporate exemplars. *Samsung.* Samsung identifies a corporate culture supporting innovation as its number one core value because the company truly believes that encouraging employee creativity is absolutely critical for corporate success. (3M does also—75 percent of all sales comes from products created in the last five years.) Samsung sees innovations as fostering, nourishing, and supporting people who are willing to champion new ideas, better services, new products, and product applications, and as creating entrepreneurial, opportunistic spirit that permits continuous adaptation to changing conditions.

PPG. Another global corporation with a powerful learning corporate culture is PPG (formerly Pittsburgh Paint and Glass). PPG's culture is based upon the following principles:

- Associates must take responsibility for their personal development.(All employees, including managers and directors, are called associates.)
- The most effective learning occurs on the job

PPG has developed a learning matrix that enables its people, by locating areas that need development, to identify the learning resources best-correlated to the employee's organizational level. PPG puts special emphasis on quality, values, leadership, and functional job skills. Emphasis is also directed to individual effectiveness. Success on that level will enable PPG people to be more innovative in their work, to lead work teams, and to facilitate learning with a variety of learning styles. In addition, PPG provides each associate with a *Professional Development Source Book* as a key to personal career planning, growth, and performance.

EMPOWERMENT

Global learning companies seek to reduce dependency and push responsibility as close as possible to the final action point. People are treated as adults with adult capabilities which include:

- The capability to learn.
- The ability to decide for themselves how to solve problems.
- The ability to expand greatly their productive, creative, and learning capacity.

The whole organization is expected to think and act directly on organizational strategy and planning. All employees are empowered to take part in and develop the strategy. Learning organizations realize that empowered workers can make better decisions than managers because they need and have the best information.

Corporate exemplars. *Honda.* There is a saying at Honda that there is more knowledge on the factory floor than in the office. Honda sincerely believes in the commitment, creativity, and intellectual capacity of its associates. (Like PPG, all employees at Honda are called associates—including the company president.) Honda doesn't just talk empowerment; it permits people to set out and create a new car. That's confidence and a whole lot more!

Managers believe that the associate is the best person to know how the job should be done. If managers see a problem, they ask the associate for his or her input, involvement, and advice. One Honda manager states the Honda attitude toward the worker-learners: "We have a goal here. If you can do it better—do it. If you fail, we'll pick you up and dust you off, and encourage you to keep trying."

Gary Vasilash believes a key to Honda's success is *gemba*. Gemba is a Japanese word that means "the place of action," commonly used to mean the shop floor. The gemba concept was reported to most English readers in Masaaki Imai's book *Kaizen*, which also describes other Japanese business concepts. At Honda, gemba brings together people involved with a particular project or process at the point at which some action needs to take place. This is more than simultaneous engineering and cross-functional teamwork on a project. Imai says, "In my opinion, better than 90 percent of quality problems in [g]emba can be solved with common sense by simply going to [g]emba at once and asking why until the root causes have been identified" (p. 251).

An example of the power and effectiveness of going to gemba occurred at the Marysville, Ohio, plant during the development of the Honda wagon. During the initial development process, it was discovered that installing the wiring harness in the tailgate required 10 minutes—too long. All the people involved—design engineers, assemblers, and people from stamping—arrived on the scene where the prototype was being built. It was up to them to make the changes needed to get the harness installed quickly and efficiently. Decisions could be, and were, made. The solution was found (it involved switching to a two-piece wiring harness and increasing the diameter of the hole through which the wiring was fed).

When talking to people at Honda, we found that "self-reliance" is a word used often. There is also confidence, responsibility, pride, and most important, accomplishment. Robert Simcox, plant manager at the Marysville assembly plant, says that Honda people are learning together because "they have been given the opportunity to use their own creativity and imagination."

Saturn. Another automotive company that sees empowerment and organizational learning critical for success is Saturn, a division of General Motors. The Saturn factory in Spring Hill, Tennessee, was conceived by General Motors to be a laboratory for innovative ideas. As *Business Week* noted in a recent issue, "One of the most revolutionary ideas is Saturn's approach to employee empowerment.'' Each Saturn work team manages everything without direct oversight from top management. This includes its own budget, inventory control, and hiring. An example is the Saturn machine maintenance team. It can order many tools and parts it needs on its own, and even choose the outside supplier for transmission components.

This empowerment helps the employees to make better, faster decisions than their office-bound managers. The added responsibility has also made workers more accountable, with absenteeism at 2.5 percent, much less than the 10 to 15 percent rate at other GM plants.

ENVIRONMENTAL SCANNING

There are three considerations regarding environmental interface:

- Scan the environment.
- Affect the environment.
- Choose the environmental target.

Scan the environment. The idea of scanning the environment is to be prepared for the changes likely to affect the organization. Those organizations best at anticipating change are the ones that are most adaptable—a key form of organizational learning. One method organizations use to anticipate change is the development of scenarios about possible futures. An example is the response of the Royal Dutch Shell Group of companies to the oil crisis of the 1980s. It shows how planning for environmental interface can facilitate learning before an actual crisis. When oil was still at $28 a barrel, the planning department of Shell created a scenario of oil at $15 a barrel. Shell managers constructed responses around the much lower price. When the actual price drop came, Shell had already visited the world of $15 oil. Shell was ahead of other oil companies in managing the crisis.

Affect the environment. Organizations have the opportunity to *affect* the environment they react to. Botkin calls this kind of organizational learning *anticipatory learning*. Anticipatory learning is the capacity to influence events environments, and experiences that are not yet inevitable or irreversible. It is not enough that Medtronic, the world's leading supplier of cardiovascular products and services, be fully aware of global health care needs, quality requirements, or medical technologies. It needs to be able to help change health care delivery systems in ways that save lives. Already, every three minutes, somewhere in the world, Medtronic enhances a patient's life. Scanning may soon make that every minute.

Choose the environmental target. The organization can choose the part of the environment with which it will interact, in this way defining what it will learn. When companies *benchmark*, they seek out the most successful corporations, in their own industry or some related industry, against which to compare themselves.

Corporate exemplars. *Xerox.* From 1980 to 1985, Xerox began an extensive benchmarking campaign. It examined various Japanese techniques to cut its unit production costs in half, and slash inventory costs by two thirds. Since then, its share of the U.S. copier market has climbed 50 percent, to over 15 percent. As Robert Camp, manager of benchmarking competency at Xerox, says, ''Too many companies suffer because they refuse to believe that others can do things better'' (*BusinessWeek*, November 30, 1992).

Rover. Rover has used environmental scanning as a primary tool to resuscitate its auto manufacturing and sales operations. The company has taken more than 3,000 employees off the assembly line and out of offices. Rover sent them to study management and assembly techniques in companies around the world. They are not just concentrating on car production. Employees have visited companies as diverse as Sony, IBM, and Honda. Rover sees the value of this expense by showing results in the production of its new Rover 800. This new version was designed and built in just 24 months, compared with Rover's usual 39-month lead time. Rover also looked at the processes needed to produce a car. The result was to scrap various functions and merge design and manufacturing processes so that mistakes are ironed out as they happen. By bringing together a project team representing all the major functions, there has been a 10 percent saving on development costs. Now Rover expects to be able to deliver this new car from assembly line to the showroom within 48 hours of an order being received!

GE. If GE is to cope with the global environment, it needs lifetime learners. GE's development efforts are dedicated to producing such people. GE is deliberatly trying to get people at every level to contribute ideas on how they and the organization can do things better. GE wants its managers, wherever they are, to open their eyes to the world from the moment they join the company. It wants them to learn from best practices, wherever they might be found, whether they reside in competitors abroad or in companies in other fields. Only by such continuous scanning can GE effectively turn that learning into organizational change. Many other global corporations, notably Corning, PPG, and Motorola, have successfully used this form of environmental scanning to learn and develop as organizations.

KNOWLEDGE CREATION AND TRANSFER

Learning organizations recognize that creating new knowledge involves not only objective, external information, but also tacit and highly subjective individual insights, intuitions, and hunches. Creating new knowledge is not only the province of the R&D department: it should instead be a way of behaving and thinking. Everyone is a knowledge creator and a worker. Creating new knowledge is as much about ideals as it is about ideas that fuel innovation. Nonaka thinks that knowledge creation should be at the epicenter of a company's corporate strategy.

The organization itself, according to Shosanna Zuboff, is, in fact,

> a learning institution, and one of its principal purposes is the expansion of knowledge. . . . Learning in no longer a separate activity that occurs either before one enters the workplace or in remote classroom settings. Nor is it an activity preserved for a managerial group. The behaviors that define learning and the behaviors that define being productive are one and the same. Learning is not something that requires time out from being engaged in productive activity; learning is the heart of the productive activity. To put it simply, learning is the new form of labor (p. 395).

The ability to "rope in" knowledge, to learn from what other parts of the organization or network are doing can become one of the principal sources of value-added for corporations. This informating of all employees and even external associates (customers, vendors, distributors, alliances) is an absolute must for global learning organizations. Sharing information on virtually a real-time basis and encouraging wider access to information includes the following:

- Creating on-line databases that can be used across functional boundaries.
- Hooking into on-line databases and electronic bulletin boards external to the organization such as universities and other learning centers.
- Installing an electronic mail culture where its use is widespread

- Using electronic data interchange to create comprehensive electronic network systems

Corporate exemplars. *Asea Brown Boveri (ABB).* When you operate in 140 countries and employ over 215,000 people and 65 different business areas, as ABB does, you have "to have your act together." The rapid and efficient acquisition and distribution of information and the creation of knowledge are absolutely critical. Many corporate leaders consider ABB to be among the very best of global learning organizations because of its tremendous ability to disseminate knowledge so well within the company. ABB pursues economies of scale in both production and learning—with an emphasis on the latter.

For example, the Power Transformer Business Area of ABB has several mechanisms, or forums for exchange, that have been created to foster learning. The area management board meets four to six times a year to chart global strategies. The five top staff members responsible for areas such as R&D, marketing, and purchasing travel constantly to move information and learning. In addition to the formal gatherings, there are highly encouraged, ongoing information exchanges. Ideas and problems are constantly exchanged by telephone, fax, and meeting.

McKinsey. McKinsey, the large global management consulting firm, is seen, at least by Tom Peters, as a company that has taken the concept of the learning organization "further than any other big company" (p. 385). This accolade is based on numerous factors ranging from having a director of knowledge management to the fact that McKinsey espouses the maintenance of a balance between "serving clients" and "creating knowledge."

In McKinsey, 31 practice centers have been created. There are 18 centers of competence for functional specialties such as marketing and organizational performance and 13 industries including banking, insurance, energy, and electronics. Each practice center has a wholly voluntary leadership and membership ranging in number from a few to a hundred, depending how hot the center's topic is.

The philosophy behind the centers is the belief that every engagement is seen as a learning opportunity. There is a new emphasis on the systematic development of consultant skills, so that McKinsey will have as much "internal knowledge on demand" as possible. The organization wants to create the ability to tap systematically into what people have learned. It is therefore critical to motivate workers to put their learning into databases within the practice centers.

Knowledge development is seen as a professional responsibility. One mechanism for building such commitment is the inclusion of knowledge development in the personnel evaluation process. Another even more powerful method is that an employee cannot establish a cost center or spend money until a two-page summary of how he or she will learn from the project has been prepared. Every three months, each project manager receives a printout of what he or she has put into the practice information system. An employee who has not helped to create the knowledge base at McKinsey is not seen as a contributor to the learning organization.

Another information tool at McKinsey is an on-line information system called the Practice Development Network (PDNet), which is updated weekly and now has over 6,000 documents. Documentation also includes the Knowledge Resource Directory (McKinsey's yellow pages), a guide to who knows what. For any of the 31 practice areas of McKinsey, you will be able to find the list of members, experts, and core documents. Finally, there is a Center Bulletin, which appears at a rate of 2 or 3 times per week for each of the practice areas, featuring new ideas and information that a particular practice area wants to parade in front of all the company's consultants.

3M. 3M is a highly diversified company with 50 autonomous product divisions and 57 wholly owned subsidiaries in 57 countries with an overlay of centrally operated activities. To gain as much information flow as possible, the company has established several councils (general managers, technical directors, marketing directors, and so on). Each council meets regularly to look at best practices within and outside 3M, to share ideas and concerns, and to bring in experts to stimulate broad-range thinking. In short, the councils ensure that information gets up and down and back and forth throughout the organization.

LEARNING TECHNOLOGY

A critical key to creating a learning organization is using technologies appropriate to support such an organization. Brian Quinn, author of *The Intelligent Organization,* calls technology "the most important" ingredient for organizational knowledge. Such technologies are broad-based and include the arts and sciences of learning, discovery, communications, information technology, and computer science

Successful learning organizations use technology to elicit, code, store, and create knowledge. Of special interest to Ernst & Young's Linda Morris is the blending of technologies now being used to design technology to support individual and group thinking and problem-solving activities. She states that it is "vital to the technology platform of the learning organizations to examine research findings and new practices related to neuroscience, adult development, and psychology. Equally vital are advances in the computer software and hardware that will help people act as teams despite geographic and discipline differences" (pp. 16–17).

The use of telecommunications in training applications will surely increase. Networked computers are increasing communications around the world, and global learning organizations use extensive electronic mail networks. Electronic classrooms are also available, allowing ongoing communication between trainees and resource people in distant locations. In sales training programs trainees can perform role playing within a digitally created situation.

Another technology, artificial intelligence, which involves replicating the thought process of the human brain, can observe, guide, and coach users and modify its instructions accordingly. It can adapt to each user's cognitive style, resulting in customized help that corresponds to the needs of each trainee. Training is shorter, faster, more interesting, more applicable, and more motivating because it presents only information needed by the user.

The use of technology to transfer learning throughout the organization is a high priority of many global learning organizations, including Samsung, Xerox, and Singapore Airlines. Corning adds a new twist to technology transfer across locations, whether across the hall or across the ocean. Corning's Bill Whitmore even created a new name, *tecknowledgy transfer*. Tecknowledgy transfer is a process designed to identify the technical experts, capture their knowledge, and then transfer that knowledge to new generations of experts. Corning has made learning technology a powerful tool in enhancing its corporate success on a global scale.

Corporate exemplars. *Federal Express.* Federal Express has made a major commitment to computer-aided training. Since its founding, the company has developed new technologies to "set all aspects of its business apart from its competitors" (Heathman, p.50). Federal Express has made a huge investment in interactive training resources—more than $40 million in 1,200 systems in 800 field locations. Each is stocked with 30 interactive videodisc programs, which have been used to train many of FE's 23,000 couriers and 2,100 customer service employees.

In 1988 Federal Express replaced some of its classroom training programs with a computer-based training system that uses interactive video on workstation screens. The training system can capture and interpret input from learners to determine whether a task is being performed correctly. If a learner makes a mistake, the system recognizes the error, points it out, and shows the proper method.

The interactive video instruction system presents training programs that combine television quality, full-motion video, analog audio, digital audio, text, and graphics using both laser disc and CD-ROM. Learners can interact with the system using a touch screen or keyboard.

Motorola. Motorola was delivering over 450,000 days of training each year to its over 100,000 employees worldwide. Still, Bill Wiggenhorn, Motorola's vice president of training and education, says that the company was falling further and further behind. We couldn't train the workforce fast enough to match the company's investments in manufacturing. It was like trying to go up an escalator that is going down. The long learning cycle time depressed our return of the investment in new technologies.'' To reduce learning time, Motorola used many of the same learning technologies as Federal Express, including computers, software, fiber-optic networks, satellite-linked intelligent classrooms, video teleconferences, and satellite distribution.

QUALITY

Quality is probably the most obvious of all the elements that global learning organizations exhibit because it is an absolute requirement for global business success. The organizations we examine in later chapters of this book universally focus heavily on quality—and several are unqualified leaders in the field. We cannot name every company, but we will name these: Corning, GE, and Xerox have strong reputations for their quality programs. It has become increasingly clear that when companies establish total quality management as a way of life, they are in fact establishing a learning organization. A learning organization takes continuous improvement seriously because one question is never far from the mind of the TQM-focused company: "How can this be done better?" TQM requires that a comprehensive learning approach is present and that everyone is learning continually to do everything better.

Harold McInnes, chairman of AMP, writing in *Electronic Buyers News*, reinforces the point that quality isn't an option. He writes, "There's little doubt that most firms still around at the end of this decade will have reached, or nearly reached, a six-sigma (three defects per million) level in the quality of most of their products and services due to the rising standards imposed by customers and the relentless pressure of global competition. Those companies not fully committed to a six-sigma goal, and that do not have a top priority program of total quality management, will probably not survive—or at best will be relegated to minor niche roles'' (p. 21).

McInnes's words hold great importance for the global learning organization concept. If near-perfect products and service were enough to guarantee worldwide business success, every company could succeed equally. Yet, we know that can't be so. The reason we see an emphasis on quality in each of the successful companies that we visited is that it is an absolute requirement for success. McInnes tells us that this is only the beginning.

Corporate exemplars. *Xerox.* The centerpiece for Xerox's re-emergence as a global leader in the copier industry was its companywide leadership through quality program that began in the mid 1980s. Gary Aslin, now director of Xerox's Document University, attributes the creation of Xerox as a global learning organization to this total commitment to continuous learning and total quality. Over a four-year period, all of Xerox's 110,000 employees worldwide received training for the quality program. The program included understanding the philosophy behind total quality management. A critical element in building learning people was the process Xerox used. Following the training in quality and application on the job, each learner was then responsible for training a successive group of employees, producing a cascading effect that immersed everyone in the new quality culture.

The results of Xerox's commitment to continuous learning and improvement has been impressive. Its highly satisfied customers have increased by over 40 percent and customer complaints have fallen over 60 percent. A recent market research survey ranked Xerox first in five out of six market segments. Xerox has received national quality awards in nine countries and recently received the European Award for Quality. Xerox leadership believes strongly in the interdependence and complementarity of a quality corporate culture and a global learning organization.

Tatung. Another global company that links quality with continuous learning on an organizationwide basis is Tatung. Tatung is a

Taiwan-headquartered corporation with operations in over 87 countries and a diversified manufacturer of electronic, computer, and communications products, as well as industrial equipment and home appliances. At Tatung quality and learning occur through the over 1,200 quality control thinking circles that focus on the improvement of quality in production and after-sale service.

STRATEGY

For many people the most critical element for becoming a learning organization is a deliberate and conscious learning strategy. These organizations consciously decide to make learning a top priority of the organization, to view learning as key to productive competitiveness, and as the *sine qua non* of learning organizations.

Learning should become a continuous, strategically used process, integrated with and running parallel to work. Anticipatory and action learning are built into the mindset of the company and all its people. There is a systems way of thinking to the degree that people see the future benefits and consequences of having a deliberate learning strategy.

All aspects and operations of the company—policy, strategy formation, implementation, evaluation—are consciously structured as a learning process. Systems are established for sharing the learning and applying it to business. Learning becomes an everyday part of the job and is built into all tasks.

Managerial acts are seen as conscious experiments rather than as set solutions. Deliberate small-scale experiments and feedback loops are built into the planning process. Continuous improvement resulting from concerted efforts to learn continuously is built into the very fiber of the organization and into the mindset of all employees.

Corporate exemplar. *Colgate.* An excellent example of an organization that has developed a deliberate strategy of becoming a global learning organization is Colgate-Palmolive. Colgate has a clearly stated strategy for developing organizational capability for continuous learning. It is a process through which "Colgate-Palmolive people continuously expand their capacity to perform, . . . expansive new thinking is nurtured, and . . . people are continuously learning to learn together."

SUPPORTIVE ATMOSPHERE

Global learning organizations are concerned not only about organizational productivity and profits, but also about the quality of their employees' working lives. They fully realize that organizational results are built on happy, productive individuals.

These organizations seek the following quality-of-worklife objectives:

- Development of the full range of human potential.
- Respect for human dignity.
- Tolerance of differences.
- Equity and autonomy.
- A humane and democratic workforce.

These organizations are conscious of the growing pressures of workers to meet family and work obligations, and thus try to be "family friendly" by offering company policies such as flexible work arrangements, dependent care services, and wellness programs. Corning and Royal Bank of Canada have made such programs an integral part of their human resource policy.

Howard Schultz, CEO of Starbucks Coffee Company, has helped his company grow at a compounded annual rate of 80 percent over the past three years. He declares that this success stems from a people-oriented strategy. Shultz says, "Our only sustainable competitive advantage is the quality of our work force. We are in the people development business almost as much as the coffee business."

Linda Morris has developed a model, represented here in Figure 4-2, that demonstrates the critical balance between the needs of the individual (for learning and other aspects of personal development) and those of the organization. To be able to perform work, the organization must continually build the performance capability of both the individual and itself. Performance and performance capability should therefore be viewed as two separate but integrated dimensions ideally in balance.

We find it interesting that several companies we visited symbolize the difference in their understanding of the employee relationship. Honda and PPG call their employees associates. At Tatung, they are called colleagues. Good employees want to do more than simply performing their work, drawing their pay, and going home. Good employees want to contribute to the success of the organization. The

FIGURE 4–2
Balance Model

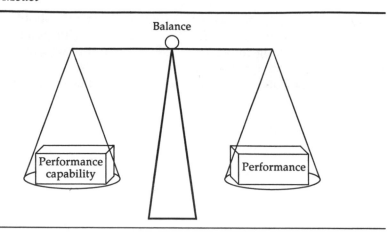

symbolism of being titled an associate or colleague is a step on the road to involvement.

Corporate exemplars. *Carvajal.* Carvajal, founded in 1904 in Cali, Colombia, as a small printing shop, is today a large global corporation of 12,000 employees in 14 countries throughout the Americas. The company has a long tradition of commitment to learning for its people, who are seen as "our most valuable asset." Diego Naranjo Meza, director of the company's Institute for Human Development, says that Carvajal has placed a priority on three key elements in building a learning culture:

- Continuous learning for all employees.
- Emphasis on maintaining and transferring information throughout the organization.
- The development of each person in the organization in an integral, holistic way.

Carvajal sees each individual as a "system of his or her own." That person's environment, family, and background must be considered in understanding and supporting his or her work in the organization. Special efforts are made to develop the entire person through training programs in self-knowledge, learning how to learn and how to be responsible for learning, English language, family life, leadership, entrepreneurship, and other subjects.

A special program for future Carvajal leaders has been established.

Carvajal wants to build leaders who "not only know how to teach and motivate learning, but also can transmit and promote organizational values and principles."

Cray Research. The fluid work environment at Cray Research has to be related to its unique founder, Seymour Cray. Cray has been called brilliant but reclusive. He invented the first supercomputer and founded Cray Research. On the other hand considerable credit must go to Cray Research's CEO John Rollwagen. He is often credited with inventing the environment in which supercomputers can be made ever better. Rollwagen describes the process by saying that he supports this environment not by telling people what to do, but by telling them what he sees. Ever modest, Rollwagen claims that Seymour Cray was very clear about the kind of environment he created for himself. He says, "Seymour never articulated any of it to me. I learned from watching him. I saw how that same environment could be created for other people—so they would function at the same high level as Seymour." People at Cray Research have evolved a statement of their "style." Because Cray Research has a unique atmosphere, it is no surprise it has have evolved a unique statement of what it is and should be like to work there. The Cray Style is reproduced here in Figure 4–3.

TEAMWORK AND NETWORKING.

Effective learning organizations know the importance of working in teams to maximize knowledge and resources. They realize the critical need to collaborate, share, and synergize with resources both inside (teamwork) and outside (networking) the organization. Many global learning organizations are considering the network form of structure, which may include global alliances, informal ties among teams that work across functions, and new ways for employees to share information. Networks use tools such as management information systems and videoconferences. According to Ram Charan, no traditional corporate structure, no matter how decluttered or delayered it is, can muster the speed, flexibility, and focus needed in today's highly competitive marketplace. Networks are faster, smarter, and more flexible than reorganizations or downsizings. A network, in effect, creates the small company inside the large company that is critical for organizational learning and global success. Networks differ from teams or task forces in three ways:

FIGURE 4-3
The Cray Style

At Cray Research, we take what we do very seriously, but we don't take ourselves too seriously.

There is a sense of pride at Cray Research. Professionalism is important. People are treated like and act like professionals. But people are professional without being stuffy.

Cray Research people trust each other to do their jobs well and with the highest ethical standards. We take each other very seriously.

We have a strong sense of quality—quality in our products and services, of course, but also in our financial results and our working environment, and in the people we work with, in the tools we use to do our work, and the components we choose to make what we make.

Economy comes from high value, not from low cost. Aesthetics are part of quality.

We look first to our customers to define Cray Research quality—and we do our best every day to deliver it.

The effort to create quality extends to our shareholders, who invest in us to see a significant return, and to the communities in which we work and live.

The Cray Research approach is informal and nonbureaucratic, but thorough. People are accessible at all levels.

Communication is key. We stop by or call if we can. Keeping people informed is part of everyone's job. People also have fun working at Cray Research. There is laughing in the halls, as well as serious discussion. More than anything else, the organization is personable and approachable, but still dedicated to getting the job done.

With informality, however, there is a sense of confidence. Cray Research people feel that they are on the winning side. They feel successful, and they are. It is this sense of confidence that generates the attitude, "Go ahead and try it; we'll make it work."

Cray Research people like taking responsibility for what they do and thinking for themselves. At the same time, we work together and are proud to share a single mission—to create the most powerful and highest-quality computational tools to solve the world's most challenging scientific and industrial problems.

Because the individual is key at Cray Research, there is a real diversity in the view of what we really are. In fact, Cray Research is many things to many people. Consistency comes in providing those diverse people with the opportunity to fulfill themselves and experience achievement individually and as part of the Cray Research team.

The creativity, then, that emerges from the company comes from the many ideas of individuals who are here and from the teams of Cray Research people who make these ideas into quality products for our customers. And that is the real strength of Cray Research.

- Networks are not temporary.
- They do not only solve problems that have been defined for them, but also take their own initiatives.
- Networks can make substantive operating decisions on their own.

Corporate exemplars. *Armstrong World Industries.* A good example of a global learning corporation using teamwork and networks for competitive success is Armstrong World Industries of Lancaster, Pennsylvania. Armstrong comprises five businesses—flooring, building products, insulation, gaskets, and textiles. In 1989, Armstrong created five cross-border, cross-functional networks as the first step in globalizing its businesses. The global teams regularly hold meetings outside the United States, identify business priorities, and problem-solve for the company.

The building products team has done several things. They visited all the company's European factories and developed sourcing plans to redesign the flow of products between Europe and the United States. They also encouraged headquarters' R&D to tailor new products for the Asian market. This global network also encouraged lower ranking mangers to emulate the network interactions. Global conferences are held regularly. These conferences are intensive sessions in which team members share technical information and operations insights and learn extensively from one another.

To share and react to various technical and management issues, all members take part in regular conference calls. The information flows well because the members have learned to trust each other. Conference calls include discussion of business conditions, of competitors, of service, and new products. For example, the 10-member building products global network conferences every other Monday at 7:00 A.M. Lancaster time. As Henry Bradshaw, an Armstrong vice-president, expresses it, "The more information we share, the more natural it becomes to share it."

Senior management at Armstrong evaluates how well the network is performing. It measures whether behavior is changing. It also measures whether the global networks are producing tangible results in four specific areas:

- Progress on global business projects.
- The quality and frequency of global communication.
- Changes in individual mindsets.
- The global team process.

The results gathered allow top management to learn quickly and to act more decisively. A recent example of learning from the evaluations was the corporate streamlining and simplifying of global reporting relationships.

Blanchard Training and Development. Blanchard Training and Development is a global supplier of training materials. It was founded by Ken Blanchard of *One Minute Manager* fame. Blanchard places a priority on networking and global learning because the evidence is mounting that each year the international business community is becoming a more interrelated and closer-knit entity. BTD has tried to take a long-term approach to building interdependent relationships with its 28 international licensees—not just between itself and the licensees, but between each of the licensees as well. In promoting a learning network, BTD finds that the benefits its licensees derive makes them both a stronger partner in acting in Blanchard's best interest and an eager partner in wanting to be more involved with BTD's international network. By taking this long-term approach to building mutually beneficial relationships, Blanchard is laying the foundation for more effective competition on a global basis in future years.

Dale Truax, president of Blanchard Training and Development International, says, "For most American business there is an impatience for more immediate results that may be due to the detriment of a long-term mutually beneficial relationship that must be developed over time with a changing emphasis and focus as needed, when both parties are ready. In many cases this means starting from a general awareness of possibilities and then over time moving to specific proposals as is appropriate, given the opportunities that evolve. It's also a challenge to keep one's organization involved and to bring management along as international business opportunities evolve. This comes both from having the organization's domestic management focus solely on their problems and opportunities in a domestic market and from being physically and mentally removed from those domestic concerns as an international staff focuses on the rest of the world."

The future direction that BTD would like to take in Blanchard's own network is the same as that the United States must take in its effort to be more of an international partner, that is, to better and more fully integrate BTD's approaches, learnings, expectations, and experiences to create tighter and more mutually beneficial bonds with greater numbers of trading partners. Truax says, "Part of this is simply coming to put aside a certain 'arrogance' that Americans, or American business is *better* than the people and business practices found in other countries. This simply is not case! We must give others the chance to tell us what they do and how they do it and appreciate what we hear and learn to be able to move closer together as equals."

Trading Partners. A primary factor influencing Blanchard's long-term approach to an international network of licensees was the free trade agreements in both Europe and North America. Truax says, "We felt that to get involved as an *insider* with countries as new trade policies evolve would be a preferred way to take advantage of the world's changing economic situation. If we could learn with them as they were learning themselves, we felt it could both help our international position and help us to truly be viewed as a partner as our relations with them solidified."

Global learning aids business success.   Truax says, "The approach we're taking, although it has taken some time and investment, has been fruitful in building our international customer base and related revenues. As we have built and maintained a strong foundation in our international network, it becomes easier both to maintain and to build upon that network with new licensees, new programs, and new opportunities."

Digital.   Digital Equipment Corporation has long been a leader in the global linking and networking of vendors, suppliers, and engineering teams. In 1989 Digital received the prestigious LEAD Award (Leadership and Excellence in the Application and Development of Computer Integrated Manufacturing). The award was given for Digital's successful integration of manufacturing activities spanning the geographic distance from the Pacific Rim throughout the United States and Europe.

The award-winning networking effort was the development of the RA90 Disk Drive program. The program combines new product innovations in recording technology and components with an integrated manufacturing automation system that put Digital to the forefront in performance, capacity, and reliability in hard disk storage devices.

Members from four different units—product engineering, manufacturing, customer service and support engineering, and product management/marketing—were on the team. They worked together from the inception of a development project, through market introduction, and onward through the whole product life cycle. The team made extensive use of electronic communications and data transfer, although it recognized that catching folks for face-to-face meetings was still important. The identity and intensity of team interactions contributed to building a climate of mutual respect and commitment in the group.

Digital has continued to develop its global integration capabilities. Today it integrates multiple contractors, businesses, and globally dispersed plants and suppliers.

VISION

A shared, challenging vision is critical to success as a global learning organization. Peter Senge has rightly noted that one

> . . . cannot have a learning organization without shared vision. Without a pull toward some goal which people truly want to achieve, the forces in support of the status quo can be overwhelming. Vision establishes an overarching goal. The loftiness of the target compels new ways of thinking and acting. A shared vision also provides a rudder to keep the learning process on course when stresses develop . . . . Shared vision fosters risk taking and experimentation (p. 209).

Shared vision is also vital for a would-be learning organization because it provides the focus and energy for learning. Powerful, generative learning occurs only when people are truly committed to accomplishing things that matter deeply to them. Vision causes people to do what they want to do. It should uncover the organization's pictures of the future and should provide meaning and value for everyone.

Jim Gannon, vice president of human resource planning and development for Royal Bank of Canada, underscores the absolute importance of vision for learning as an organization when he says that "visions are what energize the organization"; they are "the dreams that pull us forward."

A learning organization needs to be seen not as a machine, but as a living organism. Much like a human, it can have a collective sense of identity and fundamental purpose. Visions should be exhilarating. They should create the spark and excitement to enable the organization to develop renowned, visionary products.

Corporate exemplar. *Caterair.* Caterair International serves more airlines worldwide than any other airline caterer, with over 22,000 employees operating in 23 countries. Headquartered in Bethesda, Maryland, Caterair recently determined that a clear corporate vision built on corporate values would be the cornerstone of its globally expanding organization. The Caterair vision became an integral part of the company's documents, discussions, and daily life. To be the "airline caterer of choice in the world" involved a commitment to be a global leader by examining every opportunity for growth and a commitment to provide employees with all the necessary tools and resources to deliver quality, consistency, and dependability. The motto of Caterair is "Caterair People Can," and they can only if and because the organization will tolerate no blockage of essential information, drive out fear and mistrust from every corner of the organization, and always strive for world- class standards in quality and service.

Caterair's spirit is summarized thus: "Every improvement by employees will earn recognition; breakthroughs will cause celebration." David Workman, senior vice president of human resources, recounts how Caterair realized that global success depended on the "need to change the essence of how we are learning. We needed a clear mission, vision, and values that would buttress and serve as the foundation of employee development, and provide the energy and enthusiasm needed for organizational learning."

The Caterair vision is achieved only if agreement and strong support for the values underlying and developing that vision are present. And that is very evident at Caterair. The values were developed organizationwide and everyone in the organization has participated in "Mission, Vision, Values" training, discussions, and meetings. Top managers have been trained to facilitate these discussions.

We think Caterair's values are worth examining as potential examples for other organizations. They are listed in Figure 4-4.

FIGURE 4-4
Caterair's Values

Global mindset
- Communicate the fact that the airline business has become a world-as-a-single-market business.
- Every unit is a member of the Caterair global team.
- Remember that one unit's performance affects the success of all other units on the global team.
- Pursuing the world market offers the opportunity to grow and further secure our livelihoods.
- Maintain a Caterair world standard of quality.
- Pursue business opportunities with every airline.
- Look forward to and accept career opportunities throughout Caterair's world.

Continuous improvement
- Communicate the need—the intense competition in the airline business is making our customers demand more from us for the same money.
- Continually improve all that we do and how we do it—not only in big steps, but mostly in lots of little steps.
- Relentlessly pursue perfection—strive for zero defects.
- Don't think that you're the best because it's the enemy of getting better.
- Find ways to prevent problems before they happen.
- Replace "We don't do it that way" with "Let's try."
- Continuous improvement *requires continuous learning.*

FIGURE 4-4 (*continued*)

Empowerment
- Respect our people's knowledge.
- Solicit problem-solving ideas from our people.
- Listen to ideas different from your own.
- Respond in a timely way to 100 percent of people's suggestions.
- Put decision-making power in the hands of the person who knows the most about the task.
- Back up the person to whom you gave the power.
- Find out why a mistake happens, learn from it, and prevent it from recurring.
- Forgive honest mistakes.
- Provide guidance, encouragement and training.

Customer driven
- Being the best in the eyes of customers is our number one job.
- Treat each customer as if he or she is our only customer.
- There is no small customer or small customer base.
- All airline employees are our customers.
- Exceed customer expectations in all we do.
- Solve customer problems . . . *fast!*.
- Prevent problems from recurring.
- Make and meet every customer commitment.
- Do the customer's work as if you were doing it for yourself.
- Recognize improvements that lead to customer satisfaction.

People are our greatest asset
- Treat all people with respect, honor, dignity, and fairness—take care of the people.
- Live the Caterair Guarantee of Fair Treatment.
- Recognize a job well done.
- Help people feel free to ask questions.
- Supply people with the tools they need to do their work.
- Make and meet commitments to all our people.
- Increase our people's knowledge and skills.
- Encourage advancement and promotion.
- Increase confidence, self-esteem, pride, and professionalism.
- Seek out highly motivated people to join our team.

Teamwork
- Teamwork is an attitude, not a collection of players.
- Communicate team goals.
- There are no wins without the team winning.
- Solve problems as a team.

FIGURE 4-4 (*concluded*)

- Recognize team accomplishments, not just individual accomplishments.
- Argue among ourselves but act with one voice.
- Think of the next person down the line as your customer.
- Think of yourself as the customer of the next person up the line.
- Pitch in and help others, even if it's outside your usual work.

THE CRUCIAL INTERLINK

In this chapter we have examined each of the elements that comprise organizational learning. The inner sphere, learning, combined with the organizational learning sphere, describes a learning organization. It is the crucial interlink with the outer global learning sphere that provides the complexity that leads many organizations to failure. In Chapter 5 we will examine global learning, the outer sphere, in detail, and link excellence in the global elements with the standards and with specific corporate examples.

Chapter Five

Six Global Keys to Organizational Success

I n the Global Learning Organization Model, we identified six critical components in the *global* ring: acculturization, borders, globalization, language, leadership, and workforce diversity. Figure 5–1 is a reminder of the Global Learning sphere.

Let's briefly describe and then present some exemplary corporate applications of each component.

ACCULTURIZATION

This element includes the capability of an organization to convey its operations across cultures in an effective, user friendly way. Culture guides the thinking, doing, and living ways of people, is multilayered, and includes practices and values. Practices, including behaviors, symbols, and rituals, are more visible to an outside observer. They are also more easily influenced and changed than the core of culture, which is formed by values and underlying assumptions not easily recognized or understood by outsiders. Values, the inner or deeper part of culture, are less visible but influence significantly all action and thinking.

There are nine interacting factors that create the various cultures. They are religion, education, economics, politics, family, class structure, language, history, and geography. What distinguishes one culture from another is not the presence or absence of these factors, but rather the patterns and practices found within and between these factors. Our Multilayered Culture Model is shown in Figure 5–2.

Clearly our cultural background has a significant effect on how we think, act, are motivated, work, and, of course, learn. Learning habits are an ingrained part of our cultural heritage and are the result of our experiences at home, school, and work, the beliefs and behavior of par-

FIGURE 5–1
Global Learning Organization Model—Global Learning

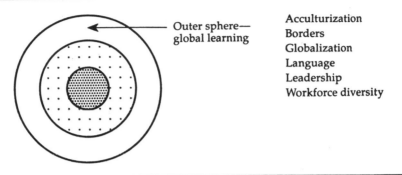

Outer sphere—
global learning

Acculturization
Borders
Globalization
Language
Leadership
Workforce diversity

⁰ Michael Marquardt and Angus Reynolds, 1992

ents, the methods used by our teachers, and the norms of our communities and businesses.

The competent global learning organization is aware of culture's effects on the work and learning habits of its employees from different cultures, and it builds training programs, interrelationships, and structures that enable all employees to participate fully in the learning processes.

Corporate Exemplar. *Motorola.* Perhaps no global learning organization has done more than Motorola to build an organization responsive to the cultural differences of its employees, customers, and vendors. And nowhere is this more evident than in the Global Design and Delivery System of Motorola University. The underlying principle of the Global System is "constant respect for people of all cultures." Says R. S. Moorthy, Manager of the Transcultural Development Center, "We question the wisdom of training and education programs whose instructional design and development focus only on the host (United States) culture and its learning theories."

The goal of all Motorola's learning programs is "to facilitate the transfer of knowledge and skills so that they can be utilized promptly and effectively in the local cultures." Therefore, Motorola's training must fit the culture and be given in the language of the learners. As of October 1992 the Transcultural Development Center had designed and delivered programs in over 30 different countries and cultural settings in some 20 languages including Bulgarian, Byelorussian, Danish, Hebrew, Hungarian, Japanese, Korean, Chinese (Mandarin), Tagalog, Thai, and Ukrainian.

FIGURE 5–2
Multilayered Culture Model

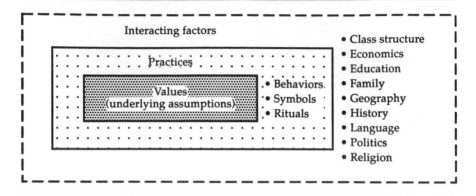

© Michael Marquardt and Angus Reynolds, 1992

The global design and delivery system consists of 14 steps beginning with a comprehensive needs analysis by region, followed by pilot testing, cultural adaptation and translation in each country, and ending only when the in-country local client or customer is satisfied with the cultural and language suitability of the materials and the trainers. All materials are developed and reviewed by cultural anthropologists and local bilingual instructors to meet the learning criteria, objectives, and habits of the local people.

BORDERS

The borders element includes the effective handling of global operations across economic, political, and geographic borders. An example of such a challenge is working with an organization in a government-controlled, planned economy. The mindset is almost impossible for others to understand, much less interact with. (This pattern is still prevalent in much of the world—China, most of Africa, Eastern Europe, parts of Southeast Asia, and the Middle East.) Yet global learning organizations may be required to deal with such organizations in an alliance or as a customer. Sterniczuk and Lis identified several economic, political, and social aspects that affect learning and interactions:

- Hierarchical relationships are critical, and these relationships dominate.

- Shortages of almost all resources exist, owing to monopolistic structures.
- Size or growth of the organization may have little to do with profits or demand.

They make these recommendations when interacting with organizations in such environments:

1. Learn and pay close attention to the political and economic environment.
2. Be aware of the economic illogic and incoherence of the state-managed system.
3. Find the delicate balance between the internal and external frames of reference.
4. Learn the best balance between change and protection of the status quo.
5. Identify ways of gaining participation in the planning, decision making, and collaboration.

Corporate exemplar. *ABB Zamech.* In 1990, Asea Brown Boveri (ABB), the world's largest producer of industrial equipment, formed a joint venture with two Polish companies to create ABB Zamech. The Polish companies lacked the key skills needed to survive in the competitive world economy they were joining. The people of the new organization quickly had to learn how to work together. A new culture of learning, competition, quality, accountability, service, and communications needed to be incorporated into ABB Zamech.

Following a structural reorganization, ABB identified key managers and began an intensive leadership development process. A team of high-level ABB experts from around the world was brought in for frequent short-term consultations. The "tiger team" consisted of authorities in functional areas, such as finance, quality, and marketing, as well as technology specialists and managers with strong restructuring experience.

Most of the Polish managers spoke little or no English, so ABB began an intensive English-language training program. Even more challenging for the new organization was the "second language barrier." This second language was the language of business. To introduce ABB Zamech to basic business concepts, a five-module mini-MBA program was established in Warsaw. The program contained modules on business strategy, marketing, finance, manufacturing, and human resources.

Within 18 months the Polish company was transformed into a center of excellence for the manufacture of gas and steam turbines. Production times were cut in half. And ABB Zamech uses about one third less electricity, gas, and water per unit of production than before.

ABB's Barbara Kux, who coordinated the turnaround process and rapid learning efforts, noted that she had never "seen so much change so quickly. The energy is incredible. These people really wanted to learn." The total commitment on all sides led to tremendous growth in technologies, skills, and responsibility. The results were truly impressive for this new global learning organization.

GLOBALIZATION

An obvious component of a competent global learning organization is its ability to function effectively as a global organization in a global economy. As Jack Welch, chairman and CEO of General Electric, said, "Globalization [of the organization] is no longer an objective, it is an imperative." Ron Allen, chairman of Delta Airlines, puts it another way: "In today's economy, you are either global or you are gone."

Employees need to understand globalization and appreciate how its complexity can enhance, synergize, and yes—even energize—organizational learning. What are the desired capacities of corporate globalization? Michael Porter sees a global corporation as one that can operate as though the entire world was a single entity and that seeks to integrate activities on a worldwide basis to link countries. Global organizations stress global operations over national or multinational operations. They pick the best people available for management, without regard to nationality, and conduct worldwide searches in recruiting personnel. Their headquarters may be located anywhere in the world. Research and development are done wherever the organization can capitalize on costs and technical capabilities. Globalization has happened when the organization has developed a global corporate culture, strategy, structure, and communications process.

Successful global corporations know how to do the following:

- Search the globe for the best opportunities available.
- Place investments around the world to achieve the highest return at the least risk.
- Purchase materials wherever in the world they are the most economical.
- Produce components or finished products wherever in the world this can be done most effectively.

- Market the product or service wherever in the world it can be done most profitably.
- Deliver products or services with global quality and service.
- Provide global quality and content in HRD.

Corporate exemplar. *Honeywell.* Several multinational organizations, including Unilever, Electrolux, NEC, and General Electric, have undertaken many far-ranging structural changes and learning activities to become effective global learning organizations. Probably no company has done as much to globalize itself and build global learners as Honeywell.

Located in Minneapolis, Honeywell is the global leader in industrial control systems. Under the guidance of Michael Bonsignore, president, and Manfred Fiedler, vice-president of human resources, Honeywell has developed its Global Leadership Center, the primary mission of which is to "spread awareness of globalization throughout the organization."

The Global Leadership Center was created after an internal status and needs analysis showed that many people in the organization were unaware of globalization and were confused about the trade-off between global integration and local responsiveness. Global management skills were scarce in the organization. Honeywell's international assignments were not appreciated as a regular part of management development, and globalization efforts varied greatly across affiliates and internal businesses. The training and efforts that did exist were fragmented. For these reasons a companywide program emphasizing communication and education on globalization was deemed critical.

The global center's mission is "to play a lead role in fostering a culture and an environment within Honeywell that promotes a worldwide business perspective, cross-cultural sensitivity, multinational experience, and global management skills at all levels and in all operations." The center provides a wide array of resources to all Honeywell employees. These include workshops, reference materials (including the company newsletter *The Global World*, videos, brochures, cultural facts, "traveler's corner"), mobility assistance (information phone line, adaptability assessment, language training, welcome package, reentry supports), global forums, and exchange programs.

The global center is highly accessible to all Honeywell workers around the world with satellite set-ups in major Honeywell locations. These resources are culturally sensitive and closely tied to business strategies. They use the best expertise around the world, and they are employee focused.

LANGUAGE

Language is a critical aspect of global learning organizations because it is indeed the carrier and conditioner of all cultures. Although English may be the common language of most global corporations, many employees speak other languages that they grew up with. These languages formed much of their thought and behavior patterns.

English is a very direct language. If you drop an object, you say, "I dropped it," implying responsibility and individuality. In Spanish, you say, "It dropped on me," implying passivity, fate, and lack of control. English is a very informal language and there is only one form of the second person for both singular and plural—"you." In many other languages, for example, Vietnamese, there are many counterparts of "you." The use is dependent upon age, gender, relationship, number, status, and so forth. It is easy to see how much more natural it is for an American manager to be informal and egalitarian than it is for a Vietnamese.

Global learning organizations appreciate the importance of language in building organizational structures, systems, and culture for learning. Communication cannot happen across language barriers if English is the only way of talking and thinking. Some of the talent and energy of worker-learners is lost if they must do strategic and major tasks in another language.

Some global learning organizations especially place a high emphasis on teaching senior managers several languages. Sumantra Goshal and Christopher Bartlett call this skill a prerequisite for a global manager. For several global companies, only people with multilingual skills are recruited and promoted. GE's Aircraft Engine unit, for example, will send promising managers overseas only if they learn to speak two other languages. "We want our people to *really* understand the global customer," says John Kinney, manager of the GE Aircraft Engine global training program.

Corporate exemplar. *Samsung.* Samsung, founded in 1938, began overseas operations in 1975 and is now one of the world's top 20 corporations with products ranging from electronics to construction. Samsung has over 235 operations in 55 countries. Samsung prides itself on being able to say, "One can find a Samsung employee virtually everywhere in the world."

With so many employees worldwide, Samsung has made training in languages and cross-cultural skills high priorities for managers. Each year over 200 present and potential managers take part in a year-long development program to prepare themselves as "regional specialists.'' The venues are in Africa, Asia, Europe, and the Americas. Aside from language training, the managers have an unfixed schedule to travel freely and meet people to learn about their customs, history, and society. Jong-Tae Kang, director of Samsung's magnificent new HRD center, cites the goal of this program as enabling ''our employees to understand cultures and people deeply, and thereby give Samsung an ability to work together with them for mutual prosperity.'' All employees are encouraged to have a ''strong sense of belonging to a global company located all around the world.'' With the ever-increasing number of non-Korean employees, the global managers ''understand the importance of global learning for corporate success.'' Part of Samsung's ''spirit'' (core values) is being an exemplary global corporate citizen, contributing to global prosperity, and giving top priority to the development and learning of its people

LEADERSHIP

Leaders in global organizations guide and energize staff who can learn and productively operate in the fast-moving and interdependent global markets of the 1990s. These organizations will depend as never before on the capacity of corporate executives who can promote organizational learning and feedback across borders, and on their ability to distribute ownership of the strategy across the entire organization.

Leaders must contribute to the creation of a corporate culture and a managerial mindset that promotes international cooperation and the flow of information throughout the organization worldwide. Leaders must devote themselves to creating an environment in which organizational learning can flourish and where the worldwide organization is involved in the continual search for learning improvement and competitive advantage.

As Manfred Fiedler of Honeywell says, ''Global leadership does not come simply by announcement. It needs the passion for world-class global excellence throughout the whole organization and a mindset that is comfortable with dealing in a global economic environment. The pursuit of global leadership requires unconditional top management commitment and significant investment. All financial costs must be considered as the inevitable price for continued competitiveness in a global marketplace.''

Corporate exemplar. *AMP.* AMP, headquartered in Harrisburg, Pennsylvania, is the undisputed heavyweight of electrical and electronic connectors, commanding about 18 percent of the $17 billion-a-year world market. AMP won nearly 300 patents in 1992, ranking in the top 20 among U.S. corporations. It puts 9 percent of sales into R&D—more than twice the U.S. average.

AMP established its international presence in Japan as early as 1957. Still, its executives believed that their managers lacked the global leadership qualities needed to build its success in an increasingly competitive global market. In 1992 AMP began an extensive program to develop what it called "globe-able leaders." These leaders must "demonstrate notable mastery of identified global business skills, and the internalization of key globalization concepts, and global competitive and organizational dynamics as well as be able to function effectively corporatewide anywhere in the world."

Among the globe-able competencies AMP managers must have are these:

- The ability to describe clearly the forces behind the globalization of business.
- The ability to recognize and connect global market trends, technological innovation, and business strategy.
- The ability to outline issues essential to effective strategic alliances.
- The ability to frame day-to-day management issues, problems, and goals in a global context.
- The ability to think and plan beyond historical, cultural and political boundaries, structures, systems, and processes.
- The ability to create and effectively lead worldwide business teams.
- The ability to help AMP to adopt a functionally global organization structure.

The AMP managers received a variety of development programs. These included briefings, global business simulations, videos, team learning activities, case studies, analysis tools, and consultations with global experts. The aim was to gain the "global perspectives, knowledge base, and skill sets" AMP determined necessary to long-term success in the global marketplace.

Global leadership workshop topics comprised this agenda:

- Globalization 101: Concepts and Realities.
- Global Leadership in the 90s.
- Cross-Cultural Skills.

- Key Management Issues in the Americas, in the New Europe, and in Asia and the Pacific Rim.

All managers are expected to remain current in global leadership areas by reading from an extensive globe-able bibliography of books and professional journals, published from around the world (*not just the United States*).

WORKFORCE DIVERSITY

Workforce diversity is about synergizing the diverse global workforce. The work force has become increasingly more diverse. In most global corporations, most of the total work force is composed of nationalities other than that of headquarters staff.

Geert Hofstede, who studied thousands of employees in over 40 countries for the past 20 years, states that the national culture explains over 50 percent of the differences in the behavior and attitude of employees. This is more than the differences resulting from professional roles, age, gender, or race.

These differences do not go away if one is employed in a global corporation. Andre Laurant discovered that the impact of culture was greater in multinational corporations than in domestic ones. As a matter of fact, a multinational environment causes people to cling ever more tightly to their own cultural values.

Global learning organizations develop programs and activities so that cultural diversity can become a strong plus and provide synergy, and not a dissipation of energy. Digital, DHL, and GE make cultural diversity training a high priority. 3M, with over 300 managers working outside their home country, has profited immensely from the cultural synergy in the corporation. The 3M staff includes an Italian as the CEO of the Japanese subsidiary, a British CEO in Spain, and a Canadian in Singapore. To increase these cultural benefits even more, a cultural synergy task force has been positioned to explore "how we can work together more effectively with our cultural differences."

IT'S NOT ALWAYS A SMALL WORLD

This is the end of our review of learning organizations and our introduction of the Global Learning Organization Model. We also examined the model's elements and cited examples from organizations that stand-out in each. Our model, like all models, is descriptive—not pre-scriptive. It is simply a representation of what is.

In Part II we will bring together what we have learned to suggest formulations for success as a global learning organization. There are plenty of problems to sort through. Chapter 6, Obstacles and Challenges, discusses the hurdles that must be surmounted to succeed.

II

BECOMING A GLOBAL LEARNING ORGANIZATION

Chapter Six

Obstacles and Challenges

B ecoming a global learning organization is a far from easy task because we are considering the multiple, interactive dynamics of three different spheres:

- Individuals and groups
- Organization systems and behavior
- The global environment

TALES OF WOE

"It's a cold, hard world out there" is the advice that has been offered by parents to children since time immemorial—and they weren't even talking about global business and becoming a global learning organization! It is difficult to come by printable stories of business that didn't go well. Here are a few glimpses how it really is.

On managing. Hector Veloso, president of Guangmei, Beatrice's joint venture in China, gave vent to his global organization frustrations in an artfully worded article for an official Chinese publication. Velasco's comments, reported in Hong Kong's *China Daily* were as follows: "Managing a joint venture in China, takes a positive outlook on life, patience, a healthy sense of humor, a willingness to learn, and a very understanding wife and family . . . . It's not so much that there are no systems in China, because there are. But it is necessary to modify existing ones to produce the desired results."

On changing. General Motors, one of the biggest multinationals in the world, has certainly had its share of difficulties. Yet the basic lesson in the GM story is about change. It would be easy to say that GM's problems are inevitable due to its sheer size—and that these problems must be shared by other overgrown American companies such as Sears and IBM. That would be misleading. Size alone is not the problem. The key, discussed throughout this book, is simply being able to learn and to change.

"Any rigidity by an automobile manufacturer, no matter how large or how well established, is severely penalized in the market." That sounds supportive of our point, but who said it? Alfred P. Sloan, GM's chief architect, wrote those words in his 1964 book, *My Years With General Motors*. Sloan went on to warn, "No company ever stops changing . . . for the present management, the work is only beginning." Time has proven him right.

On starting a new business. In his appropriately titled book, *Beijing Jeep: The Short, Unhappy Romance of American Business in China*, Jim Mann discusses the precarious future of American business in the Middle Kingdom. He chronicles the deal from hell. Beijing Jeep starts out badly in Las Vegas, where AMC executives invited their Chinese counterparts to the company's annual dealer show. The Chinese stormed out, offended by the show's Hollywood glitter (the Beach Boys, gambling, girls jumping out of Jeeps).

Mann follows the AMC executives, as well as employees of other large and small Western companies, as they quickly learned that the Chinese market was not theirs for the taking. He tells the story of their painful, often absurd, misadventures in a country inherently suspicious of foreigners. Mann describes the Chinese officials who played the Western companies to their own advantage, acquired valuable new technology, and eventually outcapitalized the capitalists. He also explains how some of the world's savviest executives completely misjudged the business climate and fell victim to stalled negotiations, stonewalling, nonconvertible profits, and often-revised contracts. Mann's book is a only snapshot in time. It ends with a startling account of the rush to leave a Beijing under siege. Life goes on and those days are receding into the past. Still, one can only wonder how many Beijing Jeep stories have never been told. An equally frank look at IBM's departure from India would make good reading—and also serve as a hair curler!

CAUTION SIGNS

Hiroshi Wagatsuma, the author of *Nihon-jin to America-jin Koko ga Dai Chigai* is right. His book is very popular in Japan. The title might be translated freely as "Japanese and Americans are Completely Different!" The truth goes much further than that— "we are *all* different." That may not sound as pleasant as saying that we are all the same, but it is far more accurate. The problem pointed out by Wagatsuma's book is that, although Japanese know that they and Americans are very different, the Americans love to believe that they are the same as the Japanese—and everybody else!

Willingness to work from a zero base of total difference will go a long way toward success. You don't have to leave your own backyard to see people who don't understand their suppliers, customers, or even their employees. They aren't going to succeed globally *either*.

Learning activity is the sole focus of Angus Reynolds' and Abdulhamid Al Romaithy's SUCCESS model. One purpose of the model is to serve as a descriptive analog of reality. Its prime purpose is to shock the reader into perceiving the potential level of complexity that must be mastered for success in global learning situations. Its relevance here is to demonstrate the high complexity we can easily observe with a close look at one global encounter. Reynolds and Len Nadler describe the model as composed of cells that represent factors in an international learning situation. Each cell represents a possible global HRD situation involving two countries at one point in time. For example, the cell "HAT" is the intersection of the Host, Area, and Training dimensions. The combinations of factors result in 81 cells to represent the potential different contexts of one global learning event. The result is a $3 \times 3 \times 3$ cube with exactly the same appearance as a Rubik's Cube. There are 81 cells. The cube is shown in Figure 6-1.

Time is also a consideration. The components of time are before, during, and after. These represent the periods in relationship before the expatriates' arrival in the host country, during the stay, and after departure. This represents 243 (3×81) possibilities for one particular project involving two countries. Reynolds and Nadler admit that they do not believe there *are* 240 possibilities on every given project. They believe that there must be many more than that! The possibilities with third-country nationals and truly multinational projects are obviously much greater.

Change.   To produce change, to transform the existing realities, to become a global learning organization is not unlike the metamorphism that a caterpillar endures in becoming a butterfly. There are many changes, surprises, and challenges to make the transition. The first step is to be aware of and recognize the real obstacles and challenges faced by companies seeking to become global learning organizations.

FIGURE 6–1
Global Learning at a Single Point in Time

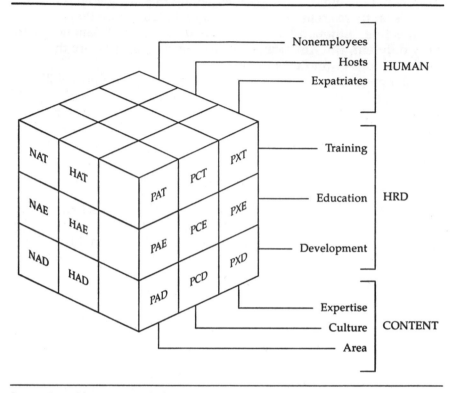

Source: Reynolds, Angus, *Technology Transfer.* Used by permission.

INHERENT LEARNING DISABILITIES OF ORGANIZATIONS

Let's begin by looking at the seven myths of learning organizations identified by Peter Senge. They are the attitudes that cause organizations to have learning disabilities so severe that most corporations die before they reach the age of 40.

Myth # 1: I am my position.   This learning disability occurs in confusing one's job title with the purpose of the organization. Sometimes people in the organization focus only on their positions, have little interest or concern for others, or do not feel responsible for the results produced when various positions interact. They wave off disappointing results as "someone somewhere screwed up." Organizational responsibility and team learning can never happen under those circumstances.

Myth # 2: The enemy is out there—or in here. There is a natural tendency for most of us to find someone or something outside of ourselves to blame when things go wrong. In many organizations, this tendency is elevated to a commandment: "Thou shalt always find an external agent to blame." Manufacturing blames marketing. Marketing blames personnel. Personnel blames engineering. All of them blame the Japanese or government regulators or banks. They blame everyone but themselves.

Myth # 3: The illusion of taking charge. To ensure that an organization is not too passive, it often takes an ill-advised stand of rushing in to handle a problem or crisis. Hasty action may prove to be much more costly than carefully and systematically analyzing the whole situation, and seeing how organizationwide wisdom might resolve the problem. The disability is thinking that an aggressive reaction is the same as being proactive.

Myth # 4: The fixation on events. As individuals and as organizations, we are conditioned to see life as a series of events, each of which has a single, obvious cause. Organizations focus on last month's sales in China, who's been promoted to the marketing post in Germany, or the delay in delivering the product to the partner in Egypt. These events distract organizations from seeing "the long-term patterns of change that lie behind events and from understanding the causes of those patterns" (p.21). The main threats to organizational survival and success do not come from sudden events. They arise out of gradual processes—erosion of the educational system, decline in design quality, ecological decay, or worker expectations (and other forces identified in Chapter 1).

Myth # 5: The boiled frog parable. If you place a frog in boiling water, it will immediately hop out. However, if you place the frog in water at room temperature and gradually increase the temperature, the frog will do nothing, seemingly enjoying himself, becoming gradually groggier, until he is boiled. Why? Because, like most organizations with learning disabilities, the frog's internal apparatus for sensing threats is geared to sudden changes in the environment. Slow, gradual changes don't set off any alarms. Learning to perceive gradual changes calls for the ability to slow down—see the subtle, as well as the dramatic.

Myth # 6: The delusion of learning from experience.   Granted, the most powerful learning does come from experience. But, when the consequences of that experience are in the distant past or in the distant future, the organization may never directly experience the consequences of its essential decisions. The most critical decisions in organizations may have systemwide consequences that can easily stretch over many years. Disabled organizations do not recognize when the consequences of their actions are too far away in time to teach them anything.

Myth # 7: The myth of the management team.   The so-called management team in most organizations tends too often to be fighting for their own turf. And they achieve the appearance of being a cohesive team only by squelching disagreement and reaching watered-down compromises. When they face complex issues, they find inquiry threatening. The result is what Chris Argyris calls "skilled incompetence"—management teams incredibly proficient at keeping themselves from learning.

Learning disabilities are tragic in children, says Senge, but they are "fatal in organizations," causing most organizations to die young, never having become a smart learner and therefore having remained uncompetitive in the global marketplace.

THE INTRINSIC DIFFICULTY

To develop a global learning organization, the organization itself must make a dramatic and extremely difficult shift, because the very fabric of the organization—the design of work, the work environment, technology, reward systems, structures, and policies—all must change. This process is intrinsically difficult, given human and organizational nature.

In our recent travels we have found that in Asia, Europe, and the United States many companies have recently decided to become learning organizations. Naturally, we applaud that decision. We also hope that, in every case, the conclusion was not reached too lightly, simply because becoming a learning organization would, in some nebulous (or magical) way, be beneficial.

Those organizations that have succeeded have found it very beneficial. As far as we know, none of them found it easy. The difficulty of making the required shifts in the fabric of the organization should not be underestimated. The competence level of each individual, as well as of the entire organization, must rise. And, of course, organizational change in and of itself is neither synonymous with, nor adequate to guarantee, organizational learning.

ORGANIZATIONAL BARRIERS TO LEARNING

Organizations—structures, people, systems—may either help or hinder learning. Too often, they hinder organizational learning and put up barriers through some or all of the following means:

- Bureaucracy
- Competitive atmosphere
- Control
- Poor communications
- Poor leadership
- Resource utilization
- Rigid hierarchy
- Size

Bureaucracy. Often, as corporations go global and continue to grow, they go from entrepreneurial to bureaucratic. Policies, regulations, and forms replace energy, creativity, and excitement. Busywork becomes more important than thinking and planning. Too much learning will only make the bureaucrats more restless and frustrated. It is much easier to refer to the policy manual than have to make a separate, new decision on every new situation, idea, or request that arises. In bureaucracies, "whack the gopher" is a popular game. Managers or fellow employees hammer down little gopher heads of differences or innovativeness that appear above the holes of the gameboard. Peter DeLisi of Digital sees this game as a metaphor for many organizational cultures that he has encountered.

Competitive atmosphere. A critical ingredient in learning organizations is the degree of collaboration and teamwork existing in organizations. Too often, however, organizations support excessive individuality and competition. Ray Stata, CEO of Analog Devices, points out the difficulty of building teamwork when he stated, "It's hard to win minds to the new importance of teamwork . . . and break down the perception that a commitment to teamwork somehow means a compromise of the individual's primacy. In the American culture, especially, it's very difficult to get people to accept their interdependence." To get them to seek collaboration with business units in other countries is sometimes well nigh impossible.

Control. Organizations love control. It is more reassuring; it offers fewer risks and more opportunity for determining where rewards and recognition will reside. Giving power to others can complicate matters, make decision making more difficult, and be more emotionally draining. Control of information, decisions, people, and technology can be a "high" for those in control, but it is always a "low" for organizational learning.

Poor communications. Communication between two individuals is difficult. Messages might not be sent or received well, with either person perhaps not caring enough to transmit or receive. Time spent on "telephone tag" with filters and unconscious biases are just a few of the impediments to effective and efficient information flow. These difficulties are multiplied by the thousandfold hurdles of organizational life. Now put all this in the global environment—distances, language, cultural values, and communication practices. It becomes almost natural for global organizations to have miserable communications. Too many organizations are stuck with rigid vertical communication structures, narrow listening skills, delayed feedback, and information that is difficult to access. Vital learning is distorted, misrouted, or concealed.

A 1991 *Harvard Business Review* worldwide survey of business leaders revealed that less than 20 percent of respondents share significant strategic information with their employees. An astounding 25 percent say they never share information with customers.

The information flow through middle management in some global corporations is so thick that, as one corporate executive put it, "even a Roto-Rooter couldn't get through to the staff below." And yet without good communications, organizations cannot get the information, the knowledge, and the enthusiastic support needed to become a learning organization.

Poor leadership. Leaders should be the models of continuous learning and should encourage and reinforce learning among their employees. However, the opposite is often the case. Traditional corporate leaders rarely attend learning activities, either within or outside the organization. They do not spend time reading the literature, benchmarking what the best companies are doing, or taking the time to promote and support staff learning. Rewards and promotions are for activity and organizational output—not for how much employees have educated themselves or analyzed mistakes for learning purposes.

Resource utilization. Many organizations have an abundance of information; they are literally drowning in it. But either the management information people do not want to or know how to disseminate it or the staff is not interested or motivated to seek and use it. Organizations have created a reward and punishment system where it is better to say "I didn't know" than to say "I took a risk and misapplied the information." Global, multicultural corporations sometimes have managers who underutilize the knowledge and skill of people of other cultures because "nothing brilliant can come from foreigners." Also, many of these people are "so doggone quiet, never volunteering ideas or information, unless you ask them directly."

Rigid hierarchy. A major organizational learning barrier is the hierarchy in which every bit of information, every decision, and every "good" idea has to go up and down the layers of management. To protect their status and turf, the hierarchy seeks to avoid risks, confrontation, and challenges. Power stays in the hands of a few people and is not shared, at least in matters of high importance. And in global companies, of course, these leaders feel that it is even more important that all senior positions remain in the hands of headquarters nationals.

Market power, according to Tom Peters, is inversely proportional to the number of layers of bureaucracy. The bureaucratic, vertically integrated firms grow sluggish, cut themselves off from innovation, and cannot shift gears quickly.

Size. We see "too big" size as one of the chief barriers to organizational learning. There is often an indirect correlation between the size of the organizations and the amount of organization learning. Small organizations generally learn much better and quicker, although they may have fewer resources, such as R&D people, information technology, and HRD personnel. Global conglomerates must work much harder in order not to become stagnant with overweight and oversize.

INSUFFICIENT ORGANIZATIONAL CAPACITY

Robert Shaw and Dennis Perkins point out that companies need to overcome three organizational deficiencies in the process of becoming a learning organization. These are the insufficient capacity to reflect and interpret, transfer and disseminate learning, and act.

Insufficient capacity to reflect and interpret. The organization may be experiencing symptoms, such as denial of problems, acting on partial information, and exploring only a limited set of choices. If it cannot correctly interpret the consequences of internal and external factors in relation to organizational outcomes, it suffers from this insufficiency. Among the potential causes are performance pressures, competency traps (prisoners of what has worked in past), or the absence of learning forums that encourage reflection and help with the complex task of interpreting outcomes.

Insufficient capacity to transfer and disseminate learning. Symptoms of this incapacity are ignorance of problems, ignorance of possible solutions, and redundancy of effort. Potential causes of this organizational learning deficiency are the presence of intergroup boundaries, the myth of uniqueness and superiority over anyone else, and narrow bandwidths for acceptable information exchange.

Insufficient capacity to act. One symptom of the incapacity to act is an organization's lack of experimentation with new approaches. In this case, organizational members embrace standard operating principles and procedures. They take for granted the assumptions underlying those principles and rarely challenge them. A second symptom is the inability to implement solutions. The potential causes for the incapacity to act include the presence of too many priorities, bias toward activity versus results, and members' perception that they are powerless anyway.

UP THE GLOBAL LEARNING ORGANIZATION LADDER

We have examined the major obstacles and challenges of becoming a learning organization. Now, in Chapter 7, we can explore the stages or levels that companies pass through on their path toward being a fully functioning global learning organization.

Chapter Seven

Stages in the Development of Global Learning Organizations

N ancy Adler suggests that corporations typically undergo four conceptually distinct, progressively more complex phases as they evolve from domestic to global status. These are shown in Figure 7-1.

In phase I, the domestic phase (in which fewer companies now exist except in some service areas), companies operate on domestic terms and focus solely on domestic markets. These companies have relatively few competitors and are structurally centralized. The perspective is generally ethnocentric and cultural sensitivity is comparatively unimportant. Training and learning programs are built around preparing staff to work effectively in the local, domestic workplace.

International, or phase II, companies are those that begin to export their products or services abroad. Usually in such companies international human resource development activities focus only on the small group of expatriate managers involved directly in foreign operations. Structurally, the company is decentralized and often forms a single international division for its foreign operations. The corporate strategy is multidomestic. Cultural sensitivity begins to be very important.

During phase III, the multinational phase, companies focus on least-cost production with sourcing, manufacturing, and marketing worldwide. The parent company operates with a centralized view of strategy, technology, and resource allocation. But at this stage decision making and customer service shift to the national level for marketing, selling, manufacturing, and competitive tactics. There are many competitors, and profit margins are low. Products and services are standardized, and the basic orientation is price. Learning programs and skills become increasingly important, and there is a greater interaction across cultures and functions.

FIGURE 7–1
Domestic to Global Corporate Evolution

Corporate Activities	Phase I Domestic	Phase II International	Phase III Multinational	Phase IV Global
Competitive Strategy	Domestic	Multidomestic	Multinational	Global
Importance of world business	Marginal	Important	Extremely important	Dominant
Primary orientation	Product or service	Market	Price	Strategy
Product/ service	New, unique standardization	More standardized	Completely customized	Mass-commodity
	Product engineering emphasized	Process engineering emphasized	Engineering not emphasized	Product and process engineering
Technology	Proprietary	Shared	Widely shared	Instantly and extensively shared
R&D/sales	High (10–14%)	Decreasing	Very low	High
Profit margin	High	Decreasing	Very low	High
Competitors	None	Few	Many	Significant (few or many)
Market	Domestic (small)	Multidomestic (large)	Multinational (larger)	Global (largest)
Production location	Domestic	Domestic and primary markets	Multinational, least cost	Global, least cost
Exports	None	Growing, high potential	Large and saturated	Imports and exports
Structure	Centralized (Functional divisions)	Decentralized (Functional with International division)	Centralized (Multinational lines of heteroarchy business)	Centralized and decentralized (Global alliance)
Cultural sensitivity	Unimportant	Very important	Somewhat important	Critically important
With/whom	No one	Clients	Employees	Employees and clients
Organizational level	No one	Workers and clients	Managers	Executives

In phase IV, the global phase, the corporation operates globally. Global thinking and global competencies become critical for survival. The company is constantly scanning, organizing, and reorganizing its resources and capabilities so that national or regional boundaries are not barriers to potential products, business opportunities, and manufacturing locations. Companies send their best, fast-track managers and senior executives for global assignments. Cultural sensitivity becomes critically important as do language skills. Products are mass customized. Imports as well as exports are part of the company's operations for manufacturing and sales. There are globally coordinated strategies, global structures, and a global corporate culture. Global learning becomes essential to remain competitive. Developing the thinking globally and acting locally mindset (a Samsung motto) is integral to operations and interactions.

THE GLOBAL LEARNING CURVE

To aid organizations in identifying their location on the road to corporate globalization, Bren White, Mike Marquardt, and Quentin Englerth have developed the global learning curve shown in Figure 7–2. The curve overlays key corporate events, activities, and strategies on Adler's four phases. As the figure shows, firms often begin their ascent toward global status by international travel and then begin to export and get involved in international law, tax, and finance issues. As a firm enters the multinational phase, it encounters new marketing quality, service, and telecommunications systems. In order to truly arrive in the global phase, a corporation transforms its structure, policies, organizational dynamics, and HRD activities. Most importantly, and with greatest difficulty, it transforms its corporate culture.

Of course, not all companies systematically and clearly traverse across each of the phases. Also, companies may operate in phase I (domestic) for some corporate activities (such as personnel) and be in phase IV (global) for other corporate activities, such as technology. As this mixed-corporate evolution exists, so also exists dysfunction and inefficient results, and finally economic downfall. Therefore, the need for organizational learning is critical, to assist and lead corporations in the journey toward globalization.

STAGES IN THE DEVELOPMENT OF LEARNING ORGANIZATIONS

In their study *The Learning Organization: A Review of Literature and Practice*, Alan Jones and Chris Hendry identified four phases of development for learning organizations:

- Foundation
- Formation

FIGURE 7-2
Global Learning at a Single Point in Time

- Global corporate culture
- Multilingual capability

Global culture
Phase IV
- Global cultural skills
- Global career planning
- Globalized training
- Global organization dynamics
- Global recruiting and assignment
- Globalized functions
- Global policies

Multinational culture
Phase III
- Global structure
- Global management development
- Global leadership
- Global market strategies
- Expatriation/Repatriation

International culture
Phase II
- World class quality and customer service
- Multinational marketing
- Global telecommunications and information systems
- International selling

Domestic culture
Phase I
- International negotiations
- International law, tax, and finance
- Export tactics
- International travel

- Continuation
- Transformation

It is important to note that organizations do not pass as a whole from one phase to another. In addition, one part of an organization may be far more advanced in its learning capacity than another.

Phase 1: Foundation stage. The initial characteristic of a learning organization, and the foundation for becoming a learning organization, is one that creates the habit of learning and generates enthusiasm for it. This is no small task, as we and most other writers have warned. For the organization, this foundation level of learning has two components:

- Basic individual learning.
- Creating new learning that moves employees' perceptions along and out of the mode of thinking of work and of learning as they do at present.

At the foundation phase of becoming a learning organization, the organization has the following concerns:

- Learning how to learn.
- Developing a natural instinct for learning.
- Creating motivation and confidence in learning.
- Showing that investment in learning can produce success of various kinds.

Typical activities include learning and working in groups and teams, personal development skill training, formal training in how to do specific jobs, and providing learning to master programs.

Measures of achievement for the foundation phase are as follows:

- The organization shows an outward commitment to learning and training.
- The training content addresses not only specific organizational production or service goals, but also focuses on commitment to personal development.
- Motivation is generated in individuals and groups by the training and learning provided, as well as the desire to continue with it.
- There is a collective opinion that training and learning pay because of personal and organizational improvements.
- Use is made of a personal portfolio of learning activities.

Phase 2: Formation/transition stage. The second stage is concerned with encouraging and developing skills for self-learning and self-development. It is also about acquiring the skills to work effectively in project teams and in a variety of situations. At this stage, the learner begins to learn more about the organization as a whole and develops a coherent, developed, and meaningful view of the organization and what it does. The organization begins to make tougher learning demands on the employee, and the employee looks to the organization to provide resources and support and information on what is available for new and added learning. Activities at this phase include the following:

- Jobs that enable the employee to gain experience of team and group work.
- Learning through job rotation and shadowing.
- More experiential learning.
- Training based on individual learning needs and styles.
- Training on how to meet future requirements of the organization.

Phase 3: Continuation stage.   In the continuation stage, the learner and organization become self-motivated, confident, innovative, and independent. In doing so, learning becomes more crucial, as the challenge is to find out how learning can be accelerated for the organization and each individual and each group of individuals. The organization is concerned with learning how to ask important questions about what is done, how it is done, when it is done, and why. People have developed a much greater ability to find answers. The organization has provided the needed vision, values, structures, technology, communication channels, and climate. Activities appropriate for this stage include the following:

- Alternative work practices.
- Development of autonomous work groups.
- Elimination of demarcation lines vertically and horizontally.
- Job enlargement.
- Organizationwide career plans.
- Shared responsibilities.

There is a greater capacity to accommodate change; change is viewed as a means of help instead of a hindrance.

Phase 4: Transformation stage.   The transformation stage is about thinking and doing things differently. It is concerned with making a complete change in form, appearance, and character. It also includes changing structures, attitudes, and perceptions; learning how to have different values; and learning how to think differently by absorbing local, national, and global cultural influences. Among the activities in the global learning organization in the transformation stage are the following:

- Change in work practices and experimentation with alternative work practices—work arrangements may start to fit the job to be done and this in turn influences recruitment, so there may be more use of outplacing, part-time workers, contract working, and flexible days, weeks, and even years.

- Concern for ethical issues related to product, service, and their production and influence.
- Everyone in the organization learning to ask, to go after the root causes of problems.
- Everyone sees the organization as a whole, and there is a willingness to learn from and with others.
- Extensive use of project modeling, simulation, and other envisioning activities.
- Flat management structures, with mangers being developed to become coaches and facilitators instead of directors of activities.
- Greater emphasis on leadership and group entrepreneurship, both based on a better understanding of what creativity is and how it can be learned and managed.
- Learning focuses on managing personal change and self-assessment.
- Organizational changes in structures and systems through the influence of technology, social change, and globalization factors.
- The organization adapts to newly emerging social and human values.
- The organization focuses on how business is acquired and assets are managed so that corruption does not happen, ethical standards are high, and strategies support community initiatives for the enhancement of people at large. (For example, Siemans has recently opened what it calls a "green" factory, where every effort to conserve energy is included in the design, electrical systems, water use, and so on).
- The organization looks at its competitive advantage not simply in commercial and monetary terms, but in social and ethical ones as well, with concern for its own people and society generally.
- The organization measures and values inputs as well as outputs.
- The social and ethical dimension underpins all organizational activity, with an emphasis on corporate responsibility.

- The whole organization is committed via personal involvement.
- Thinkers and doers come together.
- Time is given for everyone to reflect and think.

A transformative shift is ultimately fundamental and necessary for all learning organizations. It involves "readdressing the basic purpose, values, and vision of an organization and of work itself." When this transformation occurs, people will not only perform different tasks, but also "speak differently, assume different roles, and see themselves in different relationships with one another." Linda Morris gives some examples: emphasis will shift from objectives to outcomes, from testing to goal attainment, from information dissemination and recall to pattern recognition and goal attainment, and from evaluating to valuating.

ORGANIZATION BUILDING

Awareness of the process of organizational building can provide some insights on what steps, strategies, and tactics in the following two chapters might be most useful and advantageous for application. In Chapter 8 we will explore the various ways to develop organizational learning capacity.

Chapter Eight

Developing Organizational Capacity for Global Learning

W e don't believe that a manual can be written entitled *50 Ways to Create a Learning Organization* or *Creating a Learning Organization in 30 Days*. There are no such unambiguous, easy, and universally applicable steps to becoming a learning organization. If there is one principle that is obvious to learning organizations, it is that learning organizations are never fully "there," having reached perfection. As Chris Hendry says, "There is no nirvana for learning organizations." Learning organizations are, by definition, in the process of continual change.

Second, it is important to remember, that there is not a single, reliable way of becoming a global learning organization. Each organization must develop a structure and style that is best suited to its own people, history, skill base, technology, mission, and culture. Watkins and Marsick refer to it as "sculpting" the organization in the way that will best "release the inner potential of its technology, people, and resources."

Finally, learning organizations are indeed possible. In some ways they are natural since as Peter Senge declares, "Deep down, we are all learners. It is not only our nature to learn, but we love to learn." And because we are the essence of the organization, we can make learning the essence of organizations.

Therefore, what we will present in this and the next chapter are possibilities, not prescriptions. It is for you to determine what will work best in your organization. We will begin by providing 13 possible steps you can take to transform, your organization into a learning organization. These are listed in Figure 8-1.

FIGURE 8–1
Action Steps for Building the Organization's Capacity to Learn

1. Transform the individual and organizational image of learning.
2. Create knowledge-based partnerships.
3. Develop and expand team learning activities.
4. Change the role of managers.
5. Encourage experiments and risk taking.
6. Create structures, systems, and time to extract learning.
7. Build opportunities and mechanisms to disseminate learning.
8. Empower people.
9. Push information throughout the organization and to external associates (customers, vendors, suppliers, and so forth).
10. Develop the discipline of systems thinking.
11. Create a culture of continuous improvement.
12. Develop a powerful vision for organizational excellence and individual fulfillment.
13. Root out bureaucracy.

STEPS TO CREATING A GLOBAL LEARNING ORGANIZATION

Transform the Individual and Organizational Images of Learning

A clear and key strategy in moving toward a learning organization is changing the image (Senge's term is *mental model*) that most people have about learning. People tend to look at learning through the mental model of their past—school benches, discipline, control, memorization, drills, and credentials. Jim Gannon told us that Royal Bank's reluctance to use the term ''learning organization'' is caused by the negative associations employees had with their school learning experiences. The mental model for learning organizations must be revisited with feelings of energy, excitement, business success, personal responsibility, fun, integration, sharing, and personal and organizational growth. Once this image of learning is established, individuals and organizations will want to jump quickly on the bandwagon. In addition, workers need to think of themselves as not just positions and boxes within the organization, but, as Charles Savage calls them, *knowledge contributors*. That's how people in Carvajal, CNN, Honda, and other successful global learning organizations see themselves.

Create Knowledge-Based Partnerships

Encourage everybody in the organization to seek information, ideas, and momentum from other learning organizations and leading researchers. Identify successful learning organizations in your industry and others, both in your geographic region and other parts of the world. Read the growing literature about learning organizations. The Learning Organization Network of the American Society for Training and Development has compiled a list of over 150 articles and books in the field. We predict there will soon be many more. Attend conferences and workshops on the subject of learning organizations. Invite a corporate leader of a learning organization or one of the leading consultants or researchers in organizational learning theory and practice. Arrange for in-house workshops and discussions on the topic of learning organizations with a panel of people already working in recognized learning organizations or consultants recognized as leaders in the field of learning organizations. Create or become part of a consortium of organizations seeking to become learning organizations.

Ernst & Young has followed all these avenues in its efforts to become a learning organization. A recent example of the firm's efforts to glean as much as it can about learning organizations was the two-day program the company arranged called *"Valuing the Learning Organization: A Symposium to Establish the Concepts, Language, and Metrics for Measuring Human Capital in the Knowledge Era"*. Panelists and participants included many of the top business and academic leaders in the learning organization field, who gathered to discuss common perspectives and create action plans for their respective organizations.

Develop and Expand Team Learning Activities

Team learning is the capacity of a team to enter genuine thinking together, and it is vital because teams, not individuals, are the basic learning unit in modern organizations. A variety of ways to develop team learning can be used, such as new job assignments, participation in team projects, developing in-house activities, and group assessment of learning efforts. Robert Waterman sees the movement of people in and out of the various functions and businesses of an organization as a key for developing a learning organization. Calhoun Wick and Lu Stanton Leon, in *The Learning Edge,* suggest the building of "developmental learning teams," whose prime purpose is to build learning skills and learning attributes as a team.

Change the Role of Managers

Managers in a learning organization should have but one aim: pursuing improved performance by fostering long-term learning and continuous improvement. Learning organizations need the support, modeling, and involvement of management. This backing, and, hopefully, championing of the company's becoming a learning organization will happen when substantial business benefits and returns become obvious.

Once leaders have become convinced of the value of a learning organization, they must themselves become learning models, anxious to learn for themselves and encourage others to learn continuously as well. The managers should now see themselves as coaches, facilitators, and leaders who promote, encourage and reinforce learning.

Watkins and Marsick recommend some of the following steps for leadership to undertake to promote organizational learning and to create a corporate culture for learning:

- Provide opportunities for training and practice in organizational learning.
- Support and encourage staff to overcome the fear and shame associated with making errors, and set norms that legitimize the making of errors made while in search of progress.
- Coach and reward for efforts made, and set norms that reward innovative thinking and experimentation.

Encourage Experiments and Risk Taking

Meaningful learning cannot occur without experimentation—trying something new and different. Create an environment where people feel comfortable with, and are motivated and rewarded to, experiment. Have organizational heroes be those who have stretched and experimented, not those who never rocked the boat. Develop reward systems that reward learning and helping others to learn. Ideas for new approaches to products and processes will occur only in people who feel that trying something new is rewarded in its own right and not only in successful experiments. It is not enough, however, to hear about an experiment or about something someone else has learned. Real leverage and learning come from applying that learning in hundreds of different places throughout your organization. Organizations must free up and motivate people to use what others within and outside the company have learned. Reward those who can apply other people's insights, as well as those who come up with new ideas of their own.

One global company that has successfully encouraged and rewarded experiments and risk takers is 3M. It has created the Pathfinder Award for people working in the 57 countries where 3M plants are located. The award recognizes those who "develop new products or a new application of a product for a particular country or culture." In 1991 alone 67 different awards were conferred to different work teams; the value of those 67 creative ideas in terms of sales was $522 million!

Create Structures, Systems, and Time to Extract Learning

Strong global learning organizations provide an array of opportunities and situations where the results of action can be examined for learning. Some ideas include learning reflection times and learning audits.

Learning reflection can be done at regular times after meetings and during special weekly learning reflection sessions. Learning audits measure whether the structures, time, and other resources are available for learning as much as possible from organizational action. Double-loop and deutero learning are a systematic part of organization life.

Learning needs to be repositioned in the organization, with greater emphasis on individual responsibility. Top management, in collaboration with the HRD department, should expect all departments and individuals to take greater responsibility for their own learning. Organizations should provide continuous learning packages that encourage everyone to view learning as an everyday experience and actively use opportunities available for personal development.

Build Opportunities and Mechanisms to Disseminate Learning

Effective learning organizations set up times and events, including conferences and monthly programs, to ensure that the learning that has been gained through experience, reflection, and anticipation is disseminated to every appropriate corner of the organization. PPG gathers thousands of managers each year to exchange information, mingle, hold informal meetings, and share learning experiences. Xerox and Corning hold annual events linked to their quality efforts where teams of employees present their projects, experiments, and innovations. Other companies write case studies about their successes and failures and use these cases in meetings and training programs.

Blanchard Training and Development sponsors an international conference of its international licensees each spring. This conference rotates from country to country every year. Each fall BTD sponsors regional conferences in different relevant geographical areas throughout the world. One of the biggest payoffs of these conferences is the wealth of knowledge gained from exchanging business information and sharing techniques on how to help the managers in these businesses to be more effective. For example, Blanchard might have a licensee in Sweden give a presentation on how it uses one of the Blanchard program materials—and in the process learn better ways to present and integrate the concepts of the program into the working experience. Participant managers then have participants build on what they have learned with their own experiences for others in the group to learn from. "It becomes truly a mind-expanding experience," says Dale Truax.

BTD also sponsors a staff exchange in which an employee comes from a licensee's organization and works for a six-month period in a job at Blanchard Training and Development. This fosters a better understanding of Blanchard's approaches, products, and personnel. Likewise, BTD places its employees at various internships with licensees' organizations to learn more about that company, its programs and products, and the organizational and local culture.

Empower People

Judith Vogt and Kenneth Murrell, in their recent book *Empowerment in Organizations*, contend that empowerment is critical in building a successful learning environment because such action can "spark exceptional performance." If employees are offered the ability to achieve responsibility, recognition, and opportunity, they will work and learn at optimal levels. Managers should allow decision-making power and accountability to reside at the lowest possible level. They should do whatever is needed to free the worker to serve the customer, including the ability to spend significant sums and cross any functional border. Employees should be fully informed with financial, technical, and other data to help them take the initiative and to be proactive.

Companies such as PPG and Samsung have developed many mechanisms to create and sustain the freedom for employees to act. Employees are much more comfortable in carrying out the vision and plans of the company when they feel as though they have a major role to play. To work productively and creatively, the individual has to have the power to learn.

It is important, says Jim Gannon, to realize that accountability and empowerment are not correlated. Too many organizations have given only accountability with no empowerment (witness the bureaucracies of Eastern Europe and elsewhere). Empowerment, adds Gannon, is determined by the "amount of influence, trust, and ability to get exceptions that the employee has."

Push Information throughout the Organization and to External Associates (Customers, Vendors, Suppliers, etc.)

Information-powered organizations hire and enjoy having people who think in terms of the knowledge they need to deal with their responsibilities and opportunities for others and for themselves. They actively seek out and pass on the knowledge and information the organization needs to survive.

Learning organizations live on and breathe the oxygen of information and communications. Gannon thinks that information "should be shared as soon as possible if the organization is to survive." The information should be easily accessible whether in person or through information technology. It should flow up as well as down in the organization. There should be lots of open discussions and conversations throughout the company. Alan Webber goes so far as to suggest that in the knowledge economy, the most important work is conversation. Webber notes that at McKinsey "the conversation is the organization."

Develop the Discipline of Systems Thinking

Systems thinking is a vitally important skill, but so difficult for most people to apply. To become a learning organization, it is essential for more people in the organization to see patterns and interrelationships. Only by doing so can they realize the full consequences of actions and decisions. Until systems thinking is endemic in the organization, the organization will not be able to acquire the full learning that is available in the activities within and outside the organization.

Create a Culture of Continuous Improvement

Learning organizations thrive in a corporate culture of continuous improvement. In learning organizations quality is sought for every product and for every service, both within and outside the organization. Motorola started the process of becoming a global learning organization when it made the commitment to the six sigma improvement process, a level of quality that allows no more than 3.4 defects per million in manufactured goods. To reach that goal (which Motorola has now exceeded) called for constant attention to improving every action and interaction in the organization. It forced the organization to find ways to keep getting better—and that required them to be better learners and to be smarter as an organization. If you scan the organizations in Part III in this book, you will note that *all* of them have made quality a key mission of the company.

Develop a Powerful Vision for Organization Excellence and Individual Fulfillment

The people in a learning organizations strongly believe in and are committed to a common mission and a shared vision. Together, the members of the company have developed a powerful "magnetic" target that everyone wants to aim toward. Profits and market share are not enough to gain such commitment. Rather, it's excellence, sharing, and concern for the customer and for each other. It's the growing of the organization and the individual.

Root Out Bureaucracy

The bane of any organization seeking to gain the power of learning in the workplace is bureaucracy. The bureaucratic ways of thinking and operating kill the energy, creativity, and willingness to risk necessary for learning to bloom. Forms and regulations for every possible scenario choke off learning.

Tom Peters declares that an absolute priority for an organization to learn is the demolition of bureaucracies. We recommend the following:

- Build a project structure rather than functional barriers,
- Decentralize: work horizontally.
- Eliminate hard structures.
- Eliminate vertical and horizontal barriers.
- Introduce fluidity.
- Weld all former functional activities into seamless wholes.

Beyond that, we recommend that you consider doing as Royal Bank of Canada encourages its people to do with any bureaucracy that does and will appear in the bank.

- Challenge unnecessary forms and silly rules.
- Expose and eliminate systems and processes that discourage learning.
- Change what is rewarded and recognized to those things that promote knowledge development and improve quality and service.

PLACES TO BEGIN CREATING A GLOBAL LEARNING ORGANIZATION

How should one begin transforming one's company into a global learning organization? Is there a starting point?

If organizations are in fact organisms, then each small part—every department or section—has some capacity to affect the whole of the organization. Any entry point has the potential to build pockets of experimentation that can get people to work together on real problems that will release their energies, tackle flaws in the system, and simultaneously learn.

You can begin in any part that has the potential to affect the others. Start where the energy is. Consider any or all of the following sources:

- Work with the board of directors.
- Work out from the human resources department (because it may be knowledgeable and supportive of the learning organization concept and values).
- Establish a joint union-management initiative.
- Set up a series of task forces.
- Run a consciousness-raising development program.
- Work with the strategic planning cycle.
- Begin with a diagnosis.
- Start with a company conference.
- Emphasize one of the key dimensions.
- Start with one department.

The degree of difficulty in getting the organization to change also depends on one's position in the organization. If you feel that you are not in a powerful position, and that you are working in the middle and at the margins, work through committees and through other structures designed to provide an avenue for indirect influence over decision makers.

It is important for you to answer the following questions:

1. What stage of globalization and organizational learning is your organization occupying?
2. What is your position in the organization?
3. What avenues and resources might you use in transforming your company into a global learning organization?

DEVELOP THE NECESSARY SKILLS FOR WORKERS

Global learning organization people must be able to think strategically, intuitively manage information, thrive on constant change, and synergize and be energized in multicultural interactions. Samsung lists as one of its primary training goals "the cultivation of the ability to positively adapt to an ever-changing business environment."

In this chapter we have addressed the organizational elements of global learning organizations. In Chapter 9 we will explore some techniques for globalizing learning organizations.

Chapter Nine

Globalizing Learning Organizations

T o work in the global environment, an organization must prepare itself for differences and surprises in culture, language, economic and political perspectives, distances and borders, and working and learning styles. One corporation that moved quickly and successfully from primarily domestic to global learning is Whirlpool.

WHIRLPOOL

In 1989 Whirlpool, headquartered in Benton Harbor, Michigan, acquired the $2 billion appliance division of N. V. Philips Gleoilampenfabriekin, headquartered in the Netherlands. In one fell swoop, Whirlpool had gone from an almost exclusively domestic company to a 40 percent global corporation. With the Philips purchase, Whirlpool had suddenly become the largest household appliances company in the world.

The significance of the challenge could be seen by the fact that many of the U.S. senior managers didn't even have passports. Yet Whirlpool leaders were acutely aware of the critical importance of making the Dutch and American companies an integrated global corporation. The people of Whirlpool would need to quickly integrate the forces of globalization, culture, language, communications, and workforce diversity. They wanted to leverage their new resources instead of having them merely be added deterrents to Whirlpool's organizational success.

Whirlpool, under the guidance of its president and CEO, Dave Whitwam, and the human resources staff, developed several programs to globalize what now was called Whirlpool International B.V. These various strategies were so successful that Whirlpool was recognized by *Personnel Journal* as an Optimas Award winner in the global outlook category for the unique globalization efforts made to "succeed in the world marketplace."

One of the key programs that enabled Whirlpool to learn, as an organization, to become global is its annual global conference. The first global conference was held in Montreux, Switzerland, for one week in June 1990. Top executives from 16 countries in Whirlpool's European and North American operations attended. The theme of the conference was "Winning Through Quality Leadership: One Global Vision."

Let's carefully examine the planning and learning strategies involved in the design of the first global conference. The first step was to determine the worldwide conference's goals. Four major goals were identified:

- Advance a unified *vision* of the company's future. (Remember Senge's strong exhortation that shared vision is critical starting point for any learning organization.)
- Instill the idea of embracing the future as one global company.
- Establish a keen sense of responsibility within the leadership group for creating the company's future.
- Identify and initiate explicit steps toward integrating various activities and ideas throughout Whirlpool worldwide operations into a unified whole.

Another important goal of the conference was to enable the participants to think first of each other as business partners—not as *foreigners*. The conference designers also wanted to be sure that the participants' own goals and interests for the conference would be met. Beginning nine months before the conference, they surveyed the interests of all 140 managers.

Encouraging cultural mixing between the managers was deemed crucial. The problem is that at typical international meetings managers gravitate toward their own "cultural cocoons." Planners tried to build in events to help managers get beyond their own national backgrounds and people of their own language.

The well-planned structure of the conferences freed the managers to involve themselves in the true, most critical, part of a conference—and the building of a learning organization. Emphasis was on meeting, getting to know and trust, working with, and learning with their new global colleagues. Together, they could better focus on critical, challenging issues such as the Whirlpool vision, strategic planning, and quality.

One element that built powerful learning among the global participants was the conference "ground rules." Attendees were encouraged to take part themselves, and to help others participate as well, in the meetings and informal activities. They were challenged to get beyond their comfort zones with these guidelines:

- Create situations in which you can meet everyone.
- Promote an atmosphere of worldwide learning.
- Remember that the only problems we cannot solve are the ones we do not identify.
- We are all responsible for making the week productive.
- Be a good listener.

Whirlpool managers themselves prepared and conducted the various workshops. This tactic helped the leaders of the new Whirlpool become accustomed to acting as learning facilitator and teacher as well as manager.

During the conference managers were invited to identify which major areas of the company's operations could be improved. Following discussions in small groups, 200 areas were identified. These were then boiled down to 15 topics, such as global management reporting systems, global quality initiatives, development of a global corporate talent pool, and compressing consumer product delivery cycles. Fifteen cross-functional and multinational groups, called "Whirlpool One Company Challenge Teams" were then formed to examine these 15 topics and present their recommendations at the next global conference in Washington, D.C. Team members met regularly and reported their progress in *The Leading Edge*, the corporate newsletter for Whirlpool's worldwide leaders.

Whirlpool people felt that this first global conference was so successful that it "launched the company ahead in time by an estimated three to five years in the integration of its global management team, and saved the company millions of dollars in the process" (Laabs, p. 39). Now there's an example of how to become a global learning organization in a flash!

GLOBALIZATION OF LEARNING

Transforming a nonglobal organization into a global one is a challenging and formidable task that cannot happen in a haphazard or "trickle-up" manner. The top leadership must understand and value its importance and complexity and provide the comprehensive, continuous, enthusiastic support needed in building the globality of the enterprise.

In addition, global learning companies must, according to Sylvia Odenwald, "invest in a thorough selection process and an extensive

FIGURE 9–1
Global Assessment Systems

Organizationwide Components	Functional Components
Corporate culture	Human resource management
Leadership	Marketing
Workforce	Technology development (R&D)
Structure	Finance and purchasing
Strategy	Telecommunications and information systems
Policy and procedures	Manufacturing
Organizational dynamics	Sales and service
Management controls	Human resource development

training program for their human resource professionals." These organizations should employ global trainers who "know training content and understand the technologies involved, . . . who have the added dimensions of multicultural awareness and specific cultural competence and experience. Only through a continuing education process can multinational companies truly globalize learning and compete in the global marketplace"(p. 147).

In *Global Human Resource Development*, Michael Marquardt and Dean Engel present an HRD model for enabling an organization to move from a domestic company to a global corporation. Their model involves four distinct global inputs:

- Learning assessment.
- Organization development.
- Leadership development.
- Training.

Global Learning Assessment

There are many components both organizationwide and functional that can be assessed in order to determine the degree of globalization achieved and the company's rating against other global competitors in that particular industry. Figure 9–1 shows the 16 components in our Global Assessment System. In this global assessment system, each of the eight organizational and eight functional components are measured against global standards, especially with those firms considered the top global companies in the industry. The gaps identified can serve as a foundation in determining key organizational competency needs and strutural changes. Special care should be given to how learning will be achieved in each component. The following areas within each component can be measured to determine globalization and learning status.

Global Assessment System—Organizationwide Components

a. Corporate Culture

- Commitment to learning.
- Global values.
- Global vision.
- World-class standards for quality and service.
- Global teams.
- Cultural productivity.

b. Leadership

- Global vision.
- Global skills and competencies.
- Multilingual cross-cultural skills.
- Strategic understanding of global markets and finance.
- Communication and negotiation skills.
- Appreciation of global technology and people.
- Global perspective on a corporatewide basis.
- Innovation and inspiration.

c. Workforce

- Well trained, yet continuously learning.
- Globally aware, multilingual, multicultural.
- Independent thinkers with team focus.
- Customer driven, quality oriented.
- Entrepreneurial and innovative.
- Adaptable and flexible.
- Appreciative of multicultural understanding and skills.
- Committed and caring.

d. Structure

- Globally integrated and locally differentiated.
- Decentralized.
- Multicentered.
- Close to market.
- Flat layered; few boundaries.

- Matrixed, with cross-functional and cross unit coordination.
- Structured into worldwide business teams.
- Widespread decision points.
- Flexible, rapidly responsive.

e. Global strategy

- Integrated system for dealing with worldwide corporate challenges, opportunities, and problems.
- Planning and execution of business on a worldwide basis.
- Management strategy with focus on power triad of new Europe, Pacific Rim and United States.
- Leverage of local strengths in global successes.
- Global linking of functions.
- Pursuit of strategic alliances.
- Localized and tailored objectives.

f. Policy and procedures

- Culturally clear decision-making practices.
- Global coordination of activities.
- Centralized global policies and localized procedures.
- Global standards for quality, service, and design.
- Decisions made within a global context.

g. Management controls

- Globally inspiring mission and corporate goals.
- Management systems that encourage continuous improvement.
- Globally consistent performance measurement for managers.
- Reward systems that incorporate quantitative and qualitative data.
- Globally consistent business unit measurement and reward systems.

h. Organizational dynamics

- Cross-cultural, cross-organizational, and cross-national.
- Innovative and synergistic.
- Empowering.
- Adaptive.

- Standardized global communications for gathering, processing, and distributing information.
- Interdependence and collaboration.

Global Assessment Systems—Functional Components

The global audit also investigates eight different organization functions to determine how they can be regauged toward globalization.

a. Human resources management

- Worldwide human resources planning.
- Global recruitment and selection.
- Expatriation and repatriation programs.
- Global and local reward systems.
- Global succession planning.

b. Marketing

- Global marketing planning and management.
- Appropriate customization and differentiation.
- Global and local marketing team integration.
- Global product strategies.
- Global pricing.
- Global and local distribution channels.
- Culture-based advertising.

c. Technology development (R&D)

- Integration with manufacturing and marketing.
- Mass customization.
- Global quality standards.
- Shortened product development cycle.
- Centralized R&D locations.
- High investment levels.

d. Finance and purchasing

- Global financial services.
- Capital budgeting and resources.
- Global purchasing strategies.

- Taxation and currency exposure.
- Flexibility and speed.
- Global measurement and reporting.
- Degree of complexity and value added.

e. Telecommunications and information systems

- Hardware, software, and staff capabilities.
- Standards and cross-boundary interfaces.
- Global processing, transmission, and utilization of data.
- Technology connectivity and telecomputing.
- Value-added networks.
- Staff interchange capability.

f. Manufacturing

- Flexible manufacturing systems.
- Quality and continuity of products.
- Computer design and manufacturing.
- Just-in-time inventory and production.
- Self-directed work teams.
- Statistical process control.

g. Sales and service

- Global sales and promotion strategies.
- World class customer service.
- Culturally appropriate quality.
- Global customer education.

h. Training and development

- Status as a learning organization.
- Globalized company curriculum.
- Integration with global strategies, markets, and customers.
- Culturally appropriate materials.
- Utilization of learning technologies.
- World-class trainers and resources.

Global Organization Development

After a systematic global assessment or audit has been completed and the organization has become more aware of its globalization strengths and limitations, the organizational transformation process can continue. The organization should attempt to resolve the incongruity between its globalization goals and its present organizational structure and capability. Several strategies can be considered to promote the development of a global learning organization. These include process engineering, team building, and organizational mapping.

Global Leadership Development

Honeywell and AMP leadership programs were discussed in Chapter 5. A growing number of other global organizations have also developed comprehensive global leadership programs for their managers and key staff. Typically these programs include the following elements:

- Individual profiling and consultations.
- Global executive seminars.
- Formal learning exchanges with other global managers.
- Global briefings and conferences.
- Executive retreats.

Emhart has begun an executive development program on global competitiveness. Colgate-Palmolive and Cray Research give executives short-term assignments overseas to boost their global awareness. Aetna Insurance, Unilever, and Electrolux regularly rotate managers between domestic and international assignments.

Global Training

All members of a global learning organization should have the knowledge, skills, and attitudes essential to operate in settings and with people throughout the world. Stephen Rhinesmith suggests the following as basic to this goal:

- Orientation programs for people across functions, regions, and product groups to instill common global visions and global corporate strategies and values.
- Global scanning seminars to ensure familiarity with global social, economic, and political trends and to teach managers how to balance global and local integration and develop a global coordination for learning.
- Cross-cultural and multicultural skill training emphasizing problem solving, decision making, communicating, selling, negotiating, coaching, appraising, and leading in global contexts.

- Creativity and self-awareness training to help staff become better learners and become able to reframe and manage contradictions and complexities, chaos and change in the global environment.

MANAGING AND LEARNING ACROSS BORDERS

There are many important management and learning activities that should be executed differently when operating across countries, cultures, and borders, for example, administration and learning styles.

Administration

The coordination and management of learning across borders involves many administrative issues such as transportation; relocation; cultural orientation of local employees to understand the expats (expatriates), expats to understand the local employee, and third-country personnel to understand each other; language translation; host government relations; housing, facilities; and support service.

Learning Styles

People from different cultures in global organizations have, in their lifetimes, developed different learning styles, habits, and approaches, which, in turn, were influenced by their education systems at both the formal and informal levels. Some employees will be accustomed to a philosophical, didactic, deductive, collaborative, rote style, whereas others have been conditioned by and prefer a practical, individualized, inductive, questioning approach.

ACCULTURIZATION OF THE PRODUCT AND PROCESS

Acculturization is the conveying of a program (including its ideas, content, and goals) across cultural boundaries to ensure that the program is user-friendly.

An acculturized learning program in an organization will contain as few roadblocks to the learner as possible. The organization tries to ensure not only that learning happens, but that it is useful for the cultural milieu in which it takes place. The cultural adaptation is crucial. It is as important to success as language translation.

In developing and implementing learning programs for employees, organizations should factor in the influence and impact of culture in their efforts. When possible, it is highly beneficial to involve local people in the acculturation aspect of the learning program.

UTILIZING GLOBALIZED EMPLOYEES

One of the quickest and most effective ways of globalizing the learning company is to tap into the information and skills of employees returning to headquarters assignment. For global companies repatriation is an important part of global strategy and needs to be carefully considered as such. From the company's point of view, returning expatriates offer a resource that should not be overlooked. They bring back considerable experience, information, and expertise that can be applied immediately and in the future. Chapter 22 describes how Samsung manages this process very deliberately. Returned expatriates can help in the expatriate selection and training process by supplying insights into the realities that have to be faced by those on overseas assignments. They are likely to be in-house experts in the culture of particular countries and regions of their own assignment and probably have priceless contacts and tips that can be passed along. They can provide reality testing for candidates who are preparing to go overseas and give real-world credibility to the preparation and training process. They can be used to support the return of other repatriates, and act as sponsors for those expatriates still overseas. Finally, they can be a source of valuable input in both global and regional strategic planning.

LEADERSHIP IN THE BUILDING OF GLOBAL LEARNING ORGANIZATIONS

In an increasingly dynamic, interdependent, and unpredictable world, it is simply no longer possible for anyone to figure it all out at the top by themselves. The old model of organization leadership—the top thinks and the bottom acts—must now give way to an integration of everyone thinking and acting at all levels at all times. The old days when a Henry Ford, Alfred Sloan, or Tom Watson "learned for the organization" are gone.

A growing number of corporate leaders and boards realize that capturing the collective knowledge of the organization will ensure competitive advantage, yet few such organizations exist today. Why? Peter Senge's answer is that too few companies have the right kind of leadership; the leaders they have might have been acceptable in the past, but they are ineffective in learning organizations. These are people who set the direction, made key decisions, energized the employees, and were even charismatic heroes.

The global learning organization calls for a new type of global leader with new kinds of roles and skills. Christopher Bartlett and Sumantra Ghoshal think that they must have the capacity to leverage their company's learning worldwide. Now let's examine the new global roles and skills that will enable leaders to undertake such leveraging.

NEW GLOBAL ROLES

We will explore four new roles required for the leader of a global learning organization:

Teacher, facilitator and co-learner. The global leader is not there to tell employees *what are* the "correct" things to think and do. He or she should encourage and help employees gain a strong desire to learn and continuously to improve their skills, as well as their learning abilities and resources. The leader should be a voracious learner, a lover of learning, and a model of knowledge management.

Architect and designer. With the new technologies, structures, environment, and resources of the global learning organization, the leader must be an architect who can fit these elements into a system that thrives in the global marketplace. The leader has to help redefine the organization, reshape the networks and teams, and reinvent new methods for selecting, training, and rewarding people so these methods all match the continuous changes inherent in the new global environment. The leader must also design core values and visions, develop policies and strategies, and then translate these guiding principles into business decisions.

Coordinator. Like the conductor to an orchestra, the global learning leader needs to coordinate many people and operations across the room, across town, across the world. The leader must fashion a repertoire of approaches and tools from those of simple, centralized controls to the management of exceptions. Such horizontal management calls for the ability to track information, polish products and services, and energize people from within and outside the organization. Encouragement and empowerment enable each orchestra member to play the music more magnificently.

Coach and motivator.   Because the global learning organization will consist more and more of knowledge specialists, it will be an organization of equal colleagues and associates. No piece of knowledge will necessarily rank higher than another; each will be judged by its contribution to the learning and success of the organization. This information-based, more egalitarian company will need a leader who can transform individuals into a soccer-type team where every member is responsible for the success of the team, and each one can see how his or her play affects the whole game. The leader-coach motivates, implores, inspires, and promotes every team member.

NEW GLOBAL SKILLS

These new leadership roles require new skills. Lets examine the three most critical areas Senge identified: building shared vision, surfacing and challenging mental models, and engaging in systems thinking.

Building shared vision.   The leader should be able to envision the type of world the company represents, one that is varied enough to attract and retain the best and brightest global citizens. They should be able to do the following:

- Blend extrinsic and intrinsic visions.
- Communicate one's vision and ask for support.
- Encourage personal visions from which emerge shared visions.
- Keep visioning as an ongoing process.

Surfacing and testing mental models.   Many of the best ideas and visions in an organization never get put into practice because they often conflict with established mental models and ways of doing things. The new global leader has the task of challenging these existing assumptions without invoking defensiveness or anger. Specific skills in this area include these:

- Balancing inquiry and advocacy.
- Distinguishing what is espoused from what is practiced.

- Recognizing and defusing defensive routines.
- Seeing and testing leaps of abstraction.

Systems thinking.   Leaders in global learning organizations must help people see the big picture, with the underlying trends and forces of change. They need to think systematically and be able to see how culture influences every aspect of their business. For example, how do leadership styles in Asia differ from those in Latin America? Leaders need to organize and manage massive amounts of information and apply it using different cultural lenses. Some key skills to accomplish this include the following:

- Avoiding symptomatic solutions and focusing on underlying causes.
- Distinguishing detail complexity (many variables) from dynamic complexity (when cause and effect are distant in time and space, and when the consequences over time are subtle).
- Focusing on areas of high leverage.
- Seeing interrelationships, not things.
- Seeing processes, not snapshots.
- Seeing that you and the cause of your problems are part of a single system.

FASTEN YOUR SEATBLETS

We have now completed our presentation of the theory, practice, and steps for becoming a successful global learning organization. Part III provides detailed, living examples of what 16 individual companies are doing to succeed at being global learning organizations. Each offers a different focus and provides useful ideas.

The problems you have to address when becoming a global learning organization are not simple. If they were, all organizations would already be learning organizations and global projects would already be carried out correctly. We hope to have helped launch you toward resolving the problems cited. Remember the need for alertness to potential problems and doing the right things right at the right time. After that, it's time for the rubber to meet the sky!

P A R T

III

EXEMPLARY GLOBAL LEARNING ORGANIZATIONS

Chapter Ten

Analog Devices:
Executive Commitment to Innovation and Organizational Learning

A nalog Devices grew consistently at a rate of about 20 percent per year for nearly 15 years. Then five-year goals (1982 and 1987) were missed, as CEO Ray Stata says, "by a country mile." This slip could have been explained by the tough times being experienced by the entire U.S. electronics industry, but that wouldn't have been the whole story. Something was also wrong *inside* the company, but what?

Unfortunately, in the 1980s Analog's situation was anything but unique in corporate America. Companies that had enjoyed decades-long world leadership in their markets were brought to their knees. Many reasons were advanced to explain the United States' loss of competitiveness. These include the dilapidated education system, government regulations, the high cost of capital, military spending, low reinvestment, a strong dollar, and a spendthrift government. This blame was not misplaced. It was all true, and it did contribute to the business decline.

Analog had the largest share of the high-performance linear integrated circuit market—its niche. It had the best designers and technologists in the business. It had a highly motivated work force with excellent labor relations. It had not underinvested, or managed for short-term profits. Stata was wise enough to recognize that there had to be something wrong with *the way* the company was managed. He set out to understand what was wrong and how to make it better—and there began an interesting story (and one with a moral).

A COMPANY AT THE CROSSROADS

Some pundits say that the root of the problem for U.S. corporations is the declining rate of innovation. U.S. innovation has almost always

Analog Devices at a Glance

	Organizational learning	Global learning
	✔ Appropriate structures	Acculturization
	✔ Corporate learning culture	Borders
	Empowerment	✔ Globalization
	Environmental scanning	Language
	✔ Knowledge creation and transfer	✔ Leadership
	Learning technology	✔ Workforce diversity
	✔ Quality	
	✔ Strategy	
	Supportive atmosphere	
	Teamwork and networking	
	✔ Vision	

© Michael Marquardt and Angus Reynolds, 1992

Headquarters:	Norwood, Massachusetts
Founded:	1965
Main business:	Precision high-performance linear, mixed-signal and digital integrated circuits, and modular and board-level products used predominantly in equipment and systems that involve processing information from real-world sensors.
Chief executive officer:	Ray Stata
Number of countries where located:	15
Total employees worldwide:	5,200

been demonstrated as a technology that generates new products or improvements in the design and manufacture of existing products. At Analog Devices (and many other U.S. companies), technological innovation was not the real problem. The bottleneck was *management* innovation. Stata believed that many U.S. firms lagged behind in the *management innovation* needed to take fullest advantage of their technological leadership. The big difference is that Stata recognized the real problem.

What Business Is Analog Devices in Anyway?

Real-work phenomena, such as temperature, pressure, sound, images, speed, acceleration, position, and rotation angle, are inherently analog in nature, consisting of continuously varying information. This information can be detected and measured using analog sensors, which represent real-world phenomena by generating continuously varying voltage and currents. The signals from these sensors are first processed using analog methods, such as amplification, filtering, and shaping. They are then usually converted to digital form for input to a microprocessor, which is used to manipulate, store, or display the information. Often the signals are further processed after conversion to digital form using a technology called *digital signal processing* (DSP). In addition, digital signals are often converted to analog form to provide signals for analog display, sound, or control functions. These manipulations and transformations are collectively known as real-world signal processing. Analog Devices is the only Fortune 500 semiconductor company whose exclusive focus is real-world signal processing.

Background

Analog Devices has long recognized the advantages of global deployment of people and resources to best serve the needs of its customers, no matter where in the world the customers manufacture or sell.

Analog established operations in Europe in 1966 and in the Pacific Rim in 1970. Today over one-half of Analog's revenues are derived from sales outside the United States. They operate manufacturing facilities in the United States, Ireland, Japan, Taiwan, and the Philippines. This worldwide structure means that customers in each of the three major electronics centers of the world have easy access to a local source of supply.

Analog's products are sold and supported through sales offices found across the United States and in Austria, Belgium, Denmark, France, Germany, India, Israel, Italy, Japan, Korea, the Netherlands, Sweden, Switzerland, Taiwan, and the United Kingdom. Sales representatives and industrial distributors also offer Analog Devices' products worldwide.

Most of Analog's end customers are original equipment manufacturers (OEMs) who incorporate the products into equipment, instruments, and systems employed by end users in a wide variety of applications, including engineering, scientific, and medical instruments; industrial automation equipment; military and aerospace equipment; computer peripherals; communications equipment; and high-end consumer electronics products.

Over the past two years Analog has been in the throes of a wrenching transition that is molding it from a commodity analog device company serving a fragmented market to a more value-added linear and mixed signal semiconductor company that will balance its business between the stable and profitable standard linear integrated circuit (IC) market and the emerging high-growth, special purpose, system-level mixed signal and DSP market.

A New Environment

Analog's industry is undergoing massive changes as markets make the transition from a cold war to a peacetime economy and as products make the change from technology-driven, general-purpose, standard-function integrated circuits to market-driven, application-specific, system-level integrated circuits.

To adapt and respond to this new environment, Analog Devices, like many other companies in the industry, is undergoing a major transformation. In constructing the path to the future it must be willing to experiment, to take risks, and to invest significant resources to prepare for the future. Ray Stata believes that Analog Devices, more than any other linear IC company, has been making the needed investments and learning the hard lessons that are part of the transformation that industry is experiencing.

From its experience Analog believes that it sees more clearly the picture that has emerged of what it can and must do to maintain its leadership in real-world signal processing in the 1990s. Analog believes that its aggressive technical innovation, emphasizing product performance and reliability with a high level of functional integration, and its investments in advanced semiconductor processes and manufacturing facilities, will allow the company to continue to compete successfully in its chosen markets against both foreign and domestic semiconductor manufacturers.

Although growth of the standard-function linear market has been essentially flat for three years—which has certainly had a depressing effect on Analog's business—the outlook for this market is that it will continue to grow modestly in the 1990s. The number of applications emerging for these types of products will grow at an attractive rate, and Analog is giving high priority to targeting and penetrating these new opportunities.

A NEW STRATEGY FOR LEARNING

Fatefully, Stata met MIT Professors Jan Forrester and Peter Senge during this re-assessment period. He learned of their work in applying system dynamics to the analysis and design of complex social systems. Forrester had pioneered the use of feedback theory and systems analysis to examine the behavior of systems for 30 years.

Peter Senge invited Stata to join eight other organizational leaders in the "New Management Style Project." The group members met semiannually for four years. It proved a fruitful collaboration to accelerate management innovation.

As Stata says;

> Learning emerged as a fundamental concept. It not only helped us to better appreciate the power of system dynamics, but also to integrate a broader range of management tools and methods to facilitate organizational change and improvement. In an even broader context, as I come to understand this concept more fully, I see organizational learning is the principal process by which management innovation occurs. *In fact, I would argue that the rate at which individuals and organizations learn has become the only sustainable-competitive advantage, especially in knowledge-intensive industries.*

Analog Devices is undergoing a massive transformation to adapt to a rapidly changing world. As it undergos these changes, Stata says it is essential that the company retain the guiding principles that have been the bedrock of its past success. Foremost among these has been the strategic intent to *be the best*. "Being the best at what we do is the guiding principle of our business strategy, and we are proud of the leadership position we have established in our standard-function linear IC business," says Stata.

SYSTEMS THINKING

Stata notes that one of the highest leverage points for improving performance when using system dynamics to stimulate organizational behavior is the minimization of basic system delays. This seems an evident conclusion, and system dynamics is needed to prove it. What is not so clear is the resultant size of loss from excessive inventories, excessive lead time, and poor customer service that results. The question is that, if these conclusions are so obvious, then why did it take U.S. manufacturers so long to recognize the critical importance of manufacturing cycle time and to focus on reducing time to market? Stata admits that it certainly was not obvious to him in the mid-1980s that excessive manufacturing cycle time was one of the main causes of Analog's problems.

ORGANIZATIONAL LEARNING

Stata says that another important use of system dynamics is that of a training tool. His article in MIT's *Sloan Management Review* "Organizational Learning—The Key to Management Innovation," is one of the best-supported and most persuasive endorsements of the learning organization concept ever written. For example, once Analog had decided the correct policy on cycle time, it had to learn how that policy works best and why. The mental model of how the organization works or should work created a precise language through which management could share its understanding. As Stata says, "By comparing our model with others, we provide a mechanism not only to converge on a shared model, but also to communicate to younger, less experienced managers the organization's stored experience and knowledge."

To encourage organizational learning Analog formed 15 corporate product market and technology task forces that drew together professionals from throughout the company. The teams met for months. The result of their deliberations was a delineation of nine imperatives for change. They also made specific recommendations for how to produce the needed changes. Stata says, "An even more important result was that a broad cross-section of our top professionals understood that some of the basic beliefs and assumptions that had served us well in the past needed modification." For example, it became clear to management that Analog's almost fanatical commitment to decentralization was hampering progress. The company decided that it should coordinate technology development across divisions and centralize certain aspects of manufacturing. Management also, recognized the need to improve coordination of product planning, and to capitalize on the combined strength of Analog's diverse product and technology base in penetrating new markets. Management recognized that key accounts viewed Analog as a collection of autonomous divisions, often competing with each other. With this recognition, the need to learn to present the company as a single vendor to these customers was obvious.

Stata says, "We all realized that, in accepting these conclusions, we had unleashed powerful forces that would change the culture, structure, and behavior of the company in ways not yet foreseen." Events proved that the changes were wise indeed. For example, in less than a year Analog was selling digital-to-analog converters to compact audio disc player manufacturers in Japan and Korea, and the company had a research effort underway to develop a monolithic analog-to-digital converter for the coming high-definition television market.

BEHAVIORAL INFLUENCES ON THE LEARNING PROCESS

Another imperative for change at Analog Devices was to present teamwork as a virtue in the corporate culture. It had historically favored divisional autonomy but recognized that many high-priority changes call for interdivisional cooperation. With teamwork as the goal, the targeted virtues were *openness* and *objectivity*.

- Openness: a willingness to share information, eliminate hidden agendas, make known motives, feelings, and biases; a willingness to invite other opinions and points of view, thereby engendering trust in relations between people.

- Objectivity: searching for the best answers based on reasoned positions and objective criteria, not political influence and parochial interests; making judgments based on facts, not opinions or rumors.

To encourage teamwork, openness, and objectivity, Analog included these elements in the performance appraisal process and criteria for hiring and promotion. In addition, during performance reviews management collects peers' and subordinates' feedback on these competencies. Analog's management recognized the obvious. When pay and promotion are tied to certain factors, one knows that the organization is serious and begins to change his or her behavior.

Analog found that the best way to introduce knowledge and modify behavior is by working with small teams that have the power and resources to enact change. For example, the group not only develops a common understanding of new concepts and language, but peer pressure also helps bring around skeptics who might otherwise block progress. Any new knowledge can immediately be transformed into action as an integral part of training. Analog management believes that this approach, as opposed to sending employees to centralized training programs individually, highlights the difference between individual and organizational learning.

QUALITY

Analog determined to be the best at how it manages its business. Nearly every company in America today is undergoing a profound change in the way that it manages, and Analog Devices is a leader. The principles of total quality management, adopted from Japan, are an important part of the change process. For example, another imperative reinforced by the planning process at Analog Devices was the need to improve customer service, product quality, and yields.

The Center for Quality Management is a network of companies in the Boston area that—like Analog Devices—are committed to applying quality management and sharing their learning experiences. Through its affiliation with the Center, Analog has accelerated the diffusion of its internal quality revolution. Recently, 900 employees were trained in quality improvement methods and statistical process control. They and the other employees have put these tools to use in their daily work.

To guide its improvement efforts, Analog focuses on four corporatewide improvement programs:

- Improving operating profits through sales growth and expense reduction programs, especially in manufacturing sales and administration functions.

- Improving the results from the new product generation process through focus on the product definition function, time and cost to market, and design for manufacturability.

- Improving customer satisfaction through improvements in on-time delivery, product quality and reliability, and responsiveness to customers' needs.

- Improving the quality of the work environment through programs that enhance the quality of communication and education, which empower employees to take charge of their responsibilities and give them recognition and rewards for a job well done, which improve the quality of working relationships at all levels.

As a successful company, Analog thought that it was doing things right. The realization of just how much it had to improve to meet its customers' expectations and how little time the company had to do it were a shock and a challenge. As Stata observed, "We can no longer win by the sheer force of being first to market with the latest products and technology."

Stata's *Sloan Management Review* article provides a fascinating glimpse of how the company learned to apply TQM and make it work. We will cut to the chase. Ending a telling narrative, Stata writes, "In short, quality improvement is a way to accelerate organizational learning."

Analog means to be the best. As a guide, it has established the set of measures of "bestness" shown in Figure 10–1.

GLOBAL INFORMATION TRANSFER

Analog changed the way information was reported. Previously, only the corporate accountants saw the worldwide results totaled, instead

FIGURE 10–1
Analog's Objective Measures of "Bestness"

Quality	Target Group
Best Place to Work	Employees
Best Place to Buy	Customers
Best Place to Invest	Stockholders

of segmented by division and product line. Under that information system, no one in the corporation actually knew the worldwide sales and profits for any product!

Now division managers see results on a worldwide basis, segmented by territory, with direct visibility, although not complete control, of end-customer sales revenues and distribution costs. Affiliate managers also see worldwide results with profit and cost visibility segmented by product division.

Analog's management realized that it can influence others with information and reason. Stata says, "Control is an illusion—compelling in the short term, but unachievable in the long term." Since Analog started using worldwide product line information, much thoughtful discussion has occured in the company. In addition, behavior changes that top management calls "constructive" have occurred. The new information system helps managers understand their business better and make better decisions.

A WORD FROM THE WISE

Ray Stata says, "I believe our approach to planning as a learning process has greatly facilitated our ability to forge a consensus for change among those who must make it happen. It has also helped reduce the obstacles and resistance to change, that is, outdated beliefs and assumptions created by past success."

This executive's commitment to organizational learning has energized Analog's drive toward global success.

Chapter Eleven

Asea Brown Boveri:
An Organization for Global Success

I magine a company in which the organization chart looks like a steep sided pyramid—like this one:

Businesses	8
Business areas	65
Independently incorporated companies	1,300
Autonomous profit centers	5,000
Multifunction high-performance teams	50,000

All this is administered by only three management strata: the Zurich-based executive committee composed of 13 members, 250 senior executives including 100 country managers and most of the business area chiefs, and 5,000 profit center managers with their management teams.

Asea Brown Boveri (ABB) has been described by Tom Peters as "what may be the most novel industrial-firm structure since Alfred Sloan built modern GM in the 1920s" (p. 44). Why? Because this $30 billion in sales per year firm with nearly 200,000 employees is streamlined into units of no more than 50 people.

This isn't simply a curiosity in the museum of business ideas that didn't work. ABB is both extraordinarily different *and* highly successful.

STREAMLINED STRUCTURE

To expand the details of the pyramid described already, ABB is broken into eight major business segments:

- Power plants
- Power transmission

ABB at a Glance

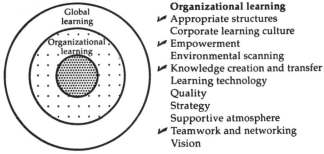

Organizational learning	Global learning
✔ Appropriate structures	Acculturization
Corporate learning culture	✔ Borders
✔ Empowerment	Globalization
Environmental scanning	Language
✔ Knowledge creation and transfer	✔ Leadership
Learning technology	✔ Workforce diversity
Quality	
Strategy	
Supportive atmosphere	
✔ Teamwork and networking	
Vision	

© Michael Marquardt and Angus Reynolds, 1992

Headquarters:	Zurich, Switzerland
Founded:	1987
Main business:	Power plants, power transmission, industry-metallurgy, process automation, mass transit rail systems, environmental control, and reinsurance and leasing.
Chairman:	Percy Barnevik
Number of countries where located:	Sales in 140 countries
Total employees worldwide:	190,000

- Industrial-metallurgy
- Process automation
- Transportation
- Environmental control
- Financial service
- Various other activities

The eight businesses are divided into 65 business areas, and these into 1,300 independently incorporated companies with an average size of 200 people, and these into about 5,000 autonomous profit centers with an average size of 50 employees each. The profit centers are reorganized into 10-person multifunction high-performance teams, for a total of 50,000 work units. Most centers have their own profit-and-loss statements, balance sheet, and assets and serve external customers directly.

ABB functions as a matrix organization composed of individual profit centers, plants and companies within a country on the one hand and business areas (for example, hydroelectric plants, financing, electric metering) on the other.

ABB did not evolve over the years into its present form. Its structure was designed from its birth as a result of a joint operation of Asea in Sweden and Brown Boveri in Germany. Each company owns 50 percent of ABB. The company headquarters in Zurich is very small. The management of the company is distributed within the companies themselves, who are closer to the local marketplaces.

In Sweden the average ABB company employs between 200 and 400 people. Many of these companies are still structured the traditional way, with functional departments. ABB plans to reorganize them into the 10-person, multifunction, high-performance teams. But they are not doing it with an iron fist. Project managers allow their employees to buy into the process at their own rate.

TRANSFERRING LEARNING

ABB's philosophy is to think globally and act locally. Learning and knowledge transfer is ABB's strategy. ABB is good at learning from its clients, but it may be the world's best company at learning from its own division. They systematically capture knowledge through their structure. The profit-and-loss centers have high customer contact. The business area structure supports sharing.

Each company has one member of senior management who oversees progress in his or her own units and serves as a liaison with the central team. The central team meets one day each quarter to share experiences. The formal gatherings are important, but ABB people think that greater value comes from the information exchange throughout the year that results from the relationships established. The system works best when a functional manager in one country feels compelled to telephone or fax the person with the same responsibilities in another country. The motivation can be either a problem or an idea.

There are other ABB forums for information exchange and learning transfer. For example, a business area management board meets quarterly, or more often, to chart global strategies.

The 65 business area chiefs have responsibility for the global strategies of their own businesses. They arrange job shifts for key people to transfer—and leverage—knowledge gained from one company and country to another. Most business area teams are pursuing economies of scale. This is not production scale, but learning scale.

Business area staff with special areas of responsibility travel constantly, confer with local unit management, and support ABB's learning and coordination goals. Functional coordination teams, composed of members who are experts in various operations, meet twice a year to work on marketing, production, quality, and other issues.

The chief of ABB's power transformers business area has described his business area as a collection of local businesses with intense global coordination. Its key to competitiveness is not based on volume efficiencies, but on tight operations. The area focuses on reducing delivery time, increasing flexibility in design and production, improving customer focus, and creating a culture of trust and exchange.

Because the ABB people work closely and continuously with customers on related problems and opportunities, they amass a huge amount of understanding. The power transformers business area is attempting to create a process of continuous expertise transfer. Success would provide an unmatchable business advantage.

Power transformers business area's chief Karlson wants his people to spend time together to get to know and understand one another better. He believes that they must see a payoff for themselves for cooperation. Once everyone sees that sharing pays, he or she will contribute his or her own idea in order to get 24 in return.

ABB Sweden's T50 program may be the most dramatic learning spearhead of all. ABB's Swedish company employs 46,000 people in 200 locations in 150 countries. The mission of T50 is to cut 50 percent from total cycle time for everything from order, through design, engineering, manufacturing, and shipping. If it is successful, T50 will increase ABB Sweden's bottom line by about half a billion dollars.

CENTERS OF EXCELLENCE

Creating value through the accumulation on knowledge across diverse, mainly locally focused businesses has other twists as well. For example, ABB's Finland group capitalized on its special talent in electronic drives. It was named as a center of excellence for electronic drives, with coordination responsibility for the rest of the ABB family. Such centers of excellence are springing up throughout the ABB family.

FLUID BUSINESS AREAS

ABB displays an unusual willingness to make changes. For example, one of the business areas was initially based in Sweden because the chief of the area was located there with his company. The business area's base later moved to Germany, and then again to the United States.

Now that's flexibility. Each of the moves was based on improved strategic location for the area's core business. It is an ABB strategy to keep the base small so that it will remain responsive to its units.

The real advantage of a business area doesn't come from economies of scale such as the combined purchasing power. A more powerful force is the global coordination between elements. There is a process of continuous expertise transfer. People at ABB speak of an atmosphere of trust. Sharing grows within the business area and throughout businesses located all around the world.

ALMOST STAFFLESS

Percy Barnevik set the pace when he became CEO. He inherited a staff of 2,000—and immediately chopped it to 200. When ABB acquired Finland's Stromberg, the headquarters staff numbered 880. Over two years the number was reduced to 25. These are not isolated examples. Staff cuts of 95 percent are routine.

ABB has demolished most of its expert staff structures. This creates a minor dilemma in its goal of building knowledge and transferring learning effectively among the 1,300 companies' 5,000-profit-and-loss centers. The problem is to succeed in meeting the goal without re-creating, even indirectly, a new and ponderous expert staff apparatus.

ABB companies try to develop and use expert power in their hierarchy-less organization in order to optimize expertise. Most ABB experts can be shifted to work teams, manufacturing cells, clusters, projects, or groups. At least 80 percent of experts at the division, group, sector, or corporate level can be inserted into these self-contained operating units.

TRAINING

Most of the companies have their own technical training function in support of their respective products and services. Two elements determine the effectiveness and success of ABB's formal training and learning. These are the company operating environment and a systematic operational approach.

The company operating environment is the one in which the technical training function exists. For example, in the ABB process automation company, the global training development centers operate in the services business unit and are found near the product development engineering centers in Rochester and in Sweden. These global training centers develop product technical training standard courseware distributed to the training centers located in the various countries in which the products are sold and serviced. The centers determine the global training policies and standards with which the local training centers must comply. The operating relationships between the global training development centers and the local training centers are conducted on a dotted-line, or informal, basis. Each country has a local ABB organization that operates on its own profit-and-loss basis. Therefore, the local training operations report directly to the local ABB company management. The local company retains any revenue from training and thus funds the local training operation.

ABB companies use a well-defined systematic operational approach within the technical training function. The main training operation requirements are training design standards and training documentation standards. An instructional design and evaluation system (IDES) defines the standards for training courseware development in the company.

A MODEL FOR GLOBAL LEARNING ORGANIZATIONS

Asea Brown Boveri is seen by more and more global business leaders as the model of the way that organizations will have to operate to thrive in the 21st century—that is, streamlined in structure, rapid in transferring information, having employees who are highly empowered, committed to continuous learning, running world-class HRD programs, and teamworking and networking globally. ABB appears not only first in the alphabetical listing of companies, but also as one of the first among global learning organizations.

Chapter Twelve

AutoMind:
Adapting to Culture

T he smallest company consciously attempting to become a global learning organization that we were able to identify is AutoMind— a small software house headquartered in Santiago, Chile, with business in Brazil, Chile, Colombia, France, Mexico, Peru, the United States, and Venezuela.

CEO Roberto Araya's belief is that knowledge is the most valuable asset in any organization. He says,

> Our mission is to provide tools to store, generate, manage, distribute and put to work 'knowledge.' This vision pushes AutoMind to learn how to handle knowledge, a very volatile and little understood asset. When I was at Bell Communications Research (formerly Bell Labs–ATT) in New Jersey, I realized that behind all products, services, and ideas, there was always a small team. What was particular to these teams was not the material resources but their motivation and willingness to try and learn. Then I thought, why not try and go for it in Santiago, where I knew valuable people and could afford to begin?
>
> When an important bank asked us why we could build and implement a corporate credit assistance expert system better than IBM and Price Waterhouse, we proposed to ask all three companies to build a small prototype within two weeks. This way each company could show its understanding of the client's needs and demonstrate its capability to translate that in a workable system. The proposition was accepted by the client and we won and got the project. I don't think we could be so successful if we weren't attempting to become a global learning organization.

TEAM LEARNING

AutoMind attempts to create an internal environment that promotes learning, while existing in an external environment that has to be understood and interacted with to be able to learn. Araya says, ''Both is-

AutoMind at a Glance

	Organizational learning	Global learning
	✔ Appropriate structures	✔ Acculturation
	Corporate learning culture	✔ Borders
	Empowerment	Globalization
	✔ Environmental scanning	✔ Language
	Knowledge creation and transfer	Leadership
	✔ Learning technology	Workforce diversity
	✔ Quality	
	✔ Strategy	
	Supportive atmosphere	
	Teamwork and networking	
	Vision	

© Michael Marquardt and Angus Reynolds, 1992

Headquarters:	Santiago, Chile
Founded:	1988
Main business:	Software applications and professional services.
Chief executive officer:	Roberto Araya
Number of countries where located:	8
Total employees worldwide:	28

sues are essential. Without the second we could go nowhere: our products, AutoMind and AutoExpert, are continuously redesigned according to experience using them in new real- world applications." Teams work around specific project- or product-related goals. "Whether it is our clients or our engineers who attempt to use AutoMind and AutoExpert, we try to learn from those opportunities. We try to improve features or introduce new ways to resolve problems they were attempting to model and solve. Even when those problems are solved and the client is happy, we look for new improved ways in order to have a product best fitted for the next time."

The company promotes learning through team building, internal seminars, readings, invited lecturers, flexible courses that include clients' problems and needs, paper writings, conference participation, trade shows, internal learning resources, partnership with other organizations (Electricité de France, Institut National de Recherché Informatique e Automatique, and other companies and universities), a high R&D to sales ratio, a high proportion of new engineers, incorporation of young but energetic researchers, important number of thesis direction, and financial support.

AutoMind spends a relatively large sum to maintain a very complete library that contains technical and commercial magazines from all over the world. This is not typical for a small Chilean company, or even for big companies in Latin America. The library is very important to team learning. The AutoMind staff conduct periodic internal seminars reviewing the literature in their library.

THE NEED FOR GLOBAL LEARNING

A company like AutoMind is forced to be competitive by the open structure of the software market. There is no other similar company for thousands of miles. Araya says,

> In our marketplace, the technology required is new, fast changing, not mature, and advances, to some degree at least, is localized in highly specialized labs and leading companies. This pushes us to be constantly alert to try new ways, to improve and reinforce what has worked, and think globally. New ideas reported by others everywhere else in the world can make a significant impact on our products and services. That is why communication is also critical. We cannot pretend to find the correct way all by ourselves. And most of the other players are far away. We produce tools to gather, discover, and distribute knowledge. We try to use these same tools in our own learning. The payoffs are twofold: we learn faster and in a more systematic way, and at the same time we test and then get ideas to improve our products.

APPROPRIATE STRUCTURES FOR VARIOUS BUSINESS CULTURES

AutoMind has a different structure in each of the countries in which it has operations. This is a reflection of the local business climate and customs of that country. Let's look at some examples.

Colombia. A year and a half after starting the company, Araya decided to show AutoMind's software at a conference in Argentina. It was the first time it had gone out of Chile as a company. More than 200 engineers saw its sample application systems. All of them belonged to big companies and were potential clients.

Fortunately, as it turned out, there were Brazilian, Paraguayan, and Colombian participants as well as Argentineans. The Argentinean economy was very bad at that time, a situation that continued for some time. However, the Colombians who went there organized a conference in Colombia a few months later and invited Araya to help them. Then he visited Colombia and presented the AutoMind products at the congress there. Exxon people were there and wanted to work directly with AutoMind. Exxon Mining operates a huge coal mine in Columbia, and several opportunities were there. Araya decided to work in Colombia directly from the Chilean headquarters. The company manages everything from Santiago, and it has done very well. With the growth of business there, Araya is thinking of opening a small Colombian branch.

France. "We started the collaboration with Electricité de France looking for their expertise, and they were looking for non-utilities applications of their research. France's basic research in mathematics and theoretical computer science is very good. Electricité de France is very strong in artificial intelligence and its applications in utilities." Electricité de France (EDF) is the generator and distributor of electric power in France. EDF is a state-owned company and has about 130,000 employees. An example of AutoMind's collaboration with EDF is provided in another section of this chapter.

AutoMind also works with France's Institut National de Recherché en Informatique et Automatique (INRIA), the state institute for research in informatics and automation. INRIA is a research institute with about 2,000 employees. It is not associated with EDF. INRIA has a strong program for basic research in computer science and automation. The AutoMind collaboration with INRIA is based on INRIA'S recent interest in promoting start-ups that apply its research. Araya says, "They are very strong in basic research and they want to go global as well. We found a good opportunity there, with mutual benefits. They get the application of their research in Latin America, and we get access to novel ideas and communication with excellent researchers."

Mexico. AutoMind's Mexican joint venture is necessitated by the different business climate in Mexico. Although Mexico is a big market, it is not enough merely to speak Spanish. You have to know how business is done. AutoMind works with Hugo Rebolledo, an ex-college friend of Roberto Araya. Rebolledo was the chief engineer of Action Technologies, a U.S. company that does all its programming in Mexico. He wanted to start his own company and was looking for partners. Mexico has almost no local development in software, despite the size of its market. Customers there need strong support for building and maintaining their systems.

In some ways Mexico is an ideal market. Human performance is often poor, but technological support, such as expert systems and performance support systems, is almost unknown. This lack of knowledge and systems provided an opportunity for the joint venture. Performance support systems should show a big payoff in Mexico.

Venezuela. One day a Venezuelan who had heard of Auto-Mind called, saying that he was interested in its product. He came to Chile to visit the company and spent a day looking at AutoMind products. He recommended a Venezuelan company to represent AutoMind in Venezuela. On his next trip to Colombia, Araya detoured to Venezuela for a meeting with this company. At the same time he visited some of his clients.

It was clear to Araya that in Venezuela AutoMind had to work with someone that knew everybody there. The start was slow. Several times the staff were ready to go and teach seminars there, and at the last minute they canceled because of military coups. Finally, AutoMind arrived and is working there through the representative company with a growing business base.

APPROPRIATE STRUCTURES FOR VARIOUS BUSINESS SECTORS

AutoMind is also exploring vertical markets. AutoMind is integrating expert systems technologies with different services. For example, it may find that a maintenance client wants a complete diagnosis of its company, not only a system. Some customers and potential customers want AutoMind to diagnose their equipment instead of providing a diagnosis system. So Araya is opening a subsidiary that does the job. The subsidiary uses expert systems and machine learning technology to be more efficient.

The company is starting another branch for financial consultancy services for small and medium companies. AutoMind has already built several expert systems that diagnose the financial health of a company and assess its short-term financial needs. The new service would insulate the client, who does not see the expert system. The client sees only the service.

At present Araya is negotiating a joint venture with a leading Chilean bank. The joint effort will provide a service to help other banks automate their audit process. AutoMind will provide the expert system expertise and the bank their expertise in risk assessment and credit. If successful, they plan to provide similar services for banks throughout Latin America. Several potential customer Argentinean, Colombian, and Peruvian banks have already expressed interest in the service.

ELECTRICITÉ DE FRANCE AND AUTOEXPERT

Shortly after the founding of AutoMind, Araya started its first project for EDF in France. The project, building an expert system to support nonstatisticians' choice of the optimal sampling in order to perform a statistical study, proved very successful.

Jean-Luc Molliere, of EDF's applied artificial intelligence research division, proposed working together on a problem of mutual interest. He was attracted by AutoMind's drive and experience in applications of expert system techniques in a variety of industries. EDF had already made several applications, but they were all company related. At the same time, EDF had been very active in developing projects with other European companies, partly because of the general trend toward unification in Europe. AutoMind provided another option, but with a company outside Europe.

A Fresh Approach

At that time EDF's Philippe Gigon, a Ph.D. candidate doing research in expert systems, was interested in traveling abroad. He, like Molliere, was interested in solving one of the main difficulties of expert systems: maintaining large rule bases. Molliere himself was very interested in this problem and in pushing the development of techniques to do automatic programming of expert systems.

Araya proposed a unique approach called *machine learning*, or *induction*. Induction mixes statistics and expert systems. Molliere, being a statistician, liked the idea very much. At the same time Araya proposed work on a diesel engine diagnosis problem, because AutoMind had a good understanding of the problem and believed that machine learning techniques could be applied to make a significant difference.

Engine diagnosis is a common problem in applied science, and it interested EDF right away. AutoMind's mining company clients in Chile and Columbia all had been working on the same problem, so AutoMind had previous data, knowledge, and access to new data, and it had already built expert systems to address this problem. This second point was very important because it allowed AutoMind to compare classical expert system tools with the new induction techniques. EDF also uses oil analysis for predictive maintenance of its own machines. Although its machines are very different from mining machines, the problems are similar.

At AutoMind the staff had been working for more than a year trying to automate expert system building (induction) with no success. The engineer in charge of the development was very discouraged and wanted to quit. At that precise moment, Philippe Gigon arrived filled with new energy.

Gigon came to stay at AutoMind for a year and a half. During the first four months no one got any results. One day, while looking at an old INRIA technical paper in the company library, the team discovered a simple but powerful idea. It tried the idea on existing mining truck oil data, which produced stunning results. The team decided to implement the new idea on the diesel engine problem. It was a success!

Adaptation

At that point Araya thought of converting the program into a product—AutoExpert. The company first tried to use AutoExpert in other problems in completely different areas and businesses. This pushed the team to redesign the program. Several difficulties and restrictions were evident.

One day while showing AutoExpert to Carlos Wilhelm, an Exxon chief engineer in risk prevention, it became apparent that greater clarity required a certain kind of graphics. Three weeks later AutoExpert produced them automatically. Representatives showed the new graphics to potential clients because the graphics provided a much better understanding of what the program was doing with the data.

The same graphics helped Araya a few weeks later to discover how to handle categorical data. This improved and generalized what the company had learned from the INRIA paper. Some weeks later Auto-Mind made a proposal to a marketing study company to analyze its data at no cost. The company used the standard techniques, and Araya's team used AutoExpert. The results were very promising, and together they sold a bank the analysis of their client database. Pablo Gonzalez, president of the marketing company, helped AutoMind figure out solutions to a few drawbacks, and the solutions significantly improved the AutoExpert product.

Four months before Gigon ended his research at AutoMind, Araya went to France to present the results. EDF was pleased with the fruits of the collaboration. After a two-hour presentation to EDF, Araya received valuable feedback. He was convinced that the new product was different from any other on the market!

A recent conference attended by more than 30 French artificial intelligence specialists confirmed this belief. Several researchers and software companies are also interested in the AutoMind viewpoint and products.

A LOCAL TWIST

Araya says,

> Our learning contributes to our success through the continuous improvement of products and services. It provides us with faster maturing of products, ones that better fit local needs in different countries. It also gives us a bigger market, and a better corporate image as a global company.

It isn't easy for any organization to become a global learning organization, no matter what its size. The usual advantages for a small company—flexibility and potential for quick reaction—are balanced by fixed costs of projects and limited resources. In particular, it is difficult to find highly motivated people who are willing to try to believe in themselves and go for long-term goals.

There are still improvements to introduce. AutoMind hopes to develop new applications of its products. Araya plans to increase the multidisciplinary nature of the AutoMind teams. This will supplement the incorporation of people from other countries, which has already brought new ideas and schools of thought, and continue AutoMind's successful expansion as a global learning organization.

AutoMind looks forward rather than back. Future global business directions supported by its global learning success include products in vertical markets such as financial services and law, expansion of its past success in predictive maintenance, growth of consultancy, and increased emphasis on long-distance support.

TOWARD A BRIGHT FUTURE

Araya tries to look beyond the horizon.

I have been for years amazed by the power of the system of numeric representation. It took thousands of centuries for human beings to understand that two horses and two cats were examples of the number two. It took another several thousands of centuries to realize how to add numbers easily. Now, with positional numeric representation, it is a trivial task.

This fact allowed the development of all our civilization. It made possible accounting, inventory management, personnel management, and all business practices. If we were able to represent and manage knowledge the same succinct and powerful way we manage numbers, we could enable a 10-year-old child to manage and use highly specialized knowledge. Theoretically a child could function at the expert level in medicine, law, and engineering. We won't see this in our lifetime, but I hope we can take the initial steps in enabling people to manage knowledge more effectively.

For global learning organizations like AutoMind, such a vision is a necessity for continued growth.

Chapter Thirteen

Carvajal Inversiones:
A Learning Family

I n 1904 don Manuel Carvajal Valencia and his sons, Alberto and Hernando, established a small printing shop in the sleepy town of Cali, Columbia. They set the type by hand and used an old-fashioned hand-operated lever press to do the printing.

All that has changed completely.

Today the Carvajal Inversiones S.A. entrepreneurial organization covers the whole North and South American continents. Carvajal grew with Cali and transformed with Colombia.

Carvajal advanced from that rudimentary technology to the most up-to-date systems of printing, paper and cardboard conversion, processing, lamination, extrusion, and printing on aluminum foil and plastic film. Carvajal also operates an area of educational publishing, and a commercial area of communications and data processing office equipment. The company is seen today as one of the vital factors of Colombia's progress and has subsidiaries and associated companies in other western hemisphere countries with exports to five continents.

Thanks to the foresight of the founders and their successors, to the tireless efforts of four generations of the Carvajal family, and to the efficiency and loyalty of its employees, the little firm born at the turn of the century has achieved a notable position in the modern communications industry. For more than 50 years, Carvajal has been committed to the creation of a community, or perhaps more accurately a family, of owners, managers, workers, and other stakeholders, all seeking to become a learning family.

Carvajal operates in a country of 30 million people, a country with serious social problems and economic limitations. In spite of these tremendous challenges, it has become the largest producer in the printing industry as well as in the book and telephone book publishing industry in Latin America. Some of its products, for instance, pop-up books, have acquired global leadership status. Carvajal is now the largest transnational Latin American manufacturing company. It has suc-

Carvajal at a Glance

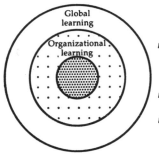

Organizational learning	Global learning
Appropriate structures	✔ Acculturation
Corporate learning culture	Borders
✔ Empowerment	Globalization
Environmental scanning	Language
Knowledge creation and transfer	✔ Leadership
Learning technology	✔ Workforce diversity
✔ Quality	
Strategy	
✔ Supportive atmosphere	
Teamwork and networking	
Vision	

© Michael Marquardt and Angus Reynolds, 1992

Headquarters:	Cali, Columbia
Founded:	1904
Main business:	Packaging, publishing, consumer goods, business forms and security printing, office automation, and storage.
President:	Adolfo Carvajal Quelquejeu
Number of countries where located:	14
Total employees worldwide:	13,000

ceeded globally while maintaining a distinctive Latin American culture. The main reason for its success is the climate of entrepreneurship, autonomy, and learning that exists consistently throughout the 40 divisions of the company.

AN IDEAL OF SERVICE

All this, of course, did not just happen. From the beginning, the zest for innovation characterized Carvajal and spurred it to explore the latest managerial, industrial, and commercial advances. With this learning spirit as a constant over the years, Carvajal reflected a permanent ideal of service to the community. Management commitment was, and still is, based on the conviction that the progress of a company depends largely on the progress of the countries in which it does business.

Carvajal anticipated the needs of the domestic and foreign markets as they developed and was ready to satisfy them with the resources of the appropriate technology. It has not only kept up to date in this area, but also in many cases pioneered industrial and commercial practices and revamped operations. Custom machinery has been built especially for Carvajal as result of its research and development. In addition, in its own workshops, Carvajal has designed, improved, and built many pieces of equipment, and produced inks and other special supplies, parts, and products.

Since its foundation in 1904 as a small printing shop, the owners created a tradition of deep respect for their employees as human beings within the company. Based on moral principles, all policies and a very particular management style reflected the tradition that has been maintained throughout Carvajal's history. It is Carvajal's conviction that people are not only their most valuable asset, but also that people are its principal strategic factor for success. As a result, Carvajal places a top priority on two factors:

- Participation as a way of maintaining up-to-date information throughout the organization and of creating a sense of belonging, and as a form of continuous training.
- Training and development of everyone in the organization from top to bottom in an integral and holistic way.

The drive to excel and the ability to create ever better and more practical ways of doing things permeates the entire organization from the top management down to the areas of production and sales. It is also the key to a future of continued progress. Amazingly, in light of the fact that many companies that redraw their organizational chart every six months, Carvajal is still guided by the document called *General Principles of Our Organization,* which was written 25 years ago. From it grows Carvajal's vision, mission, values, and principles of entrepreneurial culture. These are listed in Figure 13–1.

Carvajal has also been an outstanding example of corporate citizenship in its hometown of Cali, in the surrounding Cauca Valley , and throughout Columbia. For more than a decade, the Carvajal Foundation, established and supported by substantial holdings in Carvajal, has been a major force in collaborative community development. In the spirit of cooperation, it has worked with its neighbors to construct thousands of affordable housing units, support public health programs and institutions, train and educate entrepreneurs and small businesspeople, and provide educational and other opportunities to both children and adults.

CULTURE AND BARRIERS

One of Carvajal's main business challenges lies in managing or synergizing the culture differences it encounters in Latin America, which

FIGURE 13-1
Carvajal's Vision, Mission, Values, and Principles of Entrepreneurial Culture

---

Vision

To become the heart and alma mater of the corporate culture, through the consolidation of an integral permanent formation nucleus of excellent quality.

Mission

To be source and motivator of the strategic vision of our corporate human resources and, in consequence, to facilitate leaders, in all levels, that they meet their obligations regarding formation and development of the persons that work with them so that they contribute with effectiveness, productivity, creativity, quality, and daily practice of our culture in the way the organization requires to increase its leadership.

Values

Respect for human dignity.
An integral vision of every person.
Persons forming persons.
Quality.
Self-criticism capacity.
Loyalty.
Ethics.
Respect for the environment.
To be example and witness.

Principles of Entrepreneurial Culture

- A commitment to quality, productivity, service, imagination, and the self-fulfillment of each human being through the enrichment of his working life.
- The customer and the worker are both equally important elements.
- Their welfare as well as the company's progress depend largely on the realization of our corporate principles.

---

make it difficult to have a unified view of human resources. This includes dealing with a typically Latin autocratic view of management, even though Carvajal comes from a long tradition of participation. Yet Carvajal is determined to overcome these cultural barriers and expand in the Latin American market.

In Latin America there is a definite and firm trend toward free markets and open economies. NAFTA and the European community are stimulating the creation of several free trade agreements within the region:

Andean Pact

- Bolivia
- Colombia
- Ecuador

- Peru
- Venezuela

Group of Three

- Colombia
- Mexico
- Venezuela

The Mercosur

- Argentina
- Brazil
- Uruguay

With Latin America as Carvajal's natural market, its competitive advantage in the region will be maintained and expanded through its organizational learning efforts. Carvajal International, Inc. maintains offices in New York and Miami that render valuable services to its clients in the United States, Europe, and other countries. Carvajal also avails itself of the communication facilities existing in these cities to expedite its relations with customers and suppliers worldwide.

QUALITY ABOVE ALL

Carvajal has insisted from the beginning on maintaining high standards of quality in its own products as well as in the products it distributes. This is not only an industrial policy; it is a source of pride for all who work for the company. Years of experience have enabled the company to set and maintain high standards of operation in all departments by using the appropriate equipment to guarantee quality products. Moreover, it has a responsible technical staff, continuously learning and highly qualified in carrying out their tasks in all production and marketing departments.

Quality starts with product design, which must conform to very strict standards and to the customer's specifications in each case. Raw materials and other supplies undergo chemical and physical tests in Carvajal's laboratories. Quality control is exercised by the person responsible for each step in the production process, with the advice of the quality office in each division and the overall guidance of a central office. Similarly, through the system of quality circles, employees at all levels meet regularly to identify, select, and analyze problems of their particular area and suggest solutions to management.

Carvajal's definition of quality is as follows:

To respond adequately to concrete needs from our clients in an attractive, rapid, practical, and usable way.

Proof of its success goes beyond simple acceptance of its products by national and foreign buyers, even in very demanding markets. It has also won several international awards.

CUSTOMER-ORIENTED SERVICE

Carvajal tries to pinpoint the needs and wishes of clients in order to satisfy them. The organization joins hands on all fronts to determine the markets for its various products—who the clients are, where they are, what they want, and what services or products they may require. This attention results in an ever greater market share and a better image in the community.

All areas of company activity are responsible to the customer. They try to improve their relations with their clients to increase the volume of their operations and the clients' satisfaction with the services they render. To better accomplish this mission of keeping clients happy, management established the office of the customer representative. This office first learns what opinions customers have of Carvajal's services. Then it keeps its sales departments informed of customer reactions so that any causes of complaint or dissatisfaction may be quickly corrected and relations strengthened in the future.

THE COMPANY'S PEOPLE

Carvajal reflects its Latin American origins and business environment. One of Carvajal's operating tenets is that its people are its most valuable resource and one of its most important groups of customers. From the comprehensive hiring process that allows both potential employee and employer to understand as much as possible about each other before making a commitment, to the lifelong support and development efforts made in collaboration with, and on behalf of, each employee, Carvajal's commitment to its human resources is clear.

Emphasis on product quality has not caused Carvajal to lose sight of the fact that the company is, above all, a group of human beings. The company recognizes and respects the central role of men's and women's personal dignity, aspirations, and spiritual and physical needs.

Stemming from the conviction that mutual trust is the basis of real participation throughout the organization, managers of divisions and subsidiaries, both domestic and foreign, as well as directors of administrative areas and service centers, enjoy great autonomy and decision-making power in their areas of responsibility. Each division has its own management board with the necessary operating independence, yet each enjoys the strength derived from the administrative backing of the whole organization.

HUMAN RESOURCE DEVELOPMENT

Diego Narajo Meza, director of the Carvajal Institute For Human Development makes the following statement about Carvajal's development practices:

> One of Carvajal's main forces is its human resources philosophy and policies because of its humanistic orientation. We need, however, to go a step further in the sense of breaking our "organizational chart culture," and create a culture where status and personal mastery and development can be reached through development of each one's personal talents. Thus the Institute will put a special emphasis on the talent development of every person. We will have persons working much more happily, more productively, more realized as a person, the need for supervision will decrease, and the whole as persons and as organization will be more harmonious.

Carvajal College.   Carvajal has long been a regional leader in HRD. As a sign of its commitment to the continued development of its human resources, Carvajal has begun to create Carvajal College, a world-class corporate educational institution that will, within the next few years, become a state-of-the-art education and training institution with its own campus in Cali.

Carvajal Institute for Human Development.   Narajo says,

> We have had a very aggressive training center by Colombian standards for many years. Since July 1992 we have undertaken the creation of the Carvajal Institute for Human Development with a holistic view of training and development. Our experience has demonstrated that we have to see each person as a unique system. Employees' environment, family, and origins play heavily on the way they behave and progress. That is why the principal mission of the Institute is to create and promote a strategic vision of their human resources. We are setting up programs that strategically respond to specific needs of the company such as a school of strategic marketing, a

school of English as a second language, and a school of leadership. But we are also delivering programs that, even though they do not respond to direct needs, have a great influence on the performance of the individual. Programs such as self-knowledge that teach people to ask questions . . . are proving to be essential in our overall purpose. We are also working in certain areas on the very basics where we thought we would not need to go, such as mathematics or reading and writing, in order to level up all our 13,000 people.

Also, through our school of leaders, we are spreading multipliers throughout the organization who not only know how to teach and motivate learning, but also transmit and promote organizational values and principles. Our objective is that in four years there will be a wholly formed leader for every five persons in the company.

Carvajal makes the means of training and development for personal advancement available to all its employees. Training and instruction programs are conducted regularly, including lectures by well-known speakers who analyze current problems and their possible solutions.

Kindergarten too. In the near future, Carvajal will incorporate a kindergarten where it expects to enroll employees' children to try to detect talents and to teach parents how to help their children in the development of those talents. Indirectly, the company hopes to transmit tools for its employees to build stable and solid families. It believes that these actions create the necessary environment for learning. It also expects many of those children to be future Carvajal employees.

A philosophy of learning. Narajo told us the Carvajal HRD philosophical framework.

We must go a step further on the concept that "our people are our principal asset," which is a static and present concept, toward a conviction that our people are *the* main strategic factor for the success of our organization, which is a dynamic and futuristic concept. This must be reflected in our corporate culture.

If our main differentiation factor is our people, we will only attain that differentiation through the leadership of our managerial force. Thus special emphasis will be given to managerial development. We will obtain world leadership based upon a world-class leadership force.

AN EYE TO THE FUTURE

Carvajal wants to use its experience, know-how, and organizational learning to further develop markets in countries where it is already established, and to look for new opportunities for growth in the world market.

Diego Narajo says, ''We are still far short of the goals we have set for ourselves, and thus decided to undertake the creation of the Carvajal Institute for Human Development. I am confident that the improvements we are making will get us to the goal.'' Efforts to expand its presence in markets such as Europe and the United States will undoubtedly be greatly helped by its learning drive.

Adolfo Carvajal Quelquejeu, president of Carvajal, states,

> Our international presence grows day by day in intensity, in keeping with our purpose. Our bond of union is enthusiasm in the commitment to do things right. We want to create something lasting and valuable: a persistent tradition, in the midst of technological and management innovations, of doing things better than others, faster, at lower cost, generating productive employment and well-being. We are nearing the completion of 100 years of this effort, never before extended into so many fronts, with so vast and promising a horizon. The difference in Carvajal is our conviction that work guided by these principles will be a source of wealth and well-being for the company, our personnel, and the communities of the several countries to whose prosperity we contribute and on whose prosperity we depend.

Carvajal has truly become not only a learning organization, but also a global learning family.

Chapter Fourteen

Caterair International:
Vision and Values Elevating Organizational Excellence

I n 1991 airlines experienced a worldwide decline in business including, for the first time ever, a downturn in global air travel. The consolidation of airlines continued with the dramatic shutdown of two large U.S. carriers and a surge in the sale and exchange of airline routes worldwide. The international airline business declined because of the Persian Gulf War, as well as a persistent recession in the United States and elsewhere in the world. Many airlines were in trouble then and responded immediately by cutting the quality of food.

Who has bright prospects in the face of this environment? Caterair, who else? The airlines have come to understand that food and service are an important part of their marketing equation. A Delta Airlines spokesperson said, "You may not win customers by having good food, but you may lose a lot of customers if you have a bad meal. Meals are extremely important."

Caterair International has spread its wings in solo flight. It is the 1989 incarnation of Marriott Corporation's airline catering division. Although not an airline, its business depends on the airline industry. Caterair controls about 40 percent of the domestic aviation catering market. In addition, they have a major global presence. Forty-four percent of sales come from their international business. Caterair has kitchens in Australia, South Korea, Japan, and Taiwan. It also has joint ventures in Moscow with Aeroflot and in São Paulo with Varig. In 1991 Caterair catered approximately 200 million meals worldwide on almost 2 million flights.

Caterair inherited many sound values from its previous owners. Its new mission, vision, and values statement, however, provides a powerful directive, and the tools to fulfill its strategic plan and retain its leading position in the airline catering industry.

Caterair at a Glance

Organizational learning	Global learning
✔ Appropriate structures	Acculturization
✔ Corporate learning culture	✔ Borders
✔ Empowerment	✔ Globalization
Environmental scanning	✔ Language
✔ Knowledge creation and transfer	✔ Leadership
✔ Learning technology	Workforce diversity
Quality	
✔ Strategy	
Supportive atmosphere	
Teamwork and networking	
✔ Vision	

© Michael Marquardt and Angus Reynolds, 1992

Headquarters:	Bethesda, Maryland
Founded:	1933
Main business:	Airline catering
Chairman, president and CEO:	Daniel J. Altobello
Number of countries where located:	23
Total employees worldwide:	22,000

Our mission is *to be the airline caterer of choice in the world so that:*

1. Employees experience a quality of life resulting from an environment of growth, fair treatment, and opportunity.

2. Customers receive value and consistent, superior service for the specified products.

3. Airline passengers perceive on-board food as a necessary and valuable feature.

4. Shareholders receive at least the required return on investment.

5. The community shares and benefits from our success and perceives us as a good corporate citizen.

OPERATIONAL TRIANGLE

People at Caterair talk about an operational triangle. The triangle is formed by Caterair, its customers, and its suppliers. The goal is that Caterair people will routinely exceed their customers' expectations for quality, consistency, and dependability so that "our customers will offer us as an example to others." The standard is that "we will act as though each customer is our only customer."

Being customer-driven isn't a bad idea. Management recognizes that it is in a customer-driven business, and that "we do not so much have a product to sell as customers to be satisfied. In our quest for quality, two factors are paramount: we will strive continuously to improve, and we must be the best in the eyes of every person who works for our customer.''

The on-time guarantee program has produced exemplary service and customer satisfaction. Since Caterair began the program in 1990, it has compiled an average performance record of only one delay for every 4,424 flights catered.

INFORMATION TRANSFER

Caterair believes in getting the word around. Its *Horizons* newsletter is published quarterly in six languages. It is distributed in its global marketplace to all employees and contains information not previously shared on a worldwide basis. There are also 12 regional newsletters. These provide a more localized focus on events and celebrations of more focused appeal. Caterair also publishes a newsletter for its managers, who in addition benefit from a videotape series published for them in the second month of each quarter. The videos are distributed in French, German, Portuguese, Russian, and Spanish, covering topics related to finance, marketing, and industry news.

LEARNING CULTURE

Management is trying to create an entire new organization and learning environment so that people can constantly change, be innovative, and meet customer demands. There is also a reengineering task force focused on what Caterair's kitchens should look like. Caterair believes that in leadership and quality it has a sustainable advantage that can't be duplicated. Caterair is reengineering its units to reduce costs and cycle time while increasing productivity and profitability.

The training staff worked hard to ''change the essence of how we do learning.'' Particular attention has been directed to how adults learn and how to disseminate skill sets. The Caterair approach is to provide training targeted to each level of management. With a goal of merging specific job-related skills and leadership development training, Caterair has established two separate but complementary training programs. The concept of the Caterair Quality and Leadership Institute (CQLI) is to communicate, educate on, train about, and problem-solve business issues, thereby establishing a learning environment to sustain and support the new culture and quality process. The Caterair Leadership and Development Center focuses more on providing managers with the leadership skills to change their working environment and institute Caterair's values on a day-to-day basis. The Caterair Quality Institute concentrates on providing skills with which managers can improve individual work processes in their units or functional needs.

The Caterair approach to quality and management development provides training targeted to each level of management. The goal is to provide management with concepts, ideas, and tools that it can use on the job. The HRD staff focuses on getting the flight out, but also on exposing managers to techniques that will help them develop their subordinates into high-performance teams and ready them for more senior positions.

GLOBAL MINDSET TRAINING

Caterair has conducted global mindset training for 12 regional VPs in Canada, France, Mexico, the Netherlands, and Spain. Managers are also exposed to similar programs. They are likely to appreciate these experiences because managers' career paths must include international experience for promotion. There have been 19 such programs held in Boston, Caracas, Detroit, Frankfurt, London, Los Angeles, Madrid, Mexico City, Minneapolis, Moscow, Paris, Phoenix, San Francisco, Santiago, Seattle, Toronto, and Vancouver.

Caterair management views the institutes as the primary driver of cultural change in management, assembly management training in various departments, and in its kitchens. In an effort to streamline training and increase organizational efficiency, Caterair combined production, and food service, and transportation, and multiple and single kitchens, thereby saving $50 million and reducing hourly staff by 20 percent. David Workman, senior vice president for human resources, says, "We are trying to create an entirely new organization and learning environment. Our people need to be able to constantly change so they can be innovative and meet customer needs. To gain a sustainable advantage, we produce top leadership and top quality."

Global mindset training is supported by a series of value exhortations for Caterair employees. (These were presented in Chapter 4.) Caterair's corporate HRD group developed a vehicle to communicate the mission, vision, and values (MVV) worldwide through a series of events:

- Caterair leadership program
- Managing for quality
- Facilitating the Caterair Management Plan

The process not only communicated MVV, but also modeled behavior for Caterair's leadership, addressed implementation issues at the unit level, and provided a structured guide for managers.

QUALITY AND LEADERSHIP INSTITUTE

The Quality Institute offers 11 courses for employees ranging from new hires to future general managers. Altogether it provides a spectrum of learning opportunities tailored to the food service industry. Content ranges from statistical process control through Pareto analysis, group facilitation techniques, contamination and food-borne illness, meal load factor determination, and productivity measurement. The courses offered are as follows:

- Quality Tools
- Group Facilitation Techniques
- Total Quality Management Orientation
- Sanitation Certification
- Transportation Scheduling
- Productivity Measurement
- Quality Measurement Systems
- Customer Service Techniques
- Purchasing Management
- Production Systems
- Operations Finance and Administration

TECHNOLOGY

Caterair management recognizes that it is in a low-technology, service-intensive business. At the same time, it believes that the judicious application of appropriate technology can raise the level of service, produce higher quality, and promote lower cost throughout its worldwide network. Accordingly, Caterair has embarked on a program of technological improvement unique in its industry.

Trainees benefit from technology-based instruction. The 27-person HRD staff produce training programs using laser disk and satellite delivery as well as conventional methods. It has also invested $14 million for new technology and improvements to the existing fleet and facilities. New technology is appearing in the Caterair kitchens; a series of automated robotic systems is being phased in.

MANAGEMENT INITIATIVES

Management hopes to create empowered employees and build high-performance teams. Caterair management has developed a five-year strategic plan for the company and has formulated a new MVV for Caterair and its people. The strategic plan is both a map for the future and a blueprint of what must be done to remain the leading airline caterer in the world.

The company conducted a series of executive events to forge consensus and build its team. Management initiated a process to formalize the development of the strategic business plan, measured its corporate culture worldwide, redefined the corporate MVV, and introduced a systematic, companywide decision-making process designed to facilitate planning, problem solving, and communications and resources allocation (CMP).

EMPOWERMENT

Caterair is proud of its code of fair treatment. Management wants to ensure the same opportunities for individual growth and sharing of gain for all employees. Efforts are underway to drive mistrust from every corner of the organization and keep it out. Management has set guidelines for the empowerment of employees:

- Respect employees' knowledge.
- Solicit problem-solving ideas.
- Encourage unsolicited problem-solving ideas.
- Listen to the other person's ideas.
- Respond to employees suggestions in a timely way.
- Put decision-making power in the hands of the most knowledgeable person.
- Empower people to act when they must.

- Back up those you empower.
- Investigate mistakes, learn from them, and prevent them from recurring.
- Forgive honest mistakes.

POISED TO TAKE OFF

Looking ahead, based on several independent forecasts, it appears that the worldwide air travel market will continue to grow through the 1990s, nearly doubling in size by the year 2000. In addition, Caterair expects consolidation within the airline industry to continue for several more years. CEO Daniel J. Altobello says, "Far from being a disadvantage, we view the twin phenomena of growth and consolidation as strengthening the industry and providing additional business opportunities for Caterair. The traditional partnership between suppliers and customers will grow stronger with growth and consolidation. Caterair's global network, as well as our reputation for quality and strong bonds with many of the world's airlines, will work to Caterair's advantage in the years ahead." Caterair International has quickly become a high-flying global learning organization.

Chapter Fifteen

Corning:
Synergy and Learning Success

"**A**ll parts of our vision . . . work in harmony together. That harmony, that *synergy*, weaves our tapestry, the one big picture we share . . . a vision . . . as the very best—as *world-class*," the new CEO said. None of the top managers at the 1983 meeting yawned noticeably, but neither were they impressed. He went on to announce his plan to spend $5 million on a total quality program. The managers thought that it was the "flavor of the month." It wasn't. Later, many of the rank and file and the unions were not easily convinced of management's sincerity. The company did need revitalization; nearly 70 pecent of revenues came from slow-growth businesses in which Corning was not a market leader. Profits had declined for three years in a row.

Corning's CEO Jamie Houghton admits that, at the time his idea "went over like a bomb." They've come a long way since then and all three groups came around. Houghton and Corning are now known for the relentless pursuit of quality, defined as complete customer satisfaction. Along the way, the company that made the bulbs for Edison's electric light sold off the light bulb business, among other businesses that didn't meet standards of profitability. It also sharpened its joint venture skill, a hallmark of Corning since 1924, using its 19 major joint ventures and other alliances with external partners to develop and sell new products faster. Today, magazines such as *BusinessWeek* routinely call Houghton "visionary." His vision today is "to be the best, to be among the world's 10 most admired corporations by 1995 and unquestionably world class." There's much more to the story.

WHERE ARE THEY COMING FROM?

Beyond Edison's light bulbs, Corning produced a series of technical milestones including heat-resistant and corrosion-resistant glass, ra-

Corning at a Glance

Organizational learning	Global learning
Appropriate structures	Acculturization
✔ Corporate learning culture	✔ Borders
✔ Empowerment	Globalization
Environmental scanning	Language
Knowledge creation and transfer	✔ Leadership
✔ Learning technology	Workforce diversity
✔ Quality	
Strategy	
Supportive atmosphere	
✔ Teamwork and networking	
Vision	

© Michael Marquardt and Angus Reynolds, 1992

Headquarters:	Corning, New York
Founded:	1851
Main business:	Specialty materials, consumer housewares, laboratory services, and opto-electronics. Also has principal joint ventures with 15 other companies
Chairman:	James R. Houghton
Number of countries where located:	12
Total employees worldwide:	31,000

dar and TV bulbs, glass-ceramics, photochromic lenses, computer disks, and fiber optics. Corning was founded by Amory Houghton in Brooklyn, New York, to produce tableware and decorative glass. Its first diversification was into railway signal lenses, lantern globes, and thermometer tubes.

Today Corning remains the world's leading special glass and ceramics company. At the same time Corning's technology extends to more than 60,000 different products including plastic and metal and advanced laboratory testing instruments and procedures. Alliances such as Dow Corning (silicones), Ciba Corning (medical diagnostics), and Siecor (optical cable) add still more technical versatility. Corning's global network of businesses and alliances focuses on four market sectors:

- Specialty materials
- Telecommunications
- Laboratory sciences
- Consumer housewares

More than one employee told us, "Corning is a great place to work and to learn."

A FAMILY BUSINESS

Jamie is the seventh Houghton to hold the chief executive title. The Houghton family control of a $900 million piece of Corning—15 percent of the stock—is an unmatched, if not unique, advantage. It gives Jamie the freedom to take risks and manage for the long term. As CEO, he took them.

Houghton made the tough, costly moves that proved right for Corning. When he took over, profits had declined for the three previous years in a row. Approximately 70 percent of revenues were from slow-growth businesses. Worse, Corning was not the market leader for those businesses.

In the first six years Houghton divested marginal businesses worth $500 million in revenues. The venerable light bulb business was sold during this maneuver. Simultaneously, Houghton spent a like amount to acquire new businesses. He also established several foreign joint ventures. These moves made Corning a player in laboratory services and fiber optics. Attention to production processes resulted in increased efficiency and reduced costs. Jamie continued the company's traditional investment in research, development, and engineering at a rate significantly higher than the national industry average and supported technical commitment with hard dollars. The result was the Corning we see today—growing and leading in its markets.

BEING VENTURESOME AND BUILDING NETWORKS

"What we are seeing today is that the companies that are most successful across a broad range of industries—computers, telecommunications, pharmaceuticals, are the ones that can use alliances successfully to get access to new skills, products, or markets," says David Ernst, an international management consultant at McKinsey & Company.

Corning has the unique ability to make joint ventures work successfully. *FW* magazine picked Corning as its best practice company for joint ventures and alliances, calling Corning "by far the master of the art of partnering." This is no mean feat; a McKinsey & Co. report asserted that two thirds of major joint ventures or strategic alliances experience serious financial or managerial problems within the first two years. Yet many more alliances have succeeded at Corning than at any other firm. Over the years Corning has been involved in more than 48 joint ventures.

Today, Corning has a minority or 50 percent share in 22 ventures in 12 countries including Japan, Korea, India, Germany, and China. Corning's corporate network adds value beyond that created by its single parts. It is bound together by a dedication to total quality, a commitment to technology, shared financial resources, common values, and management links. Jamie Houghton emphasizes Corning's worldwide network of businesses, subsidiaries, and alliances—Corning's own "global village"—in recognition of the basic strength it gives the company in this one-world era. He urges Corning's worldwide network of joint ventures and alliances to share technology. Within each sector Corning uses various organizational and ownership structures, including partnerships with other companies, to best meet the requirements of its customers and to compete more effectively.

The equity alliances produced 35 percent of Corning's net income in 1991. Corning's partnerships typically produce higher returns on assets than its wholly owned units. The biggest venture is Dow Corning Corporation, a profitable maker of silicones. The alliances have greatly expanded Corning's scope. The ventures and alliances provide the means for it to leverage strengths in research, bring products to market quickly, and enter new markets more readily than it could alone.

Corning's partnership style involves sets of counterpart middle managers sitting down and discussing the problems most likely to arise in the new venture. The problems that plague many joint ventures include the obvious ones of capital commitments and management structure. Corning typically maintains oversight of its alliances through a six-member board of directors—three executives from each parent company. Participation of Corning's corporate staff and operating units is kept to a minimum. If Corning has enjoyed unusual success in its joint ventures, it may be because of its lengthy and careful preparation. Corning looks years in advance at every company in related industries to identify potential partners. Corning managers start to record detailed notes on potential partners well before any formal deal making. When the time for negotiation arrives, Corning has completed extensive research into a potential partner's background.

RESEARCH AND DEVELOPMENT

Corning invested 17 years and $100 million in fiber optics before it obtained a major order. Today, its $600 million-a-year business leads the market—which is growing at 20 percent annually. Corning's development of optical fiber helped impart direction to today's opto-electronics market. Corning's network is now a leading global supplier of fiber-optic cable and supporting components.

Corning is also the leading supplier of glass for LCDs. Still, to maintain its leadership, Corning's labs will spend $100 million on R&D on liquid crystal displays by the time it breaks even on the project, around 1995. To capitalize on Corning's heavy research and development investment, Houghton urges businesses to share technology.

TRAINING EQUALS LEARNING AND FIXING

Jamie Houghton's vision for learning is this: "I see a company whose employees pursue training and education that lead them to do the job right the first time." Bill Whitmore, Corning's guru of "tecknowledgy transfer," says, "To be successful, training must be looked upon as a strategic tool, not a necessary evil." Throughout its U.S. operations, Corning is gambling on achieving higher-quality products through a higher-quality work force. Training will continue to be stressed for all payroll groups. Technological changes alone will make continual learning a requirement.

Manufacturing organizations are generally run by people with engineering or business backgrounds. They often look for engineering or business solutions to problems. Although they know on an intellectual level that learning is important, they often don't feel comfortable investing in it because they don't understand it. We also need to note that much of managers' lingering doubts about the effectiveness of training is not unfounded.

The industrial training function has been run by individuals who have little or no professional background in training. Therefore, many training development efforts have produced dubious results. Even when professionals have been hired, these individuals sometimes come from an academic background, and shop floor training is very different from the classroom.

Manufacturing facilities could have training development teams chartered to produce measurable learning packages for all job descriptions. A key possibility is to document the fixes and create training to prevent recurrence. Potential spin-offs include opportunities for common interdepartmental tools and uses with customers and vendors.

Changing ingrained organizational cultural habits is a difficult task.

To do so, a company must develop an ongoing history of training successes that contribute to the bottom line. If persistent, these successes will become a seed crop that will germinate and bear fruit. Upper management is in the business of making a profit and will invest in proven winners if they are worth their salt. Whitmore says, "In manufacturing, much time is spent fixing and re-fixing sick processes. If the proper documentation and training development techniques are applied to the fixing process, we can begin practicing holistic training management techniques and our fixes will become permanent."

Technology. Satellite and teleconferencing can be used to bring troubleshooting teams from one location to another without the travel cost. Corning has used a closed circuit TV system to pipe an event to a group in the cafeteria. A remote feed could be established to take a group in a remote location onto the plant floor.

Whitmore says, "If Corning wants to maintain its competitive edge in this age of expanding technology and world-class markets, we must provide our workers with timely, job-specific training. If we can meet this challenge, we'll continue to outpace our competitors. If we don't, we won't."

TECKNOWLEDGY TRANSFER

Moving equipment is only half the battle—how to run it is the other half. Technology transfer is the movement of knowledge from one person in one location to another in a different location. Bill Whitmore says, "When transferring knowledge, whether it be across the ocean, across the country, or across the block, the distance between two minds is the same. Only the logistics are different."

The tecknowledgy transfer process is a straightforward, easy-to-use, cost-effective method for transferring technical knowledge from one person to another with the least error. The result is customized learning that is based upon Corning's best known expertise—and it won't retire, change jobs, or forget important details. More importantly, it works. The word tecknowledgy was coined in 1986 to differentiate between the equipment used in technical manufacturing operations and the knowledge needed to operate that equipment at optimal levels of proficiency.

Whitmore defines tecknowledgy as the state of process awareness attained by true technical experts. It is the foundation on which procedures are written and technical advances are made. And although it was usually acquired through years of hard won experience, it is transferable if the proper techniques are used.

Building on this definition, *tecknowledgy transfer* can be further defined as a training development process designed to pinpoint true technical experts, capture their knowledge, and transfer that knowledge to new generations of process experts.

For these reasons, we, as training developers, are playing an ever-expanding role in manufacturing organizations, and the tecknowledgy transfer process can be an awesome weapon in Corning's arsenal.

A glimpse. Because we are a video generation, video is a useful tool. Whitmore uses on-the-fly video production techniques. The programs are edited on camera and produced as they go. The finished tapes resemble the popular "This Old House" program's style. Video also helps to overcome literacy problems. Successful people with a literacy problem often compensate with memory. Corning finds video useful in these situations. It is also helpful in overcoming language barriers.

An international transfer to England had a team of retired people who knew the process. The aim was to videotape procedures so that the active workers would not have to return to the job site repeatedly. Whitmore made a permanent record for future learning. Video production for the project was copied and shown to local site people, who then used it to produce tapes for their customers. For example, when developing a new technology, employees used tapes of the old one as references to help gain a better insight and understanding of the capability of the particular technique.

At Corning today, 4 to 7 percent of the technology transfer budget is spent on training. Before, that figure was about 2 percent. Four percent may seem high, but it highlights hidden costs that would be spent anyway, such as those for training an engineer. The payback is great. There is significant cost avoidance because learning curves are greatly reduced, and sometimes are eliminated altogether. In the past, Corning normally asked an expert in engineering to design the training. Now it has the tecknowledgy transfer process. The subject of projects to date were complex processes, calling for specialized knowledge in many cross-functional disciplines.

Savings. Based on historical data, the projected three-year learning curve for technology transfers of this kind was estimated at 50 percent during the first year, 70 percent by the second year, and

90 percent in the third year. A target of 100 percent of the standard is possible by the fourth year.

The learning curve for the Corning's international tecknowledgy transfer is 70 percent for the first year and 100 percent by the second. One tecknowledgy transfer activity cost $190,000 but saved Corning over $655,000 in learning curve expenses.

Cloning. Now Corning needs to find a way to expand its ability to service demands. Because of the growing demand for his services, Whitmore's calendar is booked a year in advance and he's begun developing a series of courses on the tecknowledgy transfer process. He would like to see Corning benefit from an extended network of technology transfer teams. A core team could be responsible for training the extended teams, keeping them appraised of state of the art in learning.

The next step. Any project should have someone who is focused on training. To maintain a competitive edge, the process knowledge base must be expanded, and added experts must be cultivated. This allows management to expand to multishift or multisite operations. It also prevents the manufacturing process from being crippled by the loss of key individuals. Cultivating new experts also allows proven experts to spend time breaking new ground instead of fighting old fires.

QUALITY
A CLASS ∧ ACT

Although Corning is peerless in the area of alliances and joint ventures, in quality it doesn't take a back seat to any other organization. Corning's quality program has an unusual level of backing—from the very top. Jamie Houghton says that the pursuit of quality never ends. At Corning, it doesn't and he is one of the main reasons why. Dave Luther, Corning's vice-president of corporate quality, says, "I've spent time with the work force—listening and understanding what they say. There is great wisdom in the work force. They say training is important. When I say, 'I'll give you an overview of Deming or Juran,' they say, 'No. Teach me to do my job better.'"

Traditionally, Corning had used the acceptable quality level formula, like most other U.S. companies. The formula allowed a percentage of defects as the most economical way to operate. Competitors proved that as an operation approaches zero defects, it becomes more cost-effective. Not a slow learner, Houghton decided that quality was the path to success. A corporatewide change in the way of thinking and working is made up of tens of thousands of daily individual changes. Houghton needed a permanent system that would inspire such changes.

Houghton is closely identified with Corning's quality program. He preached Corning's goals at meetings at 50 company and joint-venture sites a year. He appointed the company's first director of quality and a high-level quality council in 1983 and sent every employee through a two-day quality seminar. Early on he established goals to get them to this quality level. By 1991 all employees would spend 5 percent of their time in job-related training, errors would be cut by 90 percent, and all new goods and services would meet customer requirements and competitors' quality.

Corning's quality people listened to outside experts and benchmarked companies and industries worldwide. They carefully thought about Corning's unique internal needs, and then they forged a system built on four principles and ten actions (see the "Formulas" section later in this chapter).

There is no end in sight. Houghton says, "The learning curve, industry's familiar measurement of improvement through experience, breaks the old rules here. Why? Because there is no finish line with total quality, no point at which you sit back and say, 'We're there.'"

Corning's goal is to provide end products, components, and services to meet the most demanding requirements of customers and customers-to-be. Today, all Corning employees, from plant floor to laboratory to executive office, take part in a total quality system that embraces both products and individual performance.

Houghton's efforts to improve quality are paying off. MetPath, a clinical lab testing unit, delivers 98.5 percent of its reports to customers in 24 hours or less, up from 88 percent in 1986. Optical fiber customer returns have been reduced to fewer than 1,000 parts per million from 6,800 in 1986. Houghton says, "We've progressed to the point where parts per million is a routine measure of defects, and such once-utopian concepts as continuous process improvement, or even zero defects, are goals that drive us on."

EMPOWERMENT

Another Houghton vision is as follows: "I see a company where employee groups run their own areas, solve their own problems—with supervisors acting as advisors." He understood that managers could not improve quality alone. He has given more responsibility, and a share of profits, to Corning's unionized workers.

In another step to make quality a reality, Houghton established partnerships that give Corning's unionized employees more control over how factories are run. Corning has encouraged teams of hourly workers to redesign their own factories and decide who should work which jobs. At the Blacksburg plant Corning wanted to surpass the Japanese-style teamwork system, where groups of workers perform several tasks in a specific production area but are not trained to perform all the jobs throughout the entire production process. Corning wanted a work force versatile enough to perform every task in every aspect of the production process. To ensure cooperation, an employee design team built its production line so that the entire team worked within earshot of one another, instead of the traditional long straight line. One job classification was derived from 47 folded into one. The workers perform a weekly rotation through each job. The situation just described brought a big pay-off to Corning. Defects, formerly at 10,000 parts per million (ppm), were reduced to 3 ppm.

When slack demand recently forced budget cutting, another union team decided to eliminate overtime, impose a two-week shutdown, redeploy workers, and cut travel. The employee-driven plan saved more than the $450,000 target without cutting jobs. Houghton wants Corning's 28 United States plants to operate in the same way by 1993.

Customers are also empowered. Corning's system enlists and directs the commitment of employees to achieve ever-higher levels of quality. At the core of the system is its definition: *meeting the requirements of the customer, 100 percent of the time, on time, every time.* In practice, it means understanding and agreeing on requirements with customers before the process begins. The system also involves continuing the dialogue to ensure that employees know what the requirements are, and that they are continuing to meet these requirements.

Jamie Houghton says, "The far-reaching business changes of recent years were—and are—accompanied by far-reaching cultural changes. The most profound change at Corning is visible in the companywide obsession with world-class quality."

CORNING'S FORMULAS

A top-notch quality program is more complex than a few maxims can represent. At Corning, though, much of the quality spirit has been captured in simple formulas that can be quickly studied. They are shown here in Figures 15–1, 15–2, and 15–3.

FIGURE 15–1
The Four Principles

- Meet the customer's requirements
- Error-free work
- Manage by prevention
- Measure by the cost of quality

FIGURE 15–2
The 10 Actions

1. Commitment: a continuing personal pledge of action in support of total quality.
2. Teams: the grouping of people to manage total quality at each location.
3. Education: programs to create awareness and teach the skills and techniques needed for total quality.
4. Measure and display: measurement of error rates to focus attention on the need for corrective action; use of charts and displays of those error rates to show progress.
5. Cost of quality: identifying the dollar cost of noncompliance to quality by quantifying the error, detection, and prevention costs.
6. Communication: continuous and consistent activity to inform everyone of company and unit progress and to help spur employee involvement.
7. Corrective action: establishment of systems to identify and eliminate problems. This is the powerhouse of total quality; improvement suggestions from corrective action teams or individuals must receive a response from management—usually within seven working days.
8. Recognition: recognizing individual and group participation in, and contribution to, total quality performance and results.
9. Event: an annual gathering of employees to celebrate and recommit themselves to total quality.
10. Goals: establishment of error-reduction goals by everyone.

Quality linchpins.   By the time the total quality program was in place for five years, success was already evident. The companywide attention to customer satisfaction and customer-driven results was focused like a laser beam, and the linchpins of the company's continuous quality improvement program were evident. They are as follows:

- *Benchmarking:* the process of rigorously comparing parts or all of a Corning product, service, or function against the best in the marketplace.
- *Process management approach:* a technique for improving the management of processes in nonmanufacturing environments. The approach helps identify the boundaries of an ad-

FIGURE 15–3
The Quality Structure

- Quality improvement teams, formed of a cross-section of employees in each unit, manages the quality process. The team ensures that there is a plan in place, and people assigned, to carry out each of the 10 actions.
- Corrective action teams. These teams do the actual work of tracking a problem to its root causes and finding a solution. Team members are those people best equipped—through knowledge, expertise, and ownership—to solve the problem. The teams are transient; when a problem is solved, the team disbands.
- Division quality executives are quality experts at the division staff level who help to formulate a long-range quality plan for the division and assist ongoing division programs when needed.
- The quality council, along with executives representing all departments and selected representatives from all payroll groups. The council's purpose is to find new and better ways to manage quality, and to share problems and solutions.
- The management committee, composed of the chairman and a group of senior company executives. It approves quality policies and plans, and decide on strategic directions.

ministrative process, its inflow and outflow, and its measures of effectiveness.

- *Service quality (customer action planning system):* a series of workshops teaching that the quality of service that accompanies a product is as important as the product itself. They stress reliability, responsiveness, and even empathy—experiencing the feelings of the customer.
- *Customer-supplier partnerships:* a new way to understand and meet customer requirements. In structured meetings, teams of Corning employees and customers or suppliers meet to describe, debate, understand, and reach agreement on what the requirements are.
- *Union-management quality reviews:* sessions involving approximately 15 different employees each time, led by teams of union officials and Corning managers. The purpose is to hear and understand what Corning's people say about their progress toward total quality.
- *Workplace partnerships:* a mutual recognition by Corning and the American Flint Glass Workers' Union that their shared objectives cannot be achieved unless a true partnership exists. While endorsing the continuation of their traditional collective bargaining relationship, the two parties in early 1989 forged a new partnership. It states, in part, ''In fostering this process,

trust, communication, and respect for the dignity of the individual are absolutely essential.''

- *The Malcolm Baldrige National Quality Award:* awarded each year by the President of the United States to a maximum of six companies in the United States for quality excellence. Corning's telecommunications products division, with some of its complex fiber-optic processes running at zero parts per million in defects, was the company's entry in 1989, and it received a site visit by senior examiners. The award's criteria are now Corning's template for corporatewide world-class quality.

Other notable ideas, actions, and institutions.

The quality institute.   The company's central quality process instructional institution was established in Corning, New York, in 1984. The first class was composed of the company's senior executives. Aside from training in quality, the institute contributes to overall company quality as the focus of Corning's worldwide learning network. There are facilities in 58 locations, with instruction in six languages.

The vital few.   The management committee introduced the concept of the ''vital few'' in 1985. The vital few is implemented at the unit level. Vital few is a term for focusing on what's important. The name identifies the process of identifying, ranking, and eliminating error sources. The bottom line is this: ''Decide on your top three vital issues. Pick one. Remove it. Permanently!''

Delighting the customer.   The well known author of *In Search of Excellence*, Tom Peters, introduced a needed insight. He spoke at the company's quality milestone meeting in 1987. Peters asked whether Corning was ''delighting the customer.'' After some soul-searching Corning's executives realized that the correct answer was no. They were too heavily focused on internal processes. A major change in emphasis began.

CORNING'S STRATEGIES

With the process and structure in place, the final component for achieving total quality was a set of implementation strategies. The following six strategies served as guideposts for charting the quality course and have helped evaluate progress:

- Provide visible, unquestioned leadership.
- Focus on customer results.
- Train.
- Achieve and recognize employee participation.
- Communication.
- Provide a quality process and quality tools.

The strategy statements themselves have remained essentially intact over the years. The actions taken to support each one, however, continuously evolve as Corning journeys toward total quality.

Provide visible, unquestioned leadership.   Leadership is the most important of the strategies. The presence of leadership is a must at the top of the organization and, at the unit level, is the most reliable predictor of success. The leader is expected to provide a vision or a direction, to provide encouragement, to allocate resources, and to assess results. Perhaps most important is the need to set a personal example for others.

Focus on customer results.   If total quality is meeting the requirements, then a focus on customer results is essential. A rigorous process is necessary for learning requirements precisely, and for agreeing with the customer—whether internal or external— on how those requirements are to be measured. Once agreement is reached, there is an all-out drive to achieve error-free work in meeting those requirements. Dave Luther says, ''Our workers say, 'Show me how to do today's job better.' It's a great strength of our work force.''

Awareness training.   At Corning, the culture change sparked by total quality called for awareness training, whereas the many new techniques of quality called for skills training. Phase I, in 1984 and 1985, stressed awareness and the basics of quality. Phase II, begun in 1986, added specific skills such as group dynamics, problem solving, and statistical analysis. Today, continuous job skill training to meet the company's 5 percent goal is mandatory for all employees.

Achieve and recognize employee participation.   Employee participation in solving workplace problems is the energy source for total quality. Recognition encourages people to try for improved performance. Frequent recognition—both formal and informal—by supervisors and peers reinforces that encouragement.

Communication. This is a vital part of total quality and one that is easy to underestimate. Communication is not top management talking at everybody else, but a shared activity among managers, employees, customers, and suppliers. "What's right? What's wrong? How can we improve?" Workplace communication continues to be a rigorous challenge; the dialogue must be organized and consistent.

Provide a quality process and quality tools. Total quality began by providing a framework for action. Subsequently, problem-solving methods, communication guides, employee quality surveys, customer and supplier quality programs, formulas for managing administration, and techniques for improving service to customers— the tools of quality—were developed and honed. The effort must be continuous as needs and quality standards evolve.

Jamie Houghton says, "Instead of ending, a quality learning curve keeps charting new territory. It continues to focus activity on customer requirements, employee empowerment, reduced variation, and zero errors. It makes high-quality plus lowest-cost production a reality. Goals, no longer ends in themselves, become directional signs to ever-higher goals."

WHERE DO YOU GO FROM UP?

One of Jamie Houghton's visions is this: "I see a company that is so well known for its total quality system that we are besieged by the outside world wanting to know our secret." Unlike some visionaries, Jamie has seen his vision materialize. Corning has become a total quality global learning organization.

Chapter Sixteen

General Electric
Global Action Learning for Global Brains

/ /**W**hen you've been told to shut up for 20 years, and someone tells you to speak up," Vic Slepoy told *Fortune* Magazine, "you're going to let them have it." The "it" in this case is ideas, and the program has unleashed a torrent of them at GE. The focus at multiday Work-Out sessions is to eliminate needless, mind-numbing work and to come up with ways to perform critical processes better.

Work-Out is General Electric's employee involvement program. It has been described in newsletters and academic journals, but no one has captured the essence of the program better than Vic Slepoy, an electrician for GE's jet engine business in Lynn, Massachusetts.

The head of Slepoy's organization in Lynn, Armand Lauzon, recalls he had "about a minute" to say yea or nay to more than 100 worker suggestions at an early Work-Out session. These ideas yielded improvements, but more important, showed that Lauzon's plant services organization had saved more than $200,000. One idea alone—a production employee's plan for a grinder shield to be made at the plant rather than purchased—saved $80,000.

Lauzon's organization is a small part of just one of GE's 12 key businesses. Work-Out is underway in all of them. Says GE Chairman Jack Welch, "All around this company in large plants like Schenectady, Lynn, and Louisville, and scores of smaller sites like Florence and Salisbury in the Carolinas and Decatur, Alabama and many other places, compulsive managing and mutual mistrust are giving way to real teamwork. GE has become faster and more energized than any of us ever thought possible." GE isn't an average company by any definition. And Jack Welch is certainly not an average CEO.

Vic Slepoy's statement is not a fluke. It describes a now-famous corporate technique called Work-Out. Work-Out was born at GE's Crotonville training center after a session with executives in "the pit," the

GE at a Glance

Organizational learning	Global learning
✔ Appropriate structures	✔ Acculturization
Corporate learning culture	Borders
✔ Empowerment	✔ Globalization
Environmental scanning	✔ Language
✔ Knowledge creation and transfer	✔ Leadership
Learning technology	Workforce diversity
✔ Quality	
Strategy	
Supportive atmosphere	
✔ Teamwork and networking	
Vision	

© Michael Marquardt and Angus Reynolds, 1992

Headquarters:	Fairfield, Connecticut
Founded:	1878
Main business:	GE is a diversified technology, manufacturing, and services company with 12 major businesses: aircraft engines, broadcasting, electrical distribution equipment, electric motors, financial services, industrial and power systems, information services, lighting, locomotives, major appliances, medical systems and plastics.
Chief executive officer:	John F. Welch
Number of countries where located:	150
Total employees worldwide:	268,000

classroom where complete frankness and candor is encouraged. Welch, who regularly met with trainees, was frustrated because, all too often, he heard a solid suggestion for improvement. His answer was, "tell the head of your business." Jim Baughman, who heads the Crotonville Management Development Institute, acted on Welch's determination to spread the ideas begat there to all GE's businesses. He and Welch worked out the basics of Work-Out by the end of the day.

Their concept has been hailed as one of the most innovative organization development tools. GE really has three.

THREE TOOLS

GE uses three main tools—management techniques—in its work:

- Work-Out
- Best Practices
- Process Mapping

Work-Out empowers employees to contribute to the decision-making process. Best Practices finds good internal ideas and ideas from other companies and provides the needed communication channel to spread them between one part of GE and another. Process Mapping is an old technique based on flowcharting every step, no matter how small, that is a part of making or doing something.

All three foster lots of employee involvement and combine to sustain GE's rapid growth in productivity. According to Welch, they are the key to any corporation's survival in today's competitive environment, and they form the foundation of GE's success as a global learning organization.

Work-Out

Every time he visited the pit, Welch said, "I hope you're as brave when you are back home as you are here." Initially, all Work-Outs followed the same format, which Welch likens to a three-day New England town hall meeting. A group of 40 to 100 people go to a conference center or hotel. Sessions begin with a talk by Welch or another leader, who roughs out a problem agenda for them to fix. Then the boss leaves. An outside facilitator breaks the group into five or six teams to tackle part of the agenda. The teams work using group processes to identify solutions and prepare presentations for the final day.

On the third day, whichever leader led off comes back and takes a place at the front of the room. One by one, team spokespersons present their proposals. The rules of Work-Out force the boss to make only one of three responses: agree on the spot, say no, or ask for more information—in which case the boss must charter a team to get it by an agreed-upon date. Even if the leader's boss is in the room, the decisions must be made alone. If a boss were to overrule the decision later, it would jeopardize the whole process.

In locations that traditionally have been sore spots in labor-management relations, Work-Out has begun to transform the climate into a much more productive atmosphere of mutual respect and cooperation. "We versus them" is increasingly coming to mean GE versus the competition.

Welch tells a story to illustrate how Work-Out has transformed how GE works together as a company. In 1991 at a Best Practices session at the Crotonville facility, among the key lecturers on the subject of productivity were two of the toughest union officers GE has to face. One of them told the group that he formerly had three clearly defined enemies in his life: the IRS, the Russians, and GE management. Nowadays, only the IRS retains that status.

The essence of Work-Out is that an employee is in charge of the design of his or her own job, to ensure that things get done right.

Best Practices

Welch was also the wellspring for the Best Practices idea. GE started with an initial list of about 200 companies. It screened out direct competitors and companies that would not have credibility with people at GE. Then, it chose the two dozen that had achieved faster productivity growth than GE and sustained it for at least 10 years.

GE asked to send some of its people to the other organizations to learn about their best management ideas. It promised in return to share the results of the study with participants and let them ask about GE's methods. The companies it worked with initially were AMP, Chaparral Steel, Ford, Hewlett-Packard, Xerox, and three Japanese companies.

Best Practices is not the same as the benchmarking practiced by many other companies. Benchmarking usually involves a study of companies that are the best in particular functions (GE does that too). GE's Best Practices study took a more global look at attitudes and management practices. Baughman has described GE's question as "What is the secret of your success?" It found that the successful companies emphasized managing interdepartmental processes instead of single functions. The best companies maintain close and enduring relations with suppliers and rocket past their competition in new products introductions. Another quality GE admired was their inventory management. Per dollar of sales, the best companies tied up less working capital than GE.

The Best Practices study was as momentous as Work-Out. GE realized it should focus on *how* things got done rather than on *what* got done. Best Practices provided an empirical basis for changing what GE manages. Learning came into play as GE turned the Best Practices findings into a course. The course is delivered each month to a dozen people from each of GE's 10 manufacturing businesses.

A similar course, based on research at nonmanufacturing companies, is run for the service businesses. That course focuses on issues such as managing information technology. In 1991 GE shared Best Practices with another great company. Welch says, "We learned something everywhere, but nowhere did we learn as much as at Wal-Mart. Sam Walton and his strong team are something very special. Many of our managers and teams spent time there observing the speed, the bias for action, the utter customer fixation that drives Wal-

Mart; and despite our progress, we came back feeling a bit plodding and ponderous, a little envious, but, ultimately, fiercely determined that we're going to do whatever it takes to get that fast."

In the first week of 1992, 450 men and women who lead the company convened from around the world to share Best Practices and review the course for the coming year. Jack Welch called it "a very special event, with a unique and spontaneous atmosphere—one we had never quite felt before . . . the mood at that meeting was one of exhilaration and boundless confidence. The commitment to speed and boundarylessness was at a new high."

Process Mapping

Process mapping sounds simple, but it's not. The process produces a complete, detailed diagram of a process. To do it right, managers, employees, suppliers, and customers must work on the map together to make sure that what the company thinks happens really does. When a process is mapped, GE has—often for the first time—the ability to manage an operation in a coherent way from start to finish.

GLOBAL BRAINS

Much has been written about GE's three management processes. In addition, there are three key programs leading to its global success.

- World training (affectionately called *global brains*).
- Eliminating sectors that had served as filters.
- Establishing a corporate executive council.

Global brains is the Crotonville month-long executive program. The special twist is the big decision to send the three key GE executive development programs overseas—to actually go to various countries to work on cases. Participants work on real-world problems. These are not practice drills.GE is getting very bright people to do what it might hire consultants to do. At the same time participants learn to solve real-world problems, and they build international networks together.

Much of GE's success can be traced to corporate recognition of the need for global presence in all its businesses. The domestic market had been the largest and fastest growing in the post–World War II boom era. Its domestic focus was appropriate because electrical growth was predictable. In the 1980s, if one was looking (and not every company was), one could see that Asian countries were competitors that had saturated their markets and were coming to the United States. GE's change of focus is really attributable to Jack Welch. He had built the plastics and financial services businesses. Even the previous CEO, Reginald Jones, said that big changes would be needed to continue prosperity. Welch decided to send GE's successful domestic businesses overseas. For example, GE dominated the domestic lighting market, but was not a major player overseas. It determined to be number one or two globally in each of its businesses. GE's plastic and jet engines were already strong globally, and it decided to learn from these businesses.

Along the way it streamlined reporting relationships. "Sectors," such as lighting appliances in one sector and consumer electronics in another, were done away with. This put the second key change in place. Now the head of each business reports directly to the chairman's office.

This set the stage for the corporate executive council. GE's 12 businesses meet quarterly. (There were 13 before GE sold GE Aerospace—radar satellites and so forth, not jet engines—to Martin Marietta.) The council does not review finances. Its purpose is to share information. Participants are key members of the corporate staff, and the CEO. There are no hangers-on. The result is direct sharing of ideas between people who are responsible for $5 to 7 billion businesses.

Values.   During the past several years, GE has wrestled at all levels with the question of what it is and what it wants to be. Out of these discussions, and through its experiences, it has agreed on a set of values that it believes will be needed to take the company rapidly forward through the 1990s and beyond (see Figure 16–1).

Welch admits,

> Yes, there are pockets where things haven't changed, and no, not everyone has been empowered, but the momentum is unmistakable, and we are determined to make it irreversible.
>
> This is a long road we are on, and a difficult one. Trust and respect take years to build, and no time at all to destroy. In the first half of the 1980s, we restructured this company and changed its physical make-up. That was the easy part. In the last several years, our challenge has been to change ourselves—an infinitely more difficult task that, frankly, not all of us in leadership positions are capable of.

It isn't all Work-Out. GE is a technology leader and has specific business programs that are not taught in school, for example, laser welding. The aircraft engine business has many specialized training

FIGURE 16–1
GE Values

GE Leaders throughout the Company:

- Create a clear, simple, reality-based, customer-focused vision and are able to communicate it straightforwardly to all constituencies.
- Understand accountability and commitment and are decisive ... set and meet aggressive targets ... always with unyielding integrity.
- Have a passion for excellence ... hate bureaucracy and all the nonsense that comes with it.
- Have the self-confidence to empower others and behave in a boundaryless fashion ... believe in and are committed to Work-Out as a means of empowerment... are open to ideas from anywhere.
- Have, or have the capacity to develop, global brains and global sensitivity and are comfortable building diverse global teams.
- Stimulate and relish change ... are not frightened or paralyzed by it. See change as opportunity, not just a threat.
- Have enormous energy and the ability to energize and invigorate others. Understand speed as a competitive advantage and see the total organizational benefits that can be derived from a focus on speed.

---

courses including French and powder metallurgy. GE is creating the climate in which learning is critical for success.

THE ORGANIZATIONAL CULTURAL REVOLUTION

GE's efforts are claimed by some to be one of the biggest planned efforts to alter people's behavior since Chairman Mao's cultural revolution.

It brings results. Stories about GE tell of a key part of a jet engine that formerly took 30 weeks to make. Through Work-Out, that process now takes four weeks, and the teams that run it are talking about reducing that figure to 10 days. Hardware product cycles are now down an average of 20 percent across the business, with 50 percent clearly in sight. Cycle time for some operations have dropped by 80 percent.

Corporate culture is something people talk about a lot at GE. Yet they are able to maintain an outward focus—looking for the best elsewhere. Quality is everyone's job. Although GE ranks third in the *Fortune* 500, it has no corporate manager of quality.

Has GE greased every skid on the path to becoming a perfect global learning organization? Not yet. There is still difficulty in getting Work-Out established in such a large business. Making the global part happen increases the logistics difficulty if nothing else. It is difficult to send a group of 40 people around the world. It is also more difficult to find appropriate cases for an international group. We have confidence that GE will continue to succeed.

GE has every evidence of having its act together to stand out as a global learning organization. The transformation that is sweeping GE is not complicated in theory, or even original. Much of the intellectual underpinning of Work-Out consists of ideas such as worker involvement, trust, and empowerment—well-established concepts. Welch says, "The difference is that our whole organization is, in fact, living them every day! Most of our 268,000 member company are, in fact, using soft concepts today as competitive weapons and are winning with them, rather than just inscribing them on coffee mugs and T-shirts."

Chapter Seventeen

Honda:
World-Class Learning Environment

I magine the scene. In the meeting room at the company headquarters, the chief financial officer is making a recommendation to the president of the corporation. In Japan the process of decision making is one of gaining consensus among everyone concerned and making a deliberate recommendation to the decision maker that always represents the most considered thought of the management team.

This meeting was to be momentous in any case because it concerned the decision to begin construction of a production facility in the United States. Soberly, it was reported that a financial analysis suggested that Honda could not make a profit manufacturing in the United States. Therefore, the recommendation was not to take such a step at that time.

Honda's then-president, Kawashima, speaking in the deliberate Japanese style indicating that he had considered the recommendation carefully, said, "Go ahead . . . anyway!"

Honda's corporate philosophy—the Honda Way—is an integral part of its approach to business. Part of this philosophy has always been that its manufacturing facilities should be located in the markets it serves. The decision was consistent with the Honda corporate philosophy. This also gives an opportunity to those who buy Honda products to build Honda products.

The decision to manufacture in the United States changed the company forever. No one could have expected at the time that today Honda would be the leading exporter of cars *to* Japan.

From the beginning, Honda's success can be attributed to a philosophy of seeking out the toughest challenges and applying creativity, innovation, and imagination to solve them. Soichiro Honda, the company's founder, believed that technology holds the

Honda at a Glance

Organizational learning	Global learning
Appropriate structures	Acculturization
✔ Corporate learning culture	✔ Borders
✔ Empowerment	✔ Globalization
Environmental scanning	Language
Knowledge creation and transfer	Leadership
Learning technology	✔ Workforce diversity
✔ Quality	
✔ Strategy	
Supportive atmosphere	
✔ Teamwork and networking	
Vision	

© Michael Marquardt and Angus Reynolds, 1992

Headquarters:	Hamamatsu, Japan
Founded:	1946
Main business:	Automobiles, motorcycles, and power products
Chief executive officer:	Nobuhiko Kawamoto
Number of countries where located:	39 (sales in approximately 150 countries)
Total employees worldwide:	80,000

key to Japan's future, and he sought a way to improve Japan's products.

AN INTERNATIONAL VIEWPOINT

Honda was not then, and is not now, a typical company. In 1954, when Honda was only eight years old, the company adopted an international viewpoint. Honda dedicated itself to supplying products of the highest efficiency at a reasonable price for worldwide customer satisfaction. This international viewpoint remains the cornerstone of Honda today. It recognizes that events in the world, not just events in the city, state, or country where a particular plant is located, shape its market and its products. Its products are made to compete in world markets. For example, North America Honda exported a total of 28,205 American-made cars to Japan, Taiwan, South Korea, Israel, Germany, the United Kingdom, France, Belgium, Switzerland, and the Netherlands in 1991. Plans are to increase that total to 40,000 cars exported to 17 nations. The company has several joint ventures. Its European partner is Rover Group, and it was the first Japanese auto maker to establish an office in Moscow. It has a joint venture with Auto Agro Group to distribute cars in Argentina and one with Mack de Venezuela C.A. to assemble Accords in Venezuela. It also established an exclusive distributorship in Ankara, Turkey, and the first joint venture with one of China's four local motorcycle manufacturers.

THE HONDA WAY

By establishing manufacturing facilities in the markets where the demand for Honda products exists, Honda can become part of the communities in which its customers live. Honda can give back to these communities, states, and nations something in return for the support Honda products enjoy. It is this sense of responsibility for its products and its customers that has led Honda to develop its own way of doing things.

The success of the Honda Way is based on people's feeling free to speak their minds about what they have learned. Richard Pascale, author of *Managing on the Edge*, cites a number of reasons why Honda excels at learning. Honda's decision-making process is not dominated by a single point of view. Information on an array of topics circulates widely and freely. These include performance, quality, consumer satisfaction, and competitiveness. Honda's reward distribution is more equitable than that of the big American companies. From top management on down, there is adherence to a common set of values. This consistency fosters an extraordinary degree of trust.

On the factory floor. But what about manufacturing? How does the Honda Way work in the factory? The average Japanese worker turns in between 30 and 40 suggestions per year on ways to increase efficiency and improve quality. The corresponding figure at an assembly plant in Detroit is one suggestion every seven years! After an intensive campaign, Volvo doubled the number of suggestions it received—to one per worker per year. The Honda Way is obviously different.

There is a saying at Honda that there is more knowledge on the factory floor than in the office. This means that the most knowledge can be gained from actual experience in the plant operations. The answers to problems and the improvements in quality often come from the associates who are most directly involved.

It is very difficult to recommend effective countermeasures if one spends time only in the administrative offices rather than on the factory floor. Associates at Honda with management responsibility spend most of their day on the plant floor. Their philosophy stresses that one must go to the spot in the plant and see the problem, touch the part, and gain experience in the actual job process in order to effectively solve the problem.

Honda has another very effective way of improving quality in its products and communication among its associates. A quality circles method, Honda calls it the NH-Circle.

The NH-Circle is a small group of associates—typically 5 to 10 members—who voluntarily work together on a common concern to suggest improvements in a variety of areas, such as quality, safety, communications, working environment, efficiency, and so forth. The important part of NH-Circle activity is that it is voluntary and that all members work together to achieve their results.

Ultimately, the goal of all NH-Circles is to create a better understanding of what is happening now in Honda's operations and what the future goals and tasks will be. Honda presently has several hundred associates involved in many different NH-Circle activities in all its plants. NH stands for " now Honda, new Honda, next Honda."

The Honda approach to quality is based on respect for what the individual associate can achieve. It does not mandate quality by having quality inspectors at each step of the manufacturing process. Instead, Honda teaches quality as a satisfying way of life and asks each associate to take individual responsibility for the quality of Honda products. Quality must be built in; it cannot be inspected in later. These operational standards are a key element in achieving the quality goal for each associate: accept no bad parts, make no bad parts, and pass no bad parts.

In a *Sloan Management Review* article entitled "Toward Middle-Up-Down Management—Accelerating Information Creation," professor Ikujiro Nonaka of Hitotsubashi University describes what he calls *compressive management*. It is based on observations of Honda in Japan.

Honda's top management sets tough strategic goals. On the shop floor (gemba) and in company offices, entrepreneurial individuals are learning on their own. Honda's middle managers, working in multifunctional teams, integrate what is coming from above and below to develop products and processes compressively, accelerating the creation of information. The process has been compared to a turbocharger.

THE *WE* PHILOSOPHY

There is at Honda a certain spirit with which Honda approaches everything it does. That spirit is difficult to define, but it is probably best conveyed by the word *togetherness.* It is the togetherness Honda employees have as members of a team, the togetherness Honda has with its philosophy, and the togetherness created by shared goals.

Richard Pascale quotes Pat Sparks, from the purchasing department at the company's Marysville, Ohio, factory: "The Honda philosophy is a way of life. It's characterized by closeness, communication, and frankness at all levels. Honda employs thinking people, creative people. We want people to sound off."

Visitors to Honda plants see many outward signs of its approach. Honda associates all wear the same white uniform. They all park in the same parking lot without reserved spaces. They all eat in the same cafeterias. And they have no private offices. In typical Japanese fashion, all of their desks are in one large room with no walls.

Honda believes that if it can create togetherness with its basic principle throughout its organization, Honda will succeed. For more than 30 years that basic principle has been stated as follows:

> Maintaining an international viewpoint, at Honda we are dedicated to supplying products of the highest efficiency yet at a reasonable price for worldwide customer satisfaction."

It is adherence to this principle and to its underlying philosophy that has led Honda to its present position. In the final analysis, Honda cannot be explained by mere words or numbers. The essence of Honda is a feeling—it is a philosophy—that can be understood by standing on the factory floor and by talking with Honda associates.

WHAT ABOUT OTHER JAPANESE COMPANIES?

Is the Japanese record perfect? Far from it. Current public opinion about Japanese-owned companies in other countries ranges from curiosity to admiration to resentment.

The earliest failure in Japan-U.S. globalization was the Matsushita takeover of Motorola's Quasar TV division. Unhappy stories of the lack of sensitivity to local workers abound. In that case, little attention was paid because it occurred during what were, in general, good economic times.

Often, the Japanese are in the other country but are not a part of it. Stories of separate rules for Japanese employees are heard in Taiwan as well as in the United States. Almon Clegg a former Matsushita manager, says, "They had their own company and culture . . . separate grade levels and salary structure. I reported to my manager and my co-manager reported to his. They were not the same person."

(*Frontline*, December 19, 1992.) An employee of an electronics giant tells how the most frequent complaint was expressed as, "Why are there different rules for Japanese and American employees?" Employees of a Japanese automotive giant in Taiwan echo the same complaint, substituting Chinese for American. Honda may have found the key.

A GLOBAL SUCCESS STORY

Honda's success in Ohio is not a Japanese success or the success of a Japanese company. It is the success of the American operation of an international company. What Honda has proven in Ohio is that the Honda philosophy can exist, and indeed flourish, halfway around the world from where it was conceived. It has proven that, in a global learning organization, learning can occur across borders and barriers.

Chapter Eighteen

Medtronic:
Pacesetter in Learning for the Future

D r. C. Walton Lillehei, a pioneer in open heart surgery at the University of Minnesota, was frustrated. The primitive pacemakers of the 1950s relied on external electrodes and bulky, unreliable power sources plugged into wall outlets.

There had to be a better way. Lillehei turned to Earl Bakken and Palmer Hermundslie for an engineering solution. In 1949 Bakken, an electrical engineer, and his brother-in-law, a lumberyard manager, had started in a garage to repair electrical equipment for local hospitals. Their total first month's earnings, for repair of a broken centrifuge, totaled only $8, but their local reputation had grown. In 1957 their company, Medtronic, delivered the first wearable, external, battery-powered, transistorized pacemaker—hand-crafted by Bakken on order for a single doctor!

Medtronic began implantable pacemaker production in December 1960 and was on its way to becoming one of the world's largest manufacturers of implantable devices. The company manufactures about half the pacemakers in the world, more than 1.5 million of which have been implanted. Medtronic is the world's leading supplier of products and services prescribed by cardiologists and cardiovascular surgeons to treat, and improve quality of life for, people with disorders of the heart or circulatory system. Its focus is innovation, honesty, customer service, and the relentless pursuit of quality in its products and professional relationships.

Today, Medtronic businesses circle the globe. Arthur Collins, Jr., president of Medtronic International, says, "We are continuing the transition from a Minneapolis-based, U.S.-focused company to a truly global corporation with multifunctional organizations in the major worldwide geographies."

Medtronic at a Glance

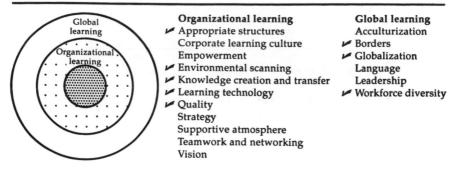

	Organizational learning	Global learning
	✔ Appropriate structures	Acculturization
	Corporate learning culture	✔ Borders
	Empowerment	✔ Globalization
	✔ Environmental scanning	Language
	✔ Knowledge creation and transfer	Leadership
	✔ Learning technology	✔ Workforce diversity
	✔ Quality	
	Strategy	
	Supportive atmosphere	
	Teamwork and networking	
	Vision	

© Michael Marquardt and Angus Reynolds, 1992

Headquarters:	Minneapolis, Minnesota
Founded:	1949
Main business:	Cardiac pacemaker systems, tachyarrhythmia management systems, implantable neurological pain management systems, prosthetic and bioprosthetic heart valves, angioplasty catheters, implantable drug administration systems, disposable devices for handling and monitoring blood during surgery, and pacemaker monitoring services.
President and CEO:	William W. George
Number of countries where located:	80
Total employees worldwide:	8,300

Statistically speaking, every three minutes, somewhere in the world, Medtronic enhances a patient's life.

GETTING STARTED AND ADVERTISING AT THE SAME TIME

Lillehei tells it this way:

> We had found a young man with an electronics repair business and gave him a part-time contract to repair our devices. I remembered Earl Bakken always got the job done right away, so I described the problem to him and he said sure, he thought he could do it. So I arranged for him to see the heart block procedure. Six weeks later he was back with a box four inches square by two inches high, and it worked great in the dog laboratory. We were soon equipping all our heart-block patients with the device, which they wore in a holster. As I went around the country describing the low

mortality rate we had established in our open-heart surgery programs everyone wanted to know what we were doing for heart block. I'd tell them, "Call Earl Bakken, he'll help you."

ORGANIZING APPROPRIATELY

The outside forces affecting Medtronic's business today and in the years to come include the following:

- The global health care needs of quality, access, and cost control.
- A changing and increasingly unpredictable worldwide regulatory and political environment.
- Demand for technologies that demonstrate cost effectiveness, while proving through outcomes measurement that a patient's quality of life is enhanced in the long term.
- Changing health care delivery systems that place new demands on medical professionals and create new requirements and needs for education.

The six strategic businesses, in each of which Medtronic will attempt to establish a leading or near-leading position, are as follows:

- Bradycardia pacing
- Tachyarrhythmia management
- Cardiopulmonary
- Heart valves
- Interventional vascular
- Neurological

In addition to reorganization into these six businesses, Medtronic has established a global management philosophy to govern day-to-day operations. Individual locations have autonomy to make changes as needed to be effective and operate in their situations. They have broad direction and goals for accomplishment but are expected to do things as best they can to attain the goals that fit their environment. In this way, the culture of the company can be continuously adjusted to meet new needs.

GOING GLOBAL

The basic international nature of the medical community facilitates Medtronic's globalism. To reinforce this, a European service center was established in 1967; a European manufacturing facility began production in Kerkrade, the Netherlands, in 1969; a research center was opened at Maastricht, the Netherlands, in 1987; and a technical center in Chitose, Japan, was announced in 1990 and completed in 1991.

In Europe, Asia, North America, and Latin America, Medtronic employs local scientists, technicians, and representatives who are committed to the company's worldwide mission and who share the specific language, culture, and national environment of Medtronic's customers. Through these thousands of dedicated employees, Medtronic enhances patients' lives where they live and work. Art Collins says, "It is clear that many creative ideas and a great deal of technological talent reside beyond our shores. We believe that a strategic advantage will accrue to those companies which are able to tap into those resources and take advantage of the exciting laboratory and clinical research which is now taking place around the world."

A global advantage.   Because of the more restrictive regulatory process in the United States, clinical trials often can be conducted more efficiently and new products launched earlier outside the United States. Because of this, Medtronic has shifted resources to take advantage of international opportunities.

Medical companies work on issues with the U.S. Food and Drug Administration (FDA) every single day. Often the implementation of objectives based on caution results in delays in getting new therapies and products to patients who require them. Because of the long FDA regulatory time cycle needed to win approvals and meet regulatory milestones, Medtronic increasingly does initial development and testing outside the United States. It is essentially a learning process. As each new milestone is passed, the information is fed back to the countries. For example, clinical trials may first be conducted in the Netherlands. The information comes in a constant stream to the people working in the United States. They work with the company's people in the Netherlands to solve problems and send the pertinent data back there.

Global business.   Medtronic's president and chief executive officer, William W. George, says, "Our second major strategy is global expansion. As this is a global business, it is important that we serve not only the industrial world, which we're serving very well today, but the developing nations as well. We will put more emphasis on those even though the payout for those areas such as Asia, India, Greater China, Eastern Europe, and the Latin American countries like Mexico and Argentina, may be some years away. There is a great potential for us to have significant gains as the medical systems of these companies come up to speed and we participate in that process."

CUSTOMER-FOCUSED QUALITY

Quality is nothing new to Medtronic. Because of the life and death nature of its business, Medtronic has focused on quality longer than most other industries. Medtronic's corporate mission statement says in part, that its good is "to strive without reserve for the greatest possible reliability and quality in our products; to be the unsurpassed standard of comparison; and to be recognized as a company of dedication, honesty, integrity, and service."

Although means of ensuring it have changed over the years, a companywide insistence on quality is the primary focus at Medtronic. Every employee is aware that lives depend on it. The result of this zeal for quality can be summed up simply: physicians and their patients know they can depend on Medtronic.

Customer-focused quality embraces all Medtronic strategies, programs, systems, and procedures, and it links product quality with the quality of the company's customer relationships. As such, it provides a constant reminder that quality has a real and profound effect on the lives of patients everywhere.

Customer-focused quality means that Medtronic employees—whether they are managers, scientists, sales representatives, or support staff—meet and exceed customer expectations. It means that Medtronic representatives respond to specific needs and desires in their respective parts of the world, understanding and appreciating variations in medical practice styles, customs, and demographics, so that each product and service provides the most effective possible therapy for individual physicians and their patients, wherever they may be.

Art Collins says, "It is important that we not only listen carefully to what our customers a saying, but also then move quickly to meet their existing and future requirements once they are identified. To this end, cycle time reduction will be stressed not only in new product development and manufacturing, but in every part of our organization."

Medtronic products are designed to strengthen the expertise of the medical professionals who choose them and to improve the lives of the diverse patients who use them. Today, as in the past, producing defect-free products for patients while maintaining quality relationships with its medical professional customers are Medtronic's most important responsibilities.

In years past customer-focused quality was typified by Palmer Hermundslie's piloting his own plane to deliver a pacemaker to a hospital operating room three states away. Today it's exemplified by company technicians testing new mechanical heart valves through a billion cycles—far beyond U.S. Food and Drug Administration guidelines—or a sales representative delivering a specially adapted device and technical support to a surgeon in a remote location in the middle of the night.

A notable example of customer-focused quality is the company's customized tubing pack operations. Working to the precise specifications of individual perfusionists, Medtronic technicians configure and deliver these tubing packs for specific surgical applications in another part of the world, often on very short notice.

Still another example is the swift customization of a heart valve sewing ring for a patient in rapidly deteriorating condition. Within 24 hours of the initial call to Medtronic, a model of the sewing ring can be rushed to the patient's physician. With the physician's approval, a clinical prototype can be produced and promptly delivered, ready for surgery.

World-class manufacturing. At these facilities Medtronic employs world class manufacturing programs and procedures, including just-in-time manufacturing techniques and total employee involvement, to ensure consistently top-quality, cost-effective, and customer-focused products and services.

Medtronic manufacturing facilities build products on demand when they are needed—a system that encourages the timely correction of design or production problems, reducing overall waste and cost. Total employee involvement encourages employees to help make decisions that improve their work and the quality of their products and services. Employees on a Medtronic product line have the authority to stop the activity if they spot a problem.

Medtronic products are rigorously tested with computer-based inspection procedures ensuring that those products are defect free when they leave the plant. To help keep track of product quality, once the products are in customers' hands, Medtronic is one of the few medical-technology companies in the world that regularly compiles, and publishes product performance reports based on clinical experience.

From design through manufacture and delivery, today's Medtronic insists that customer quality demands are met and exceeded, that quality is measured, and that quality improvements are unending.

Leading by following. Medtronic is also a good follower when it comes to quality programs, benchmarking, and statistical procedures control techniques. It doesn't suffer from the "not invented here" syndrome. Although Medtronic leads in some of its markets, it is constantly interested in and participates in events that are happening elsewhere. It has a science and technology unit, the primary function of which is to learn what is going on in other areas of medical technology. The unit also monitors what is published in journals and presented at meetings. It learns what new companies are being formed, and who the new people are in the industry, and it questions what it is learning. The key is that people at Medtronic know they don't have a monopoly on good ideas, and they are interested in ideas wherever they may come from. Medtronic uses benchmarking to maintain overall quality. It makes comparisons to some companies that are different, as well as to some that are similar. For example, it benchmarked with 3M. The result was the collection of several ideas for new techniques to discuss and consider, adapt, or try outright.

Flexibility. A company needs a certain degree of flexibility to respond to what is learned. For example, Medtronic had a line of prosthetic heart valves called the Hall Mechanical Valve. This valve was a standard for many years. Radical change in an area such as heart valves would seem unusual because there is strong tendency not to change one once it works well. Many other companies would go on to something else. But based on customer feedback, Medtronic made changes and extensions to the line to adapt to the needs of the customer. If its corporate culture was not to "mess with success" Medtronic wouldn't be doing these things.

As Medtronic grows and its markets expand, customer-focused quality keeps all eyes on the company's essential mission: helping its customers improve patients' lives.

GETTING THE WORD OUT—AND IN

Like any other company, Medtronic uses a mix of methods to communicate. There are several types of meetings. Various corporate divisions hold meetings to share worldwide communications. The relevant people come to Minneapolis from all around the world. These opportunities provide a rich atmosphere of sharing directly between those who are in the best position to benefit directly from the new ideas. Such meetings are costly and held only infrequently, based on the need.

A distinctive Medtronic opportunity for sharing occurs when one business, laboratory, or region visits another to interact on a particular project. These groups use the opportunity to interact, share, and learn from one another about things other than the specific project involved.

A distinctive opportunity also exists in the medical field. In the global medical community, international conferences are quite common. For example, Medtronic recently participated in the First Cardiostim Pan Slavian International Congress on Cardiac Pacing and Electrophysiology in St. Petersburg, Russia. Medtronic's people meet their customers, as well as each other, at these meetings. Aside from the basic learning inherent in the conference itself, much is accomplished when Medtronic people from different countries meet in the hallways and at informal evening gatherings.

Glen D. Nelson, M.D., vice-chairman of Medtronic, highlights another avenue of communication: "We listen carefully and frequently to what our customers are saying—we listen in the laboratories, in the operating rooms, in key opinion leader sessions, and in our education centers. The results have been the identification of new indications."

Additionally, word is spread by Medtronic senior managers when they travel. In the course of their global business travels, they spread ideas and learning to everyone they meet.

EDUCATING EMPLOYEES AND OTHERS

Medtronic develops its people. Nelson says, "Our employees are key elements in our growth strategy, and we understand the importance of training and development programs to support and enhance their performance and career progression at Medtronic. We strive to provide a climate that attracts scientists and technical experts, and that supports the continued pursuit of technical excellence—encouraging new ideas while recognizing and rewarding the technical achievements that support Medtronic's mission and strategies."

Customer education plays a critical role in proper application and use of Medtronic's products. In addition, Medtronic's customer education programs provide the latest data and training for physicians and other medical professionals both on-site and at seven specially equipped Medtronic Bakken Education Centers in the United States, Germany, the Netherlands, India, and Japan. Hundreds of doctors and other paramedical professionals visit one of the centers every year for conferences, seminars, and new product orientation.

Thousands of medical professionals from around the world visit Medtronic offices, laboratories, and manufacturing plants to exchange information and techniques, and thousands more attend seminars and symposia in major international locations. Hundreds take part in company-sponsored symposia in various settings around the globe. The programs are all part of a corporate emphasis on medical education, one that Medtronic believes is second to none in its industry.

The medical industry is entering a new era in which companies will have to continually justify the value of their products to third parties, who are increasingly highly skilled in assessing them. New groups will participate in the decision to buy. Medtronic will respond to this changing situation by learning and figuring out ways to produce quality products cheaper or justify the higher price that must be charged. Insurers will make sophisticated distinctions. Medtronic will have to learn how to respond. It will have to enable reimbursement community decision makers to learn about each device with a goal of reducing the number of hospital visits over time and shortening necessary visits.

REINVENTING MEDTRONIC

Dr. Glen Nelson states, "At Medtronic, we're actively involved in creating our future today. Our strategy is to 'reinvent Medtronic,' doubling our size in the next five years and essentially creating a new company with new products and revenue equal to our current company." Considering the company's current success and market leadership, this is no small goal—but it may be a necessary one.

Compared to other industries, the medical field has enormous lead times. Research and development have to start now if the payoff is to be realized 5, 7, or 10 years hence. This is the key factor that will make Medtronic continue to be a very significant growth company for the next decade.

CEO Bill George details the strategies for future growth in words that echo General Electric's successful strategy. "We have talked a great deal for the last five years about going from one business to six businesses, growing our market share, and establishing ourselves in each of the six strategic businesses, so that we had a leading or near-leading position in each of those businesses. We have very significant challenges as we look ahead. One is staying innovative. You see many companies that really stagnate when they get to be multi-billion-dollar companies. Keeping ourselves small, flexible, fast on our feet, and innovative is critical to what we want to do in the future. We believe we are doing that today."

Bill George plans nothing less than to "reinvent Medtronic." Here are a few of the steps he has in mind that relate to this chapter:

- Listen and respond to the needs and wants of our customers. Look to them as the best source of new ideas we could ever find.
- Provide our customers with products and services of unsurpassed quality.
- Expand Medtronic's global reach, building share in developed markets, creating the market in developing countries, and tapping into the creative talents of other nations by expanding our research and development and manufacturing operations outside the United States.

LOOKING TO THE FUTURE

There are great opportunities for Medtronic in the industrialized world as well as in the developing world. Medtronic plans to be a truly global company and to take full advantage of participating in the world market, not just by exporting its products or doing second-source manufacturing of those products. George states,

> We really have to take full advantage of the innovation, the ideas of Japanese doctors and German doctors and Spanish doctors, and get them into the Medtronic fold, bring their ideas, their patents, their new inventions, and get them testing our products on a broad basis. That's an important part of our global thrust and that's why we have research centers in the Netherlands and in Japan. That's why we have factories in about seven or eight countries outside the United States so that we have contact with the key technical people and the technologies of those countries, as well as with the medical community. I think we as a company need to be in sync with the changes in health care reform. We believe we've operated in as wide a variety of health care systems as you can imagine, from Canada to India to Germany to the United Kingdom to the United States. We feel that we can adapt to these changes, but we really need to be in sync with the changes as they're taking place. Finally, we need to continue to have a company that thinks and acts globally —not as a Fridley, Minnesota, company, but as a company that has strong roots here but operates on a global basis all over the world.

Already, Medtronic has set the pace as a healthy global learning organization.

Chapter Nineteen

Motorola:
Transcultural Learning and Global Alliances

"**T**en is what percent of 100?"
At one Motorola plant that question stumped 60 percent of the employees. This was not a happy event for Motorola's new management. The early 1980s were a busy time in industry. The rules of manufacturing were changing. Aged plants were going through a process of reindustrialization. Old electromechanical equipment was being supplanted with new digital electronic replacements. How was Motorola to compete globally in new technologies with an infrastructure peopled with workers who couldn't read adequately?

For more than 50 years, three generations of Motorolans had shaped the evolution of electronics as creators and as consumers. This commitment made Motorola one of the world's leading manufacturers of electronic equipment, systems, and components. From the first commercially manufactured car radio to advanced state-of-the-art microprocessors, Motorola had been a leader.

One might wonder how the company had sunk so low. A better question is how did Motorola rise to become synonymous with quality and innovation today?

HUMAN CAPITAL VALUED AT THE TOP

Motorola's earnings dropped from $349 million in 1984 to $72 million in 1985. Motorola puts the year in perspective by pointing out that it was the *only* company in the semiconductor field to have any profits at all in 1985.

To address the problem, Motorola came up with a major blueprint for learning over 10 years. Motorola is known for its reference to human

Motorola at a Glance

Organizational learning	Global learning
Appropriate structures	🖊 Acculturation
🖊 Corporate learning culture	Borders
🖊 Empowerment	Globalization
🖊 Environmental scanning	🖊 Language
🖊 Knowledge creation and transfer	Leadership
🖊 Learning technology	🖊 Workforce diversity
🖊 Quality	
🖊 Strategy	
🖊 Supportive atmosphere	
🖊 Teamwork and networking	
Vision	

© Michael Marquardt and Angus Reynolds, 1992

Headquarters:	Schaumburg, Illinois
Founded:	1928
Main business:	Semiconductors, two-way radios, paging systems, equipment and systems used for information processing and handling, data communications, aerospace defense electronics, and automotive and industrial electronics.
Chief executive officer:	George Fisher
Number of countries where located:	150
Total employees worldwide:	107,000

capital as a strategic resource, sometimes claiming that its employees are the ultimate high technology. Motorola is known for developing employees' skills to meet company goals. Bill Wiggenhorn, Motorola's vice-president of training and education, claims that Motorola's training and development programs are an investment in the employees that pays off in greater productivity, performance, and quality.

Motorola has a long-standing tradition of training. It was one of the organizations to pay the college tuition of employees who took courses in engineering. In the 1960s Motorola offered executive development courses, and sent traveling trainer teams to give courses in its European and Asian locations. Former CEO Bob Galvin often said, "Learning is a lifetime investment. Learning is a continuous process; we urge all of our people to learn every day. Learning cannot be perceived as a cost, but as an investment."

Motorola's training and development solution was mandated from the very top. A major training plan instigated by a CEO was almost unheard of in 1980. Bob Galvin told personnel vice-president Joe Miraglia to come up with a training plan. Miraglia produced a five-year plan for training at Motorola with the help of a task force from manufacturing, sales, engineering, and marketing, and the Forum Corporation. The plan called for the establishment of the $11 million Motorola Training and Education Center (MTEC) to focus training corporationwide and serve employees at all levels from the production line to the executive suite. Commitment to training by Motorola's top policymaking group was clear, and that has been the key to the success of its training effort. The chief executive officer and chief operating officer both serve on the advisory board for the MTEC.

MTEC provides the full range of services to support Motorola's business objectives. Those include research, planning, evaluation, course design, seminar delivery, instructional preparation, and staff development.

Motorola's ambitious education and training strategy was to reach all of its employees. The program was eventually extended to include all Motorola employees worldwide. It also includes the employees of suppliers, of Motorola's principal customers, and even of its educational partners. Each of Motorola's five businesses—communications, semiconductors, automotive electronics, government electronics, and information systems—has its own training department. The various business groups can deliver their own training, or purchase it from outside vendors and institutions such as colleges. Business groups are not required to use internal training; internal training must win its way by delivering higher quality programs at less cost.

William Weisz, Motorola's COO, is the chair of Motorola's policy committee and is a strong training advocate. He deserves much of the credit for helping achieve the mandated 1.5 percent budget commitment to training. Weisz visits people after a training program for a face-to-face check of results. His visits make the message clear: management supports training and is strongly interested in its effectiveness.

Top Motorola executives also act as instructors. For example, Bob Galvin would spend a day and half with executive development institute participants, and at the end of the monthly senior executive development programs, either he or Weisz would attend the final session. When the results of the training are discussed, the CEO and COO participate, challenge, and question.

TRAINING FOR BENCHMARKING

Motorola conducted a 16-hour competitive awareness program for 2,500 of its U.S. managers. The program's purpose was to make managers aware of who the competition is and what Motorola can do about it.

The program emphasizes asking who is best among Motorola's competitors or best in a particular class of activity. Motorola looks for the organization in the world that is best at one particular thing. The target organization does not have to be a competitor. It could be a retail chain or a steel company that is best at one particular thing. Motorola's goal in benchmarking is to look at its position relative to the targeted best company—then develop a plan to better the best.

GETTING THE PRIORITIES RIGHT

Motorola uses a top-down bottom-up methodology to determine training priorities. From the bottom up, it asks what people think the priorities should be for their areas. From the top down, the executive management looks at its strategies and goals. For example, if a strategy is to use teamwork, management looks at what training will make that happen. Over time these priorities have included global strategy, sensitivity to the marketplace, cycle time reduction, quality improvement, manufacturing technology, and participative management.

ACTION LEARNING FOR EXECUTIVES

Three years ago Motorola changed its executive learning model to action learning. (This is described in Chapter 2.) The program is based on the idea that the best way to learn a management skill is to do it. CEO George Fisher wholeheartedly supports the program to enable executives to develop on-line skills—a major shift.

The new executive learning model puts together 25 group senior executives (VPs) for three years. The first team was created in January 1991 and *may* complete its work by December 1993. By that time Motorola will have three teams running simultaneously.

The charter.   Each Motorola executive learning team receives a three-point charter. The teams are urged to take incidental learning and perform double-loop learning to make the learning intentional. Motorola believes that the double-loop change will get the maximum benefits. Here are the three points of each team's charter.

1. Address a real business problem that requires cultural change. There are goals, milestones, and quarterly update meetings. The teams come up with a variety of solutions. Very seldom is

it possible to resolve a problem that requires cultural change with only one intervention. There must be multiple interventions.

2. Learn to effectively manage change. This is key to Motorola's long-term plans. It's where the on-line real-time learning takes place.

3. Learn to learn.

Global learning. The program is not just domestic. It has international teeth. All three teams have international membership. The criterion for selection of the team's business initiative is that it must be companywide. Team two's charter was a global business problem. The problem it had to solve was how Motorola should enter new geographic regions on an accelerated basis.

Action learning models: GE versus Motorola. The obvious question is this: how does this action learning scheme compare with GE's well-known model? Motorola's scheme is for executives at an organizationally higher level than GE's which targets upper-middle management. Of course, Motorola's three-year team commitment is much longer. Also, Motorola's executives must not only determine a solution to the problem; they must implement their own plan.

HOW MUCH OF AN INVESTMENT?

Motorola adapted a strategy similar to the levy system laws in some countries. Each Motorola business sector budgeted 1.5 percent of its total payroll for training, although more can be spent if necessary. Actual expenditures for training have exceeded the targeted 1.5 percent of payroll in some years.

Payback came quickly. Sectors were quickly able to demonstrate big dollar savings and the return on investment in training; for example, $5.7 million was saved in two years through the application of statistical tools at three Florida facilities, $1.5 million was saved at the electronics materials origination in Phoenix, a 22 percent increase in qualified maintenance people was achieved, and 79 percent more new customer orders were received.

The heavy training investment in people at Motorola and its participative management practices have had another payoff. These strategies have promoted the already visceral loyalty among its employees.

TECHNOLOGY MANAGEMENT

At Motorola, leadership means creating an environment that enables the individual to succeed, to generate ideas that evolve into innovative technologies. It manages those technologies and develops electronic products of excellent value and quality. They benefit customers, reward investors, and improve everyone's lives.

Motorola tries to go beyond teaching people how to respond to new technologies, it tries to commit them to the goal of anticipating new technologies. Through research and development, Motorola draws on the expertise of the scientist and engineer. By managing technology at every level, it transforms laboratory discoveries into the useful, high-quality products and services that are touchstones of the information age.

EMPOWERMENT

The definition of company training changed. Its purpose was to improve not just the company and the job, but also the person. Motorolans at every level participate in the management of their work. Every person involved can identify with the success of a product or business. Employees share the profits and the pride of reaching out to achieve their potential.

GLOBALIZATION

Today, Motorola's 100,000 employees speak at least 25 different languages as their native tongues. They work in manufacturing plants and sales offices located throughout the world. As leaders, they are committed to the highest standards of quality and excellence in serving customers.

Motorola's approach to operating in an international environment is supported by learning. The strategy to be competitive globally is supported by courses in benchmarking and competitive intelligence gathering. Although the company has done business in the Asian Pacific for years, executive seminars focused on the problems and opportunities there helped to improve activities and set new targets.

Motorola believes that a skilled and educated work force is a competitive weapon in an increasingly treacherous global marketplace. As Bill Weisz said, ''We have put a lot of emphasis on strategic thinking, so that each of our businesses will continue to look at itself in different ways. By continually asking where we are strong and where we are weak, we have moved in and out of different businesses and learned how to operate internationally. I won't say we wouldn't have done these things unless there had been training, but training increased our competence and efficiency to accomplish our goals and to do them faster and smarter."

Deborah King, director of executive education told us, "As a company, we believe that to compete in a global marketplace, while technology is essential, it is not sufficient. People are what is going to make a difference. People only contribute for as long as they continue to learn."

CULTURAL SENSITIVITY

"Motorola believes that sensitivity to cultural, religious, political, and social differences of our worker population is of paramount interest" says Bill Wiggenhorn, vice-president of training and education. For Motorola the parameters of the learning content must be established on a country-by-country basis. Specifically, these parameters include the following:

- Social contact with worker, family, and country or region.
- Cultural acceptance of the learning technology.
- Ability to network electronically within country or region or globally.

Motorola University is an ideal model of how a corporation has acculturized all of its training programs. (This is also covered in Chapter 5.)

NETWORKING AND ALLIANCES

Motorola has developed an extensive network to meet the educational and training needs of its employees and external associates. An example of this cooperative spirit is Motorola's global networking with key institutions of higher learning worldwide. These partnerships exchange educational resources, such as instructors, courses, and research; learning innovations; and, cultural competencies. Presently, Motorola has partnerships in Asia, Europe, and North America with over 20 institutions of higher learning.

SUGGESTIONS FOR TRAINING AND LEARNING

Bill Weisz suggested the following words of wisdom to the CEOs of other companies several years ago. It is still sound advice from a successful top executive.

- You and the rest of your senior management must commit yourself personally to training. You must be a driving force for it.
- You must be visibly involved, perhaps as a participant or an instructor, because people learn very quickly that what you are involved in is what is important.
- You should be focused in your training, whether it's teaching people how to strategize or how to be better in manufacturing.
- You should train your senior managers and not just those people down in the organization.
- You should audit the results of training, not necessarily by looking at the numbers, but by going down into the organization yourself and asking people face to face what they got out of the training and if they are implementing it. Senior people should audit training results this way at random to validate that something is coming out of training.
- You should recognize that training is a good communication vehicle in both directions. Top management can use it to reach specific groups brought together for training, and participants can use it to tell you what is really happening in the company (Gallagan, 1986).

These are not empty words. Motorola has taken each of these suggestions to heart and has truly become a leader among global learning organizations.

Chapter Twenty

PPG:
Developing Leaders
for the Learning Organization

P PG faced tremendous pressures to become a learning organization. Much like the situations experienced by Xerox and Corning
described in other chapters of this book, PPG had forgotten the core
competencies. While the competition moved to produce a low-cost
product with high quality on a continuous basis, PPG lost its focus.
It forgot manufacturing in the push to focus on finance and marketing.
In the end, good people were leaving because of the low value placed
on them. As Stephen McIntosh, PPG's director of training, development, and education (TDE) says, "We had forgotten our core competencies and had lost our way. Our core competencies are manufacturing and auto industry, not marketing and finance. We had too many
micro strategies, not a macro strategy." PPG placed a priority on
becoming a global learning organization because it recognized that
was the only way it could make it to the next century.

BENCHMARKING

PPG management knew that it needed a model to check its success
against. It benchmarked Ford, GE, Motorola, and the Baldridge award
winners with focus on customer and direct line learning. Steve McIntosh recounts, "We have had much success in learning across businesses." And it has benefited PPG, especially in its quality efforts.

QUALITY

The payoff for the PPG quality process stems from the application of
staff on four key principles:

PPG at a Glance

Organizational learning	Global learning
Appropriate structures	✔ Acculturization
✔ Corporate learning culture	Borders
✔ Empowerment	Globalization
✔ Environmental scanning	Language
Knowledge creation and transfer	✔ Leadership
Learning technology	Workforce diversity
✔ Quality	
✔ Strategy	
Supportive atmosphere	
Teamwork and networking	
Vision	

© Michael Marquardt and Angus Reynolds, 1992

Headquarters:	Pittsburgh, Pennsylvania
Founded:	1893
Main business:	Glass, coatings and resins, and chemicals
Chairman:	Vincent A. Sarni
Number of countries where located:	11
Total employees worldwide:	33,000

- Focus on customers: understand their businesses and needs, forge strong communication links, and develop partnerships.
- Meet customer requirements by supplying the exact product or service desired.
- Look continually for improvements; apply problem-solving techniques to increase productivity, and make operations more cost-efficient.
- Do it right the first time, every time, to eliminate the cost of rework.

A TOUGH SCENARIO

When Steve McIntosh was picked as training director for PPG, he was new to the training field. Management had not assessed its training needs; Steve made many calls. He discovered that the plant's employees needed a wide array of training and that high value had to be added to that training. Steve took eight key managers for a retreat to look at what would make PPG a successful global competitor. The group agreed that it would take two complementary elements: people and competencies, or sets of skills. The group then developed career

FIGURE 20-1
PPG's Professional Development Principles

Principles for Professional Development

- Associates themselves must take primary responsibility for their personal development.
- Training and development must be focused on identified competencies, which will improve PPG's market performance.
- The most effective learning occurs on the job.
- Classroom training is only one of several alternative methods for learning.
- Development-based interaction between the manager and associate is the most important factor in professional improvement.

---

steps and produced individual career plans. The result was the beginning of the *Professional Development Sourcebook*. The *Sourcebook* would soon be seen as the foundation for every individual employee's success. Each employee would have individual responsibility for self-development. The *Sourcebook* would force them to think about training for themselves.

AN INTEGRATED INDIVIDUAL DEVELOPMENT SYSTEM

The *Sourcebook* allowed for and created a completely integrated individual development system. It is based on PPG's principles for professional development shown in Figure 20-1.

The individual development system links separate items such as the individual development plan, learning matrix, and training courses with the all-encompassing *Professional Development Sourcebook*.

Individual development planning. The individual development plan (IDP) is the link between personal performance needs and improved effectiveness on the job. A useful IDP begins with evaluation of strengths and weaknesses based on the nine PPG competency areas. Many found the competency development worksheet to be a helpful tool both in identifying areas for improvement and in creating logical action plans. Copies of the competency development worksheet are found in the *Sourcebook*. The competency development worksheets (CDWs) are also distributed in a pad similar to the lined yellow pads used for most business note taking. The cover of the pad includes directions for completing the CDWs. Each item is already marked, or not, as critical to job effectiveness. Blocks remain to be checked for individuals as a strength or development need. The items are listed in Figure 20–2.

PPG learning matrix.   Setting the nine competencies into seven levels in the organization produced the PPG learning matrix. The intersecting cells of the matrix outline skills and behaviors to be mastered in order to successful at that level. Once certain skills and behaviors noted in the cells are identified as areas for performance improvement, a reference is listed under the competency heading that refers to a particular page in the *competency development guide* (which is also a section of the *Sourcebook*). The *guide* may be the most valuable part of the *Sourcebook* because it allows the individual to take control of an action plan for competency improvement. PPG learning matrix items are as follows:

- Quality
- Safety and health environment
- Blueprint values
- Supervision
- Leadership
- Planning
- Business knowledge
- Individual effectiveness
- Functional job skills.

Training courses: one tool.   Because greater awareness, enhanced skills, and changed behavior can be established through training, a course description provides information on each TDE product, appropriately cross-referenced to designated competencies. A section of the *Sourcebook* details each course's purpose, the major training objectives, the course components, special features, scheduled dates, locations, and fees, and the TDE product manager who is responsible for the course and who can provide additional information.

Professional Development Sourcebook.   The *Professional Development Sourcebook* has moved PPG from a focus on training to an acceptance that effectiveness, growth, and continuous personal improvement come from an integrated education process. The key to the *Sourcebook* is that managers must not send their people to training for fixing, but instead train on the job. The essential competency is on-the-job learning. Effective behavior is a necessary element of

FIGURE 20–2
PPG's Competency Development Worksheet Items

Quality
- Clarifying customer and supplier requirements.
- Describing one's own requirements to customers and suppliers.
- Satisfying customer requirements.
- Creating partnerships with customers and suppliers.
- Implementing quality improvement actions.
- Selecting and applying meaningful measurements.

Safety, health and environment
- Supporting PPG safety and health policies and conforming to environmental regulatory requirements.

Blueprint values
- Acting with integrity.
- Demonstrating commitment to PPG blueprint values.
- Conforming to legal and ethical requirements.

Supervision
- Conducting performance planning.
- Conducting progress reviews.
- Conducting performance appraisals.
- Conducting individual development planning.
- Delegating.
- Treating others fairly and equitably.
- Coaching.
- Supporting ongoing customer communication processes.

Leadership
- Inspiring a customer orientation and adherence to the PPG quality process.
- Enabling others to succeed.
- Adapting leadership behavior for each situation and person.
- Celebrating successes and recognizing achievements.
- Leading group meetings.
- Resolving conflict.
- Initiating and implementing change.
- Leading teams.

Planning
- Planning to meet customer requirements.
- Using PPG business planning, budgeting, and reporting processes.
- Following up to ensure plans are implemented.

FIGURE 20-2 *(concluded)*

Business knowledge

- Demonstrating an understanding of work topics related to but outside own specialty or technical area, including markets, customers, and competitors.

Individual effectiveness

- Implementing innovative ideas.
- Problem solving.
- Making decisions.
- Displaying initiative.
- Dealing with peers, superiors, and customers.
- Using time.
- Handling emotional or stressful situations.
- Working effectively with a variety of people.
- Participating in teams.
- Negotiating.
- Writing.
- Listening and speaking.
- Making presentations.

Functional

- (Blank lines to fill in as needed for individuals.)

productivity. PPG's CEO Vincent A. Sarni describes the *Sourcebook* as "our true competitive advantage."

PPG Pocket Sourcebook for Professional Development. The *Professional Development Sourcebook* has been internally recognized as a key to career planning, personal growth, and individual performance. This *Pocket Sourcebook* is designed as a quick reference to provide an overview of the complete PPG *Professional Development Sourcebook*. Because the long-term success of PPG Industries is based on the abilities of its people, all PPG associates should have access to the *Sourcebook* to find continuing opportunities for performance improvement. Human resources representatives or facility managers make copies of the *Professional Development Sourcebook* available for individual use.

BUILDING CORE COMPETENCY LEADERS

Whereas PPG is now cultivating very capable functional specialists, it is obvious that in the past PPG had not produced a cadre of broadly experienced leaders. That realization prompted the creation of the strategic unit leader development process. Now well under way, it is composed of the 16 highest potential PPG managers worldwide who are not currently running a PPG business. McIntosh was given the latitude for 48 months to do whatever it took to turn the group into a pool of general manager talent ready for the company's core competency areas. The resulting leadership development process redefines the boundaries of creating and accelerating the evolution of PPG's general management team.

PPG's senior management group is visibly involved in the week-long quarterly meetings. These meetings are held at various manufacturing sites that provide rare opportunities to learn about diverse PPG technologies, markets, customers, and strategies early in the professional development process. Steve McIntosh is confident that "people here are willing to learn."

As one might expect, PPG places a strong focus on strategic advantage through general management skills and effective leadership. It also set to work on strategic questions. For example, how can we improve our speed to market for auto painting and what should be our global market strategy?

The design contains a number of very unusual experiences as well. For example, the high potential group completed a week with Habitat for Humanity in North Carolina. The positive community image it offered the local plant, and the community insight it accorded the individuals, are nothing compared to the team dynamics that emerged. Forcing the participants to learn to lead without their base of technical knowledge proved a powerful growth experience. As these 16 managers progress into situations where conflict is a virtual certainty, they will always have that unique frame of reference in dealing with one another.

Another session deals with the topic of manufacturing excellence. McIntosh structured this as a joint session with Motorola. The two companies matched their similar high-potential groups. An unusual event was a three-way session with Coca-Cola and Champion International. That session focused on global strategic planning. PPG is nearly unique as a driving force for joint corporate learning experiences of this type.

Spouses were invited to the winter session. It was devoted to social skills and the family traumas associated with fast-tracked careers. The regular high-potential group gatherings are supplemented with continuing assessment and developmental planning using external psychologists. In addition, PPG has implemented a formal mentoring process using members of the chairman's council. This may provide the most beneficial insights of the entire four years. Each session concludes with the presentation of a critical issues "white paper" to senior managers. The papers are prepared as a team effort in the three months between sessions.

TRAINING AND LEARNING METHODOLOGIES

PPG's managers, not just its trainers, are responsible for the learning and do the training delivery. The focus is on real needs. They also use nontraditional training and learning methods. For example, in an unusual program, PPG logs community service time as training leading to self-awareness. The learning network couples all PPG's businesses through monthly staff meetings. These events provide insight into shifting priorities and outright changes.

PPG people are willing to learn, and they display a sense of urgency. Their attitude is that the need is now. The result is a bottom-line approach to learning. PPG has developed learning partnerships with many other corporations. There is still room to grow elsewhere, for example, in PPG's joint ventures with Japanese companies.

EMPOWERMENT

PPG's people have become more empowered. For example, the training development group bids against external consulting firms on projects. It regularly proves its cost-effective approach and has underbid consultants by hundreds of thousands of dollars. As Steve McIntosh says, "Our driving force is high quality and low cost." PPG's groups have partnered with other firms and chosen preferred suppliers based on qualitative measures.

A TOUGH COMPETITOR

More than 100 years old, PPG means to be in business for the next hundred years as well. CEO Vincent Sarni says, "Intensified competition worldwide demands constant change to satisfy the evolving needs of our customers. I therefore have called upon our people to make fundamental changes in the way the company does business." Becoming a global learning organization is one of the most important fundamental changes PPG is undertaking.

Chapter Twenty-One

Royal Bank of Canada:
The Learning Work Force

"Hello. I'm John Cleghorn, president of the Royal Bank of Canada. This is Bob McKenzie, the manager of our branch bank around the corner. I thought it would be good for you to get to know one another." Thus began another unusual encounter between the manager of a local branch of a competitor bank and the Royal Bank of Canada's president and local manager. The manager of the other bank was always surprised. One doesn't expect to meet the president of the largest bank in Canada in a small Canadian town without leaving your own office. Cleghorn also wants to know what the best organizations in other countries are doing.

John Cleghorn thought it would be good to know the competition. He often took his branch manager to talk with a competitor. He was also following a long line of top Royal Bank executives who made their mark with proactive policies and innovative ideas. The 1960s era president, Earl McLaughlin, became a leading spokesperson for Canada in financial matters. It is a tradition carried on today. Recently today's CEO, Alan Taylor, was seen in that role on national television.

The Royal Bank of Canada was started by seven merchants in Halifax 125 years ago in 1869. The bank quickly went international by following the trade routes of Canadian businesspeople to the Caribbean. It was expanded significantly by the paternalistic president James Muir. He said that the Royal Bank would become "the bank with 1,000 doors," and so it did.

In Canada, as elsewhere, it is prestigious and difficult to become a banker. In the early days, only a high school education was required, but candidates were scrutinized carefully. Many character references were required with attention to traits such as punctuality. Those that were selected served a banker's apprenticeship. They expected to be moved—and were. The idea of "see the country, if not the world" described their experiences. The CEO traveled as much as one third of the time.

Royal Bank at a Glance

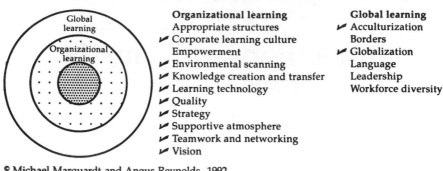

	Organizational learning	Global learning
	Appropriate structures	✔ Acculturization
	✔ Corporate learning culture	Borders
	Empowerment	✔ Globalization
	✔ Environmental scanning	Language
	✔ Knowledge creation and transfer	Leadership
	✔ Learning technology	Workforce diversity
	✔ Quality	
	✔ Strategy	
	✔ Supportive atmosphere	
	✔ Teamwork and networking	
	✔ Vision	

© Michael Marquardt and Angus Reynolds, 1992

Headquarters: Montreal, Canada
Founded: 1869
Main business: Corporate banking, investment banking, and treasury products to institutional clients as well as private banking services to individuals.
Chief executive officer: Alan R. Taylor
Number of countries where located: 33
Total employees worldwide: 56,000

Royal Bank began to assume its present configuration in the 1960s. Today Royal Bank is active in commercial retail banking in 33 countries. Its focus is something like the spreading ripples created by a stone thrown on the surface of a pond. Royal Bank's focus of operation spreads from Canada, throughout North America, to Central and South America, and onward to the world.

Royal Bank has three key visions:

- Global perspective (or mindset).
- Culture (to be open, quality, integrity, learning, and so forth).
- Education of the world's population, the Canadian population, and its own work force.

When asked about the company's culture, James Gannon, vice-president of human resource planning and development, says, ''The bank culture is a learning culture.''

ROYAL BANK FOSTERS LEARNING

There are several ways in which Royal Bank of Canada has fostered learning inside and outside the bank:

- McLaughlin created the James Muir Memorial Scholarship—full tuition of up to four years, opportunities for junior Royal Bank employees, continuing a tradition of providing learning for employees.
- Royal Bank helped establish the Institute of Canadian Bankers for professional education of bankers.
- Taylor was a founding member of Canada's Corporate Higher Education Forum, composed of 25 CEOs of corporations and 25 presidents of universities, trying to get Canadian leaders to think more globally.
- Club Bonne Heure is a learning idea. It has 800 members in Toronto and 400 in Montreal. The clubs meet at 7:30 A.M. to hear speakers who are Royal Bank leaders sharing their experiences. There are plenty of questions and answers. Employees are on their own time, but the room is usually packed.

Strategic management conference. Another learning idea is the strategic management conference. It grew out of executive conferences that had been held annually with 10 to 75 people, with a continuous learning theme. The motivation was to get new strategic ideas from all across the organization, from British Columbia to Europe. Eventually this forum grew to 175, too many people to be effective. The strategic management conference now includes the 50 top people from around the world. With a belief that they must learn from their mistakes, they attempt to consolidate the best ideas.

On one occasion the 50 invited 300 others. The strategic management conference provides the opportunity for managers to have conversations with the top two people with all other layers of management present. It serves at least two functions: introducing new strategic ideas and delegating the implementation. (It is difficult to do strategic development in groups of 50.) The conference has used electronic feedback, and it provides an opportunity for those who are geographically remote.

Other learning ideas. Another idea is the employee attitude survey, which is limited to the top 150 employees. The employee attitude survey provides an enormously powerful opportunity to provide people with information. In effect, it democratizes the organization because everyone has data.

A unique institution at Royal Bank are the CEO's roundtables. These events may include tellers or whoever fits into the travel plans. All new management employees must attend. On the executive management end, one of the top four people is required to attend. Participants have a preassignment to read the corporate strategic plan and interview co-workers. The CEO's roundtables are an attempt to tie the corporate plan to reality. There are always straight talk sessions with a quality leader format. A phrase often heard around the bank is, "We need to get out of the nine dots." This is a reference to a creative problem-solving exercise often used in management circles to get people to think of fresh ways to solve problems.

Changing silly rules.   Royal Bank believes, with Deming, that 85 percent of errors result from the system itself—not the individual. Mangers are encouraged to change silly rules. This is brought home by reference to a character from the popular British television Monty Python comedy series —the Minister of Silly Walks. Royal Bank believes that the real power in a large bureaucracy is the ability of its people to competently and quickly operate across all functions and boundaries.

Three-way partnership for learning.   Royal Bank of Canada is the largest bank in Canada, with over 7.5 million customers. To better serve these customers, Royal Bank offers its employees over 230 different workshops and seminars, as well as 60 self-study courses covering management, computers, and banking. In addition, the bank encourages staff to take advantage of various outside training and education programs.

The Royal Bank views learning as a three-way partnership among the employee, the manager, and the bank. Learning opportunities have become ever more flexible, accessible, and individualized as the banking environment changes rapidly. In such an environment, success, according to Jim Gannon, "depends on the ability of all bank people to learn quickly and continuously."

A wide array of resources is available to Royal Bank employees on an ongoing basis, including the following:

- Audio tapes
- Classroom instruction
- Computer-based training courses
- Mentoring
- On-the-job learning
- Self-completing workbooks
- Videos.

Throughout these activities, the learner is responsible for determining his or her learning needs. Each employee is given a *Learning Resource Guide* listing courses and other resources. Using this as a starting point and foundation, the employees create their own individual learning plan.

Royal Bank believes that, as a learning organization, it should be concerned with the long-term career development of each employee. There are many career paths available within the bank. With the flattening of the organizational structure, however, a career in the bank can no longer be thought of as rapid and regular movement through the bank hierarchy. Gannon says that employees must prepare for jobs that "change as people in them respond to emerging conditions and challenges. To become an asset to Royal Bank, employees need to master a unique set of skills, knowledge and relationships. And to stay at the cutting edge requires ongoing effort and attention. Learning has become *a way of life* rather than a once-in-a-while type of event."

A high-quality workbook guide, *Planning Your Career*, is completed regularly by employees. It helps them take stock of who they are, where they want to go, and what skills and abilities they possess, and develop a plan of action with priority goals and time frames.

COMMUNICATION

There are numerous other communication devices used to foster the learning culture:

- A video conferencing facility between Montreal and Toronto.
- Conference calls, for example, quarterly reviews of business groups worldwide and the operation committee worldwide conference call.
- The president's forum, a weekly worldwide conference call.
- Corporate video network.
- Exchange of video cassettes every 7 to 10 days.
- Quarterly newsletter.
- New products.
- E-mail exists worldwide.

Systems and technology executives travel the world to collect the best ideas and solutions. This systematic way of seeking innovative information has saved Royal Bank money by avoiding reinventing the wheel. For example, Jim Grant learned new insights on a recent busi-

ness trip through Denmark that ultimately saved the bank $10 million.
He is now an expert resource to the bank's business groups.

A PRIORITY ON GLOBAL LEARNING

Royal Bank has placed a priority on global learning because of its education initiatives over the past 12 years. It now has a global mindset, which is one of five characteristics listed in its corporate mission. The global mindset matches the strategic mindset. Royal Bank management uses the job as the driving force to develop the mindset. Management is convinced that education by itself doesn't work. Corporate VP of Human Resources John Gannon says, "Both sides have to learn something—and they're learning it in spades."

"It seems to me that when we talk about learning organizations it is unnatural. If learning is such a natural thing, then how is it that more organizations are not learning organizations?" asks Gannon. Difficulties encountered in becoming a global learning organization include the difficulty in bringing about change when you are successful domestically. In addition, if the domestic economy is strong, it is difficult to be interested in countries far away. The driving force that makes it happen is insecurity based on the possibility of failure. Gannon states that "change is most likely to get lost in the middle management levels of an organization."

AT LEAST ONE FOOT FIRMLY IN THE FUTURE

One Royal Bank executive likes to start discussions with employees by saying, "There are three banks here." At this point the audience thinks he will continue by mentioning retail, corporate, and investment banking. The surprise comes when he finishes the statement by saying, "the bank of the past, present, and future." The point of the story is that an organization can place its feet in only two of these at one time. Royal Bank of Canada certainly has one foot in the future as a global learning organization.

Chapter Twenty-Two

Samsung:
Targeting Globally, Acting Locally

S amsung is determined to become one of the world's top 10 corporations in the early 21st century. Lee Kun-Hee, Chairman of the Board of the Samsung Group, states,

> I have made it my personal philosophy and commitment to establish a tradition of people-oriented management and to bring about the ideal of lifetime employment for employees of the Samsung Group.
>
> A company tradition where trust and common sense prevail and where personal ability and effort are fairly evaluated is the true foundation of company management. Moreover, personal growth is company growth, which is in turn connected to social growth, and investing more resources in developing human assets will form the cornerstone of a people-oriented management.
>
> Over the past half-century, Samsung has become the leading diversified business enterprise in the Republic of Korea. With our experience and vast potential, we now seek to reach even greater heights, to become one of the world's premier business organizations.
>
> This goal, to surpass the success and growth of our initial 50 years, had its genesis in 1988. While celebrating the 50th anniversary of our founding, we instituted the "spirit of the second foundation." This spirit mandated that each affiliate place the highest priority on three key missions—human-oriented management, technology-oriented management, and self-regulated management.

Can Samsung climb that high? How is it possible for the company to succeed all around the world? We think it deserves a closer look.

WHERE ARE THEY COMING FROM?

In 1938, Samsung's founder, the late Lee Byung-Chull, set up a small firm in Taegu with the initial capital of $2,000 and 40 employees. The

Samsung at a Glance

Organizational learning
⮕ Appropriate structures
   Corporate learning culture
   Empowerment
⮕ Environmental scanning
   Knowledge creation and transfer
   Learning technology
⮕ Quality
   Strategy
⮕ Supportive atmosphere
⮕ Teamwork and networking
⮕ Vision

Global learning
⮕ Acculturization
⮕ Borders
   Globalization
⮕ Language
   Leadership
⮕ Workforce diversity

© Michael Marquardt and Angus Reynolds, 1992

Headquarters:	Seoul, Korea
Founded:	1938
Main business:	Electronics, chemicals, financial and information services, consumer products, and social services
Chairman:	Lee Kun-Hee
Number of countries where located:	69
Total employees worldwide:	180,000

company grew rapidly by actively engaging in trade with partners in Manchuria and Beijing and later by venturing into manufacturing. In 1948 Samsung moved its headquarters to Seoul and expanded its scope of activity to include Southeast Asia and the United States, thus transforming itself into an international trading house.

The 1950s. Samsung began to build up its manufacturing capacity in earnest immediately after the end of the Korean War and led national postwar efforts for economic reconstruction. In 1953 it constructed a sugar refinery, the first large-scale plant in Korea built by a local company with its own in-house technology. The next year, Samsung ventured into wool processing, a field requiring a level of technology and quality control that was considered highly sophisticated in Korea at the time. In the latter part of the decade, Samsung also branched out into banking to become Korea's leading corporation, with major business interests in trading, light industry, and finance.

The 1960s. Samsung contributed to Korea's drive for economic modernization by carrying out ambitious projects in key industries and by diversifying its range of business lines, thereby taking firm root as a nationally based corporation. It built a paper plant in 1965 and two years later completed the largest fertilizer plant of its kind in the world at the time. Through this localization of fertilizer production, Samsung laid the foundations for Korea's self-sufficiency in rice production, as well as for the steady growth of heavy and chemical industries. In 1969 Samsung mounted a challenge to enter the electronics industry, the leading new-growth business of the day. From the start, the Samsung Group placed primary emphasis on technology accumulation and penetration into overseas markets.

The 1970s. The Korean economy continued to grow rapidly during the 1970s, based on the strength of such industries as steel, petrochemicals, and shipbuilding. The Samsung Group's investments placed it the in the forefront of Korea's heavy and chemical industrial drive. Samsung led this sustained growth with its trading and electronics branches and provided Korea with a base for continued advancement in the engineering and chemical industries. Following the setup of Samsung Heavy Industries in 1974, the Samsung Group established several new companies to venture into shipbuilding, petrochemicals, aerospace, and precision industries.

Meanwhile, the Samsung Group's electronics subsidiaries rapidly diversified their product lines and enhanced their technological expertise. Samsung began fabricating silicon wafers in 1974 and producing electron guns for cathode ray tubes (CRTs) in 1975. Before the decade was out, the company was also developing or manufacturing video cassette recorders and integrated circuits for TVs and telephone exchanges. In a bid to transform itself into a world-class corporation, Samsung began its advance offshore in earnest in 1975 when its trading arm, Samsung Co., Ltd., became the first government-designated general trading company (GTC) in Korea. The trading arm strengthened its trading operations and extended its business interests to overseas resource development and plant exports.

The 1980s. Samsung entered the high-tech field in earnest, with a massive investment in a VLSI project in 1983. The timely development of 4M and 16M DRAM semiconductor chips demonstrated that its technology had become an international player.

The sophistication of its in-house chip technology enabled the Samsung Group to commence production of application-specific integrated circuits (ASICs) and microprocessors used in a wide variety of consumer and other electronic products. Samsung also achieved technological breakthroughs in other fields. For example, in genetic engineering it developed interferon, and in the precision industry it developed industrial robots. Since establishing consumer electronics plants in Portugal in 1982, Samsung has steadily built up an impressive overseas production presence. Most recently, has been actively making investments and establishing footholds in China and the former Soviet-bloc countries, which have emerged as fast-growing new markets.

Samsung, one of the world's top 20 corporations in terms of sales volume, is always on the lookout for joint ventures abroad or other strategic business ties with foreign firms. In Korea, Samsung operates a host of successful joint ventures with leading multinational corporations. Its business partners include Corning, Amoco, General Electric, Hewlett-Packard, General Dynamics, and Pratt & Whitney of the United States; British Petroleum of the UK; and Toray, NEC, and Seiko of Japan.

Chairman Lee Kun-Hee says, "This offshore commitment is significant, requiring the strategic cooperation between our home office, regional headquarters, and localized overseas operations. This involvement will continue through the ongoing enhancement of our current foreign ventures, along with additional joint partnerships and strategic alliances as market conditions dictate."

Through these joint ventures, Samsung has gained international recognition for its business management and reliability. Based on its domestic experience, it is seeking diversified strategic business ties abroad. It has so far built 236 overseas operation bases, including 35 offshore production facilities in 55 countries. Therefore, you can find a Samsung employee virtually anywhere in the world.

Samsung's corporate philosophy is deceptively simple.

- Contribute to global and national prosperity.
- Give top priority to human resources.
- Continually strive to fulfill customer needs.

We will explore the different ways in which Samsung tries to carry out its philosophy.

ESTABLISHING A GLOBAL PRESENCE

Samsung has long pursued globalization with an ambitious long-term vision. Its management goal is to take advantage of the world's most competitive resources and secure a competitive edge in every market of the world. Being known is a necessary prerequisite for such success.

Samsung set up large neon-lit advertisement boards along the roads to airports or in the centers of such major world cities as New York, Tokyo, Beijing, Barcelona for the 1992 Olympic games, and

Seville for the 1992 Expo. It also provides pushcarts bearing the red-and-white Samsung logo to over 70 major airports around the world, for the convenience of air travelers. In addition, Samsung seeks to be an active sponsor of the 1994 Asian Games in Hiroshima. All these activities are designed to further raise awareness of the Samsung name throughout the world.

As a multinational corporation with an expansive global network, Samsung is an active patron of culture. At the same time, it supports various activities as a means of implanting its own image in the minds of its customers. An example of its role as a cultural patron is the provision of £430,000 for the opening of a Korean gallery in the Victoria & Albert Museum in London. Dedicated at the end of 1992, the hall is named the Gallery of Korean Art. This civic arts project will contribute to the introduction of Korea's traditional culture and arts to a European audience.

Since 1988, Samsung has sponsored, jointly with FEI (Federation Equestrian Internationale), international equestrian and steeplechase competition tours, helping to enhance equestrian sports and contributing to the worldwide promotion of horse riding. In 1991 alone, equestrian events were held in 26 countries and steeplechase events in 44 countries. The competition, together with the equestrian events in the Olympics, is the biggest of its kind in the world.

Samsung also plays a key role in promoting other sports. It sponsors soccer teams in Germany, Hungary, and Chile, and the Dynamo ice hockey team of the former Soviet Union. Samsung is also working to popularize Korea's traditional martial art, Taekwondo. It is inaugurating its own Samsung Cup Taekwondo competition.

In the United States, Samsung has supported a fund-raising campaign jointly organized by the Alzheimer Association and Youth Hostel to help the victims of Alzheimer's disease.

Samsung's commitment to provide lasting benefits to the economies of its host nations has been favorably acknowledged. Its electronics plant in Portugal has helped the country emerge as an important exporter of color TV sets to Europe and Africa. The Portuguese government, in recognition of Samsung's contribution to the creation of jobs and economic vitalization in that country, awarded Samsung Electronics Co. the Order of Industrial Merit in 1991. The firm was the first foreign enterprise in Portugal to receive such an award.

CONTRIBUTING TO THE LOCAL COMMUNITY

Samsung's entry into the development of socialist countries tends to be dictated not by short-term profits, but rather by prospects for long-term and comprehensive cooperation. It has a policy of locating promising local firms, promoting joint ventures with them, transferring to them technology and management know-how, and sharing with them Samsung's experience in exploring new foreign markets. Its investments are not limited to local assembly plants and include projects that comply with specific local programs for economic development. Samsung is also keen on helping host countries improve their industrial structures by building a mutually beneficial international division of labor.

Samsung's contributions to the economies of host countries have been well demonstrated by various projects. In the Philippines it is creating an industrial complex in cooperation with a local firm, Solid. Samsung has been asked not only to give advice on the selection of firms applying for admission to the complex, but also to serve as the export outlet for the products to be produced there. It has helped China produce TV tuners under the OEM (original equipment manufacturer) formula by transferring its technology; and, through its joint color TV plants in Hungary, Turkey, and Thailand, it provides its accumulated management know-how and production technology to local partners.

Samsung also transfers its technology through plant exports. In assisting India's Baroda Rayon Co. to build a synthetic resin plant and Indonesia's Yasonta Group to set up a spinning mill, it provided not only major facilities but also production technology and business experience. Today, the two plants churn out the best products available locally. To impart its state-of-the-art men's suit production technology to Thailand's Asia Vivat, Samsung invited local Thai engineers to a Cheil Industries Inc. plant for training, while sending experts to Thailand. It has exported an MSG plant to China and built an MSG/lysine plant jointly with Indonesia's Astra Group.

To promote technological exchange between developing countries, Samsung set up SFOTS (Samsung Foundation for Overseas Technical Scholarship) in 1983. SFOTS has since been offering technical training in such fields as electronics, machinery, construction, and trading to engineers from Malaysia, India, China, and other countries. This program continues to win favorable responses from the recipients.

ESTABLISHING A TRULY GLOBAL MANAGEMENT TEAM

When entering a foreign market, which poses new challenges in terms of different cultures and customs, Samsung first cultivates personnel who can perform the services requested by local customers. At the same time, Korean staff to be posted abroad undergo language courses and overseas training programs so that they can accumulate knowledge about the countries where they are to work. Emphasis is placed on creating international businesspeople who can adapt to and work comfortably with their local partners.

Jong Tae Kang, Director of Samsung's HRD center, says, "As the company develops to the global company, it requires many global managers to operate business units overseas and manage locally hired employees. In addition, as the number of foreign employees increases, training and education for them becomes the major issue in our company."

Samsung also sends its managers to foreign universities or academic institutions in a bid to foster experts in international law, patents, financing, and other specialized fields. These trainees are expected to cultivate an ability to recognize international trends and devise strategies accordingly. In 1989 Samsung introduced a program designed to develop regional or national experts who "think and act as local residents." Under this program, an employee is sent to a foreign country for a year and is expected to master the language, experience the local culture, and become an expert in the affairs of that country. Currently, Samsung targets 45 countries for this program.

Samsung operates regional research centers in Korea to systematically collect and use foreign market information. All the employees returning from overseas are assigned to these centers for a short period to write reports on the business customs, culture, and value systems of the countries where they worked. Meanwhile, Samsung's overseas offices throughout the world employ people with diverse ethnic and linguistic backgrounds. These people are fostered as full members of the corporate family. To train them as such, Samsung invites them to Korea to learn its management philosophy. For example, Samsung's globalization efforts include dispatching experts in certain products to major branch offices. They are to provide more adequate service to local consumers and send more up-to-date information about the local market response to the product back to the headquarters in Korea.

Samsung has set up IPOs (international procurement offices) at its major branch offices around the world as a means of linking resources abroad and its own technological expertise. IPOs provide plants at home and abroad with reliable and competitive parts available in foreign markets. At the same time, they reinforce the Group's ability to gather accurate international procurement information, contribute to overall cost reduction, and help locate and foster promising local parts suppliers.

Samsung also seeks to more efficiently tailor its management systems to overseas markets, emphasizing planning and development of products that cater to the tastes of consumers abroad. At the same time, it is forming a network that can strategically link together its branches around the world. While respecting the special conditions, culture, and expectations of local populations, Samsung looks for universal elements that it can accommodate and apply globally. Practicing its motto of "targeting global, acting local," Samsung seeks to be an example of the international corporate citizen who works hard for the welfare of all members of the global community.

HUMAN RESOURCES AS THE BASE OF POWER

Samsung's reputation as a good neighbor and responsible corporate citizen springs from the human resources it fosters. The Group's creed states, simply, "An enterprise is an organization consisting of people, and its future depends on them." Speaking on developing resources, the late founder Lee Byung-Chull once recalled, "Eighty percent of my life has been devoted to gathering and training competent people." This conviction that the men and women of are the essence of the Group is alive and well in Samsung today.

In 1957 it began to recruit employees through its first open examinations, a practice that had not been attempted by any Korean firm before then. Samsung takes care to select talented employees and assign them to the jobs in which they can do their best. It has cultivated the tradition of nurturing its human resources by respecting individuals, offering quality educational programs, and instilling the concept of lifetime employment.

Samsung encourages its employees to realize their own potential. There are eight group-level educational and training centers that offer programs focused on strategic R&D, and centers at each member company concentrate on task-specific, specialized programs.

Samsung's human resources development system is multifaceted. It includes on-the-job training programs in which superiors become teachers and jobs become textbooks, self-development programs that take advantage of intracompany "technology universities" or seminars, programs designed to foster regional experts, and the sending of employees to domestic or overseas research institutes. At each company, diverse study groups are organized. Those at Samsung Co., for example, are noted for their development and commercialization of new products.

Jong Tae Kang says, "We have a one-year-long training program to cultivate regional specialists all around the world. About 200 trainees have completed or are taking this program in Africa, Asia, Europe, and America. We have a plan to expand the program to train 300 more young employees by 1995 to prepare for the future. This program is composed of two subprograms. One is a local language course for six months, and there is no fixed schedule for the remaining six months. During this time, trainees can travel freely and meet people to learn their customs, history, and society. We expect that through this program, our employees can understand cultures and people deeply, and this will give us an ability to work together with them for mutual prosperity."

Samsung's learning programs are effective. As one might expect, they have a Korean style. The official goals of a Samsung education are as follows:

1. To instill the spirit and a clear sense of mission in all employees.
2. To improve managerial capabilities and specialized job skills.
3. To cultivate the ability to positively adapt to an ever-changing business environment.
4. To develop active, highly educated members of society.

The characteristics of Samsung education and training are shown in Figure 22-1.

CULTIVATION OF A TECHNOLOGICAL LABOR FORCE

Recognizing that the systematic rearing of a technological labor force is the bedrock of corporate management, Samsung invests 13 billion won ($100 million) annually in the cultivation of technical and scientific personnel. This budget includes the operation of the Advanced Technology Training Institute, in-house "technology universities" run by individual firms, overseas training programs for employees, and other activities.

The Advanced Technology Training Institute was set up in 1990 at the R&D complex in Kiheung to train employees in the most advanced technologies. The institute is staffed with 340 research personnel and trains 1,500 employees annually. It is committed to research and training in such key technologies as semiconductors, mechatronics, and instrument design. The teaching staff is composed of the institute's own researchers who have doctoral degrees, as well as professors

FIGURE 22–1
Characteristics of Samsung Education and Training

---

1. *Disciplined education*

• Spiritual education (strong corporate culture).
• Proper mode of conduct and a sense of mission through disciplined education

2. *Senior-led training*

• Well-systematized courses where lectures are mainly done by seniors with relevant field experience and knowledge.
• Course material developed by training center.

3. *Strengthening organizational solidarity*

• Sharing vision of group and sense of values.
• Strengthening feeling of togetherness.

4. *Coordination with group-level and affiliated company-level training*

• To provide basic and advanced courses required for all employees.
• To provide highly sophisticated manufacturing and management technology.

from Seoul National University and the state-run Korea Advanced Institute for Science and Technology.

Most of the Group's member companies have established in-house technology universities to enhance their particular technological expertise and to encourage the self-development programs of researchers. They also offer various training programs including phased TP (training path) courses, special training in core technology, and participation in domestic and overseas seminars.

Technological innovations are essential to successful technological management. Therefore to advance its technological management ability, Samsung strives to cultivate able R&D managers and to improve its overall information-gathering and planning capabilities.

The Advanced Technology Training Institute also offers courses on technological assessment and forecasting, analysis of competitiveness, management of technical labor, R&D management, technology-related contracts, technological information gathering and analysis, and patent management.

The Group's Technology Assessment Center at SAIT evaluates Samsung's overall capacity to develop new technologies, defines future target areas, and suggests Group-level technological strategies. It also analyzes and evaluates the effect that the development of certain technologies or products might have on the company.

Furthermore, every Samsung company has consolidated its own support system under which all sections cooperate closely in developing new technology, assessing consumer needs, maximizing technological and competitive advantages, and ultimately, succeeding in the commercialization of developed technology. Under this system of coordinating the functions of R&D and production, each affiliate strives to develop at least one world-leading product. In some cases, the development team for a product is improved into the independent business division, taking full control of production and distribution of the product on its own. For example, this was the case with the team that developed the magneto-optical disk.

COMMUNICATION FLOW

To ensure smooth communication between management and labor, and to pool the creativity of employees, each member company holds the following forums:

- Open Door sessions in which workers are encouraged to speak freely to the managers on any topic of concern.
- Young board sessions, in which young employees make proposals for management improvement.
- Top-bottom communication sessions, in which free dialogue is held between the company president and its workers.
- The 21st century committee, in which visions for the coming century are formulated.

SUPPORTIVE ATMOSPHERE

In addition to the emphasis placed on the development of human resources, Samsung has created a tradition of respecting individual employees. It has attempted to create an atmosphere in which employees can work comfortably, offering affordable housing, free dormitories, and welfare benefits.

Samsung's management philosophy is characterized by respect for basic human rights and for individuals, fair treatment of employees, and active accommodation of opinions from below. All these combine to invigorate organizations. Samsung's successful management style is founded on this philosophy, which generates among workers the shared feeling that the corporation is a familial community. There are no trade unions at Samsung. By successfully transplanting its

Korean-style business management to the countries where it operates, Samsung plants enjoy lower worker turnover rates and higher productivity than other foreign enterprises.

Jong Tae Kang says, "We think that it is not easy to find out the way to measure the improved portion of business performances through training and development. However, we can say that training is one of the important strategic tools to attain business goals. Every executive and manager in Samsung fully understands this."

A friendly neighbor and a responsible corporate citizen, Samsung lives in the minds of the Korean people as a corporation that emphasizes human resources and respect for individuals. How Samsung is perceived by the public is demonstrated by the fact that for five consecutive years it was the preferred employer among career-bound university seniors. They cite Samsung's growth potential, opportunities for self-development, and job stability as reasons for their preference.

PREPARING FOR THE 21st CENTURY

The source of Samsung's progress is organizationwide learning and sustained technological innovation. In its major business lines (electronics, engineering, and chemicals) Samsung has sharpened its technological edge. In the words of chairman Lee Kun-Hee, "Samsung realizes that to maintain a global competitive edge, it is vital to develop and manufacture specialized yet diversified products to fulfill consumer and industrial needs. However, technology and manufacturing are only part of the business education; we must put our clients first— in terms of product quality and effective service delivery." Jong Tae Kang adds, "It is expected that in the future our company will be operated in more competitive situations, and strategic alliances and partnerships with other companies may be an issue in the global market. This business situation requires excellent global managers who have international perspectives and flexibility. Training and cultivating excellent global managers will be one of major tasks for our HRD practitioners." Samsung is rapidly becoming a global leader in all aspects of learning and technology.

Chapter Twenty-Three

Singapore Airlines:
Flying High on Worldwide Learning

C an an airline from a small island state really be a "Great Way to
Fly"? You'd better believe it. Many travelers to Asia do. Singapore Airlines (SIA) is known for distinctive in-flight service second to
none. It consistently wins awards for its outstanding record for superb
passenger service—in an area of the world where airline cabin service
excels above other regions.

SIA's trademark Singapore Girl, accompanied by the "Great Way to
Fly" tune, has remained the basic theme in SIA's advertising campaign
for almost 20 years. The Singapore Girl image became SIA's unique
selling proposition. The *sarong kebaya*-wearing flight attendant has become the symbol of SIA's philosophy and has appeared in countless
advertisements in all media forms and promotions worldwide.

The Singapore Girl flight attendant in the ads, a personification of
oriental charm and friendliness, has always embodied the best for air
travel to Asia. When you fly Singapore Airlines, she promises, "We
offer in-flight service even other airlines talk about." Such pampering
has helped to make SIA not only award winning, but the most profitable airline in Asia. Organizational learning has been a key to this success.

A MATCHLESS REPUTATION

In 1947 refreshments for crew and passengers consisted of ice water
from a thermos, which was replenished at each stop. This is a far cry
from the in-flight service for which SIA is known today. SIA's commitment to service excellence has earned the airline many international
awards. The important triennial Intramar survey, an attitudinal study

Singapore Airlines at a Glance

Organizational learning	Global learning
✓ Appropriate structures	Acculturization
Corporate learning culture	Borders
Empowerment	✓ Globalization
Environmental scanning	Language
✓ Knowledge creation and transfer	✓ Leadership
Learning technology	✓ Workforce diversity
✓ Quality	
Strategy	
✓ Supportive atmosphere	
✓ Teamwork and networking	
✓ Vision	

© Michael Marquardt and Angus Reynolds, 1992

Headquarters:	Singapore
Founded:	1947
Main business:	Scheduled and nonscheduled international airline services, aircraft engine overhauling services, simulator training, airport terminal services, tours, property development, aviation and general insurance, and related services.
Managing director:	Cheong Choong Kong
Number of countries where located:	34
Total employees worldwide:	15,000

that evaluates passengers' reactions to airlines, consistently confirmed SIA to be the leader in service.

CORPORATE PHILOSOPHY

In the complex aviation environment, the need for clear, visible objectives to give direction to the company's progress is evident. Singapore Airlines has adopted four corporate goals:

- To deliver the highest quality of customer service that is safe, reliable, and economical.

- To generate earnings that provide sufficient resources for reinvestment and satisfactory returns to shareholders.

- To adopt human resource management practices companywide that attract, develop, motivate, and retain employees who contribute to the company's objectives.

- To maximize the utilization and productivity of all resources.

THE FORMULA FOR SUCCESS

SIA Deputy Chairman Lim Chin Beng gives the following formula for the airline's success:

> The cornerstones of our philosophy and drive serve not only as motivators for our staff, but also as trademarks that set the airline apart in the highly competitive airline industry.

- *Growth*. We are committed to growth and expansion, with a view to eventually moving ahead of our competitors.
- *Strategic location*. We realized that we can capitalize on our strategic location to make it an important aviation turnstile at the crossroads of the world.
- *Service*. We exploited our capacity to offer the best equipment and service to our customers.
- *Consumer*. Our basic commitment is to the consumer with emphasis on value for money and good service. Feedback from customers is quickly reported to top management for appropriate action.
- *Liberal environment*. Singapore's aviation policy of allowing any country and any airline to fly in on the basis of reciprocity has been good for Singapore's tourism and trade.
- *Modern fleet*. To us, it means cost savings, on-time departures, lower maintenance costs, fuel savings, higher market profile, and improved staff morale.
- *Marketing*. Our advertising strategy centered around the airline's image with heavy emphasis on our hostesses and in-flight service. We are now the established leaders in advertising and marketing of the airline product.
- *Human resources*. Our loyal and hardworking staff are our greatest asset. Their efforts have not been unrecognized. Our personnel policy has allowed staff to be rewarded by advancement as well as by monetary compensation.
- *Excellence*. Since our inception, we have continually espoused excellence, even before "excellence" became the accepted vocabulary in management circles. Our corporate publication *The Pursuit of Excellence* spells out our aims, objectives, and achievements. It spurs us to greater heights and accomplishments as it serves to motivate management and staff alike.

> The real test of entrepreneurship in any business is how we serve the consumer or the user of our products because that is what we are in business for.

A STRATEGY FOR SURVIVAL AND SUCCESS

To prosper—indeed, to survive—the airline had to be clear about its goals and the strategies needed to fulfill them. First, in the minds of its managers were the words of the Prime Minister, who declared that SIA would have to make it on its own merits, for it could expect neither favors nor subsidies in times of trouble. The plan that SIA management evolved to guide development into a major international airline, successful and respected, was centered around service, growth, staff development, a commitment to free enterprise, and a willingness to make bold yet judicious investments.

In the early years growth was pursued relentlessly. Rapid expansion kept unit operating costs low, and the economies of scale that it engendered made modern equipment and facilities affordable. As the number of destination points served by the airline increased, so too did the effectiveness of Singapore as a distribution hub. A bigger network also reduced the dependence of the airline on any particular sector.

SIA also knew that to meet its goal of becoming a major, successful international airline quickly, it had to invest heavily, not only in modern aircraft, but also in people.

HOW TO KEEP YOUR JOB

The airline industry is a service industry. The product, whether a seat or cargo space, has an extremely limited shelf life. It expires on takeoff, and whatever seats are left unsold cannot be recovered or stored away as inventory. The offer of a seat or space is open only at a certain time, making the product highly perishable.

On international routes, most carriers resemble each other closely in what they have to offer to the consumer. The basic product—a seat on a plane—remains unalterable. What the airlines try to do is to produce a unique version of the total product. This takes the form of giving the consumer an entire range of services, such as reservations, ticketing, airport check-in, baggage handling, in-flight service, and arrivals handling, to set the airline apart from its competitors. Only then will an airline be able to clinch a competitive edge. The clear marketing strategy for an airline is to provide a level of service to the customer, such that the airline's seats and space will be fully utilized. Research studies on air travel show that, when all things are about equal in aircraft type, fares, frequencies, and reliability, travelers respond warmly to the appeal of high-quality, personalized in-flight service.

Since its inception, the airline's appeal is based on the high standards set by its cabin services. By concentrating on personal service, the fledging international carrier penetrated the international market, as other carriers emphasized network schedules, reliability, and competitive fares. Little premium was placed on service innovation.

Another reason for SIA to project itself as a service-oriented airline was that Malaysia Airlines (MSA), the carrier's predecessor, had already acquired a reputation for good service. The new management at SIA continued to develop and project the airline along this tradition after SIA separated from Malaysia Airlines in 1972.

SIA's employees receive attention from the top. Lee Kuan Yew, Singapore's prime minister, said,

> Passengers are disturbed when they see poor standards of cleanliness and, worse, slovenly service in the aircraft—no smartness in the bearing, dress, and behavior of air crew and cabin crews. They wonder if these are not also the standards of the maintenance staff and ground crew. I have stressed again and again the constant need to ensure that what passengers can see of SIA aircraft and air crew and cabin crew reassures them of our attitude of mind, our zeal for tip-top standards of safety, efficiency, and courtesy which prevails over all sectors including the maintenance and ground crew. Maintaining these high standards is not a favor SIA workers are doing to management or the government. It is what you have to do to keep your jobs in a very competitive industry. In the airline business, to stay still is to stagnate, and to stagnate is to be overtaken. We must press forward to ever higher performance.

THE BEGINNING OF AN AURA

The first Singapore Girl flew in October 1972. Then, SIA was an airline indistinguishable from other carriers in equipment, schedule, and reliability. What SIA needed was a separate identity to make itself stand out from all other airlines. To the new team leading the "new" carrier, the Singapore Girl became the promotional vehicle by which the SIA product could be launched into the world market. Since then, the Singapore Girl has remained synonymous with SIA.

The Singapore Girl was conceived as a personification of oriental charm and friendliness that the airline realized through careful recruitment and painstaking training. Pierre Balmain, a renowned French couturier, was commissioned to design new uniforms for cabin crew and ground staff. His creation of the *sarong kebaya is* another symbol of SIA today.

Word-of-mouth praise from satisfied passengers created an aura of superior service and style. The aura, once established, had to be sustained through constant training, clever advertising, and ingenuity in the cabin. Staff training then became crucial. Considerable attention was devoted to training, developing, and motivating frontline and

cabin employees to give their best to serve the customer. In 1979 a new
$2 million cabin crew training center was opened. It houses three air-
craft mock-ups in which aspiring Singapore Girls learn the basics of
in-flight service. It also incorporates a training pool in which technical
and cabin crews undergo safety and emergency drills.

THE ORGANIZATION

The chairman, deputy chairman, and managing director comprise top
management. However, SIA is not bound by hard and fast rules gov-
erning lines of communication, allocation of duties, and authority. The
structure of formal committees is kept to a minimum. The key committees and their functions in SIA are as follows:

- *Management committee.* A weekly meeting chaired by the managing director and composed of all divisional directors to discuss
  corporate problems and issues. However, matters arising from
  the various divisions that may have a corporatewide effect are
  also discussed.
- *Company planning committee.* Headed by chairman or deputy
  chairman, developmental issues of fleet planning, traffic rights,
  strategic marketing and the like are discussed.
- *Human resources committee.* Headed by chairman or deputy
  chairman to discuss issues about personnel policies and human
  resource development. It oversees the changes in personnel
  processes, the rate of change, and sets strategic guidelines.
- *Finance committee.* Presided over by the chairman, its main functions are to review general financial performance and to oversee
  funds and treasury management.

A SPIRIT OF DEDICATED TEAMWORK

SIA's goals are based on a corporate philosophy of all-encompassing,
dedicated teamwork. SIA's spirit has been summarized as follows:

- We are above all a democratic organization, not in the sense of
  "one man, one vote," but in the sense that we are not authori-
  tarian, autocratic, or paternalistic.

- SIA strives to create the smallest possible units to carry out required tasks.
- There has to be delegation of authority down the line.
- We endeavor to create an environment in which responsibility, within the authority delegated, can be exercised effectively at all levels.
- Training and retraining are the unwavering object of the group.
- Because of the tightly integrated nature of our operations, there is no question of one department being more important than another department. There are frontline activities and backroom activities. Whereas the backroom activities may not face the same type of pressure as frontline operations, any failure is bound to have serious long-term consequences. So the acid test is utility and relevance, not relative importance.

INVESTING IN HUMAN RESOURCES

Singapore Airlines runs one of the top global leadership programs anywhere. SIA spends over $80 million a year in employee training and development and has won many awards for its learning programs, as well as its airline service superiority. At its Management Development Center, established in 1987, leadership training helps give future SIA leaders the skills and values shown in Figure 23–1.

SIA Managing Director Cheong Choong Kong says, ''SIA annually spends substantial sums on staff training. Job specific training is, of course, essential, and there are well-staffed and well-equipped training departments in each of the divisions of engineering, cabin crew, flight operations, marketing, and management services to train the maintenance engineers, cabin crew, cockpit crew, reservations, ticketing and airport services staff, and computer professionals. General, non-job-specific courses are also conducted regularly in areas such as people management and performance appraisal. Senior staff from managers upward are sent to executive- development-type courses in such places as MIT and Harvard.''

Singapore's Prime Minister Lee Kuan Yew declares, ''When I get on board an SIA aircraft I shall see and feel a representative flavor of Singapore. SIA should be representative of what Singapore is, a society based on a man's or woman's worth and performance, qualities which

FIGURE 23–1
SIA Skills and Values

Skills or Characteristics	Values
1. Strategic orientation	Long-term outlook, being prepared for change, future-oriented, ability to network
2. People approach	Leadership, committed to ongoing learning, effective communications, teamwork
3. Global outlook	International awareness, political and cross-cultural awareness, concern for global environment, willingness to learn from others
4. Commitment to service excellence	Concern for total quality management, customer-oriented
5. Creativity	Innovation, imagination, entrepreneurial, adaptable, responsiveness to change, versatility

have nothing to do with a person's race, language, religion, or family status, or connections.''

PEOPLE AS ASSETS

Singapore Airlines has come a long way since its humble origins in 1947. It has grown from operating a twin-engined Airspeed Consul to operating the most modern fleet in the world with legendary in-flight service. Top-quality service is about putting people first. An airline may have a modern fleet, a well-balanced route network, and an effective marketing strategy, but what gives it an edge over its competitors is the skill and discipline of its human resources. SIA's admirable record in the service sector is due to its unswerving commitment to its most important asset—its human resources. SIA recognizes that people are the driving force behind the organization's success. SIA has excelled by recognizing the value of its human resources through comprehensive staff training and development.

Throughout its history, SIA has constantly sought to ensure that staff are trained regularly to improve their efficiency. In the early years, the company spent about $3,000 a year on staff training. Today, on average, SIA spends a total of 70 to 130 million dollars a year on training and development. The group's leadership in training and development was acknowledged in 1990 when SIA was awarded the National Training Award in the service sector category for its ''outstanding record in employee training and development.''

Chairman J. Y. Pillay states, ''We train and retrain our employees.

We do not treat our employees as mere economic digits. Our objectives are to enable each of them to develop through training and career development his full potential." In early 1974 SIA invested $1 million in a flight crew training center. Then one of the most advanced training centers in the world, today it houses the latest aircraft simulators, with computer-generated images. These machines faithfully reproduce aircraft movements and thus provide realistic and relatively inexpensive technical crew training. The center now houses five aircraft-specific simulators.

Other training centers. These include a commercial training center opened in 1971 that runs a variety of courses in such diverse subjects as ticketing, traffic, cargo, and human relations, and a computer training center, established in 1980. Today more than 4,000 SIA staff members have completed computer-related courses. SIA is self-sufficient in engineering capability, due largely to its engineering training school.

Developing staff. The training and development needs of staff are reviewed and worked out carefully so that staff can be developed to function effectively at their optimal potential. During the annual appraisal exercise, the employee's specific training and development needs are identified. The emphasis on staff training will be focused on helping staff members to function effectively today and also on preparing them to face the challenges of tomorrow. Training and development programs for senior staff are broadly categorized under four groups: core, complementary, optional, and specialized.

Core. Core programs are the mandatory and sequential training programs that a staff member has to complete during the various stages of his or her career with SIA. To start with, a new entrant to the company will be put through a one-week residential new entrant program to develop self-discipline, confidence, leadership, and teamwork and to instill a sense of belonging. This is followed by a two-week residential basic management program and a one-week residential airline industry course to equip the young executive with basic people management concepts and people-handling skills and to induct the new entrant into the airline industry. Senior staff will complete broadening programs such as the Middle Management Programme, Senior Management Programme, Managing International Business Programme, and Individualized Advanced Management Programme as they progress up the SIA hierarchy.

Complementary.   Complementary programs are skills based, and staff complete these courses as needed.

Optional.   Optional programs are generally self-development programs to help staff improve themselves in areas such as coping with stress, understanding business protocol, and so forth.

Specialized.   In addition, staff also attend specialized or job-related programs to help them function effectively in their current jobs.

TRAINING FOR TOMORROW

Learning is a cornerstone of SIA's human resource development process. This was shown in 1987 by the establishment of the management development center (MDC). The MDC is responsible for the training and development of the 20,000 staff in the SIA group. Since then, it has progressed into a professional center for management education. Besides training the staff in the SIA group, MDC is pleased to share its executive programs with other organizations in the region.

The principal mission in the SIA MDC is to enhance the long-term effectiveness of management. The center aims to increase the capability of businesses in the region to manage their present and future performance in an increasingly complex world.

MDC does not aim only to develop managers to run today's businesses, but also to prepare them for the future. It provides the opportunities to share knowledge through experience, to develop skills, and to generate new ideas. In this way, it aims to encourage businesses to manage their own corporate culture to meet the challenges of the future in a highly competitive global environment.

MDC's management development programs are available on a cost-sharing basis. One aim of this policy is to reduce training costs throughout the region. This forum provides, for management staff and executives in the region, a wide scope for discussing current and future problems and opportunities. The rich mix of participants stimulates interaction and exchange of ideas among corporate executives around the region and is a notable ingredient in the seminars' continuing success.

SIA believes that management development gives the cutting edge to international competitiveness. MDC aims to develop managers who can succeed in today's business environment and are ready to face tomorrow's challenges.

SIA's management development curriculum is drawn from a conceptual framework based on the vision of the future and the characteristics a successful manager needs to face the challenges of this vision. The programs are targeted progressively at each crucial stage in a manager's career. They are divided into three categories: management development, management skills, and self-development.

Management development programs.   These programs cover generic management skills ranging from basic management to strategic management.

Management skills programs.   These programs include vital management skills, such as negotiating, problem solving, and decision making.

Self development programs.   These seminars focus on areas to develop oneself, such as in business and social etiquette and stress management.

The faculty is drawn from centers of higher learning and experts in Europe, the United States, Australia, Japan, Hong Kong, and Singapore. Participants come from Singapore and the region, and from SIA's international network. Case studies, computer simulations, role playing, experiential learning, group discussions, and, where applicable, hands-on practice complement lectures. The seminar size is well controlled. It is small enough to promote personal participation, yet large enough to provide a variety of outlooks.

PEOPLE-CENTERED ORIENTATION

On people management, SIA management's mission is to encourage the change from task orientation to people-centered orientation. The change is being completed in various ways. At the formal level, staff are encouraged to change through people management courses. In order to give expression to the change, more authority and responsibilities have been delegated to line management on personnel matters. Line management is, in turn, asked to encourage its staff to take part more actively in decision making. Simultaneously, communication channels were improved through regular news bulletins and notices to keep staff informed of developments in the company.

CLOUDS ON THE HORIZON?

Competition in the world's fastest-growing air travel market is brutal. Profits have fallen. The competition comes from the West. Western airlines have focused on the Asian market with new long-range jumbo jets and added flights. United, for example, has more than doubled its service in the region. Others such as British Airways and Delta have targeted Asia aggressively.

They are attracted by what appears to be a gold rush in a struggling industry. Asian passenger traffic is increasing by almost 10 percent a year. This looks mighty good beside rates that are below 7 percent elsewhere in the world. McDonnell Douglas forecasts that, by the year 2010, well over half of all international passengers will connect with one or more Asian Pacific cities.

The Asian-based airlines worry because the Western airlines can bring passengers out of their extensive domestic routes while Asian airlines don't have access to local feeder networks for their international flights. But the Asian market is tough for everybody. Delta has delayed opening of an Asian hub. American Airlines has reduced Asian service to only Tokyo. The rugged competition has obliged Singapore, Cathay, and Thai Airways International to consider a new joint frequent-flier plan to match the Westerners. The Asian airlines are preparing for further acceleration in competition, consolidation, and possible steep fare cuts and over the next few years.

SIA's managing director Cheong Choong Kong told *Newsweek*, "It's not as easy these days as it was when we pioneered features like free drinks, free headsets, and a choice of meals in economy class" (November 16, 1992). SIA has a vision of the potential future. They believe the business environment of tomorrow will encompass the following elements:

- It will be increasingly competitive. Competition for market share can only be keener, and organizations must aim for a strong competitive edge.
- It will be less predictable. The environment will be more turbulent, indicators more complex and harder to read.
- The environment will be faster changing. High technology has introduced new rules, and the rules of the game will change ever more rapidly.
- It will be increasingly interconnected. The end of the cold war has broken up political barriers; and with swifter communications the world has become a global village with a single market. Thus, the need to be global in outlook is an inescapable fact of life.

LOOKING AHEAD

Given this scenario, SIA realizes that, to sustain the business of today and survive in the environment of the future, there are certain rules that it should imbibe now. This is vital in ensuring that corporate strategy is coherent with the demands of the environment. SIA believes that an organization's strategy is therefore both the product and function of its staff, whose value and knowledge base can be nurtured. It further believes the characteristics of the successful worker of today and tomorrow, as well as the values needed to sustain these characteristics, are best nurtured through an enlightened human resource development policy, of which learning must play an integral part.

This will enable SIA, with it modern fleet—one of the youngest in the world, with almost legendary in-flight service, supported by an equally proficient ground service, a sound financial base, a balanced route network, and a highly qualified and disciplined workforce—to maintain sustained growth. SIA realizes that only through innovation, imagination, prudent risk taking, and the entrepreneurial drive can it stay competitive, keep abreast of the latest in technology, and provide outstanding service. SIA is confident of its success in the next decade.

Chapter Twenty-Four

Tatung:
Turning Talent and Technology into Organizational Learning

S an-Chih Lin founded Tatung in 1918 and served as its chairman until his retirement. His motto was "honesty, integrity, industry, and frugality." He believed that talented people are the most important asset of a business and that the education of industrial talents can facilitate industrialization. He donated 80 percent of his property to support educational efforts, including the establishing of the Tatung Institute of Technology and Tatung Senior Vocational School. Today, the first clause of Tatung Company's articles states, "To carry out an industry-education cooperation program with Tatung Institute for Technology and Tatung Vocational High School for Industry."

This tradition of support for learning continues today. The president of Tatung, the founder's grandson Wei-Shan Lin, is a strong advocate of continuous learning.

TATUNG INSTITUTE OF TECHNOLOGY

Organizational learning is the center and keystone of all of Tatung's operations. The pride of the company is its Institute of Technology. In 1956 the Tatung Institute of Technology, also called Tatung Tech, was formally established to implement the cooperation program between education and industry and began to offer three two-year programs: electrical engineering, mechanical engineering, and business management. The Institute was accredited as a four-year college in 1963 with these three departments. Additional departments of chemical engineering (1970), industrial design (1970), information engineering (1982), materials engineering (1983), applied mathematics (1984), and bioengineering (1986) were added.

Tatung at a Glance

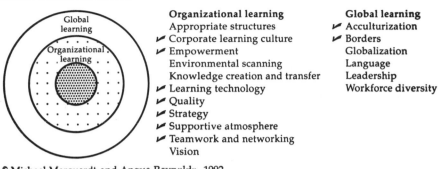

Organizational learning	Global learning
Appropriate structures	✔ Acculturization
✔ Corporate learning culture	✔ Borders
✔ Empowerment	Globalization
Environmental scanning	Language
Knowledge creation and transfer	Leadership
✔ Learning technology	Workforce diversity
✔ Quality	
✔ Strategy	
✔ Supportive atmosphere	
✔ Teamwork and networking	
Vision	

© Michael Marquardt and Angus Reynolds, 1992

Headquarters:	Taipei, Taiwan
Founded:	1918
Main business:	A diversified manufacturer of electronic, computer, and communication products; industrial equipment; and home appliances.
President:	Wei-Shan Lin
Number of countries where located:	20 (sales in 87 countries)
Total employees worldwide:	25,000

Faced with the quickening pace of Taiwan's economic development and the ever-increasing demands for highly qualified professionals, the Institute began to offer two-year master's degree programs in business management and electrical engineering in 1976. Other master's degree programs include mechanical engineering (1980), chemical engineering (1982), information engineering (1983), and materials engineering (1984). The doctoral programs were also established for electrical engineering (1982), mechanical engineering (1984), and chemical engineering (1986). The expansion of Tatung Tech into Tatung University is now in the planning phase.

Students are matriculated after passing a very competitive entrance examination. They receive assistance and support from the company but are not obligated to work for Tatung after graduation.

Tatung Tech recruits and maintains a strong faculty totaling more than 200 members. It consists of both full-time professors dedicated to teaching and basic research and part-time professors drawn from Tatung Company who help give students the necessary practical education from industry. Scholars and outstanding entrepreneurs, many from foreign countries, are also invited to serve as visiting professors.

Tatung Company and Tatung Tech complement each other. Tatung offers workshops for Tatung Tech's students to gain hands-on experi-

FIGURE 24-1
Tatung Institute of Technology Objectives

1. To nurture in students the spirit of honesty, integrity, industry, and frugality.
2. To inculcate in students the strong feeling and high standards of ethical responsibility to society.
3. To create through the process of industrialization a new society, in which everyone possesses a steady and secure job, serves the public, and enjoys a happy life.
4. To constantly strive for excellence in teaching and research.
5. To contribute to global progress by strengthening its industry.

ence. The overall objective of the workshops is to enkindle in the student an initiative spirit, develop qualities of leadership, and cultivate a deep sense of responsibility and self-reliance. Tatung also is able to provide practical work experiences for its students at all the company's factories and offices, like the internship of a medical school's students and its affiliated hospital. This permits students to integrate classroom theories and internship opportunities.

In order to develop internationally minded managers and engineers with global vision and capability, Tatung Tech has also placed great emphasis on foreign language training, particularly in English and Japanese. The idea of globalization is reflected in the institute's objectives, which are listed in Figure 24-1.

The school also offers the company's personnel a wide variety of practical courses, specialized programs, seminars, and off-the-job training. The results of Tatung Tech's professors and students in different departments and graduate programs are employed in solving problems in product development and manufacture. Continuous research and development achieved through industry-education cooperation enables Tatung to keep renovating itself as well as to design and produce important new products and services, all essential elements of organizational learning.

INDUSTRY-EDUCATION COOPERATION AS A RESOURCE

The formal joint goal of "self-standing academic research through full development of human character" has a practical result. Tatung benefits from its own industry-education cooperation in two forms: basic and applied research. The Institute conducts applied research under contracts offered by the Tatung Company in order to meet the

FIGURE 24-2
Changes over 10 years

	Fiscal 1981	Fiscal 1991
Industrial equipment	26%	13%
Home appliances	33	15
Electronics, computers, and communication	32	66
Trade sales	8	4
Others	1	2
Total	$794.8 million	$2.1 billion

needs of the company to keep pace with technical advances in the modern industrial world. The hand-in-hand cooperation between Tatung Tech and Tatung Company has the added advantage of contributing significantly to the development of technical knowledge in the Institute.

The development of new products is done jointly by the company and its subsidiaries, Tatung Science and Technology Inc. (TSTI), the R&D laboratory at Tatung Co. of America, Tatung Telecommunication Co. (TTC) in California, Tatung Tokyo Engineering Center, and the R&D laboratory at Tatung UK Ltd.

CONTINUOUS LEARNING

Dr. T. S. Lin, chairman of Tatung Company and president of Tatung Institute of Technology, also serves as a professor and personally conducts major Tatung Company learning activities. For example, he takes charge of the orientation of new employees, meeting with each new group. Company executives are invited to attend these sessions, thereby providing for continuity and cross-fertilization.

REINVENTING THE COMPANY

An educated workforce was essential to the company's evolution into new business areas during the 1980s. This shift is illustrated in Figure 24-2.

Quality control thinking circles. Tatung is a strong advocate of quality. At Tatung the quality circles movement is called quality control thinking circles (QCTC). Movements for making suggestions for improvements have been launched both in the school and in every plant and center of the company. QCTC meetings are held at regular intervals to check results and ensure effective performance at every level.

Each year the participation rate and number of improvement suggestions made has increased. Currently there are 1,200 Tatung QCTCs. They range from the production units to the district offices. Everybody joins in the team activity of thinking and acting in the pursuit of zero-defect quality.

EMPOWERMENT AND SUPPORTIVE CORPORATE CULTURE

Each new recruit becomes a member of the Tatung family. Tatung employees are called colleagues (as Honda's are called associates). Colleagues are given a job assignment and are helped to grow through on-the-job training. During work hours colleagues are trained to respect, trust, and cooperate with other colleagues in the pursuit of their goals.

Tatung corporate culture respects its employees and works to help them in their lifetime career development to nurture their welfare and foster their independence. Each day after work, colleagues are encouraged to reflect on what they have accomplished to see whether they have done well and improved their knowledge and abilities. The objective of this corporate culture is to enable colleagues to stand on their own two feet and make continuous contributions to the school, the company, and the nation in a quickly advancing world.

Tatung employs a shared management concept. Work is divided appropriately to attain a simplified organization. Tatung management style emphasizes clear-cut accountability and facilitates two-way communication. Decisions are made promptly at each level and consistent actions are taken effectively to reach the desired goals.

The company also tries to maintain a basis of mutual trust, reciprocal help, and shared responsibility in close ties with suppliers and distributors, both of which keep abreast with Tatung in equipment, know-how, and product quality centrally with Tatung's assistance. As a result, Tatung raises its productivity, improves its competitive ability, and provides customers with high-quality products and the best possible after-sale service.

A CARING EMPLOYER

Tatung has been a pioneer among companies in the so-called Asian dragons (Hong Kong, Korea, Taiwan, and Singapore) in empowering workers. Tatung was the first organization in Taiwan to implement the idea of social investment, in which a publicly owned company's employees own shares of the company. San-Chih Lin, Tatung's founder, also donated 10 percent of his estate to all Tatung employees so that they were able to become employee stockholders. A generous gift at any time, his was an unusual bequest at that time.

In 1967 the Tatung Cooperative Employee Fringe Benefits and Welfare Committee was established to take care of the colleagues' livelihood. The committee provides various kinds of subsidies, scholarships, financial aid, and medical care to Tatung colleagues. It has its own library and offers courses in languages, painting, flower arranging, and computers. The committee also directs many recreational activities such as photography, mountain climbing, picnics, and ball games, as well as jogging and mass birthday parties for employees.

REMAKING TATUNG THROUGH *MING-WU-YUAN*

Tatung is remaking itself through a spirit of best service called *ming-wu-yuan*. This maxim might be translated as "battle against red-tape bureaucrats." Ming-wu-yuan means putting the general interest above personal gains and utilizing tangible and intangible assets and human resources. Tatung, like Asea Brown Boveri, McKinsey, and other global learning companies, realizes that bureaucracy is the scourge of learning. Therefore, its leadership is continuously seeking ways to streamline its structure and policies so that communication, networking, and action can proceed. Ming-wu-yuan is a way of working and learning that has lifted Tatung into the elite among global learning organizations.

Chapter Twenty-Five

Xerox:
Continuous Learning through Quality Culture

T he natural tendency of institutions is to recall the shining moments in their history when they and their members were at their
best. Later descriptions may gloss over or even completely forget those
occasions when they did not fare quite so well. This is an unfortunate
phenomenon. Failure, more often than not, is a breeding ground for
lessons that can significantly affect future performance. Although the
near disaster we are about to describe did not reflect well on Xerox,
it is perhaps as valuable a part of its legacy as its better-remembered
successes.

Xerox introduced the world's first plain-paper copier, Model 914, in
1959. It was an astounding success and created a new industry. The
demand for convenient plain-paper copying was enormous. As shown
in Figure 25–1, Xerox grew from a small company with revenues of $33
million in 1959 to a major corporation with revenues of $176 million by
1963 and $4 billion by 1975.

Competition was weak and fragmented. By the 1970s the Japanese
were attacking the low end of the market, IBM the middle, and Kodak
the high end. Initially Xerox ignored its low-end competitors. This allowed them to build on market share and strengthen their hold on that
market segment. The Japanese appealed to consumers with their low-
cost, reliable copiers. Efficient design and manufacturing capabilities
enabled the Japanese to price their copiers at about half of what it cost
Xerox to manufacture its products.

From the mid-1960s to the mid 1970s, Xerox revenues grew at an average annual rate of about 23 percent, and profits increased at an average rate of about 20 percent. Meanwhile, efforts to manage the explosive growth made cost control far less important than it is today. Xerox
was free to offset inefficiencies by increasing prices. Between the mid-

FIGURE 25–1
Xerox Revenues from 1959 to 1975

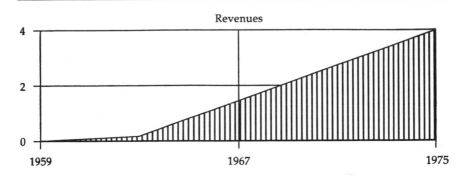

1970s and 1980, revenue growth slipped to an average annual rate of about 16 percent. During the same period, the average profit growth slipped to about 14 percent.

The Japanese were able to get their products to market in half the time it took Xerox and were about to eat Xerox's lunch. The signs were unmistakable. The examples set by other corporations in similar situations were not encouraging. The historic pattern had been good growth, a dip in the rate of growth, and then a drop like a stone. Xerox's market share dropped to less than 50 percent by 1980. From 1981 to 1983, revenues flattened, and net income in 1983 was 17 percent lower than it had been in 1980. The corporation's return on assets reflected the same downward trend. As shown in Figure 25–2, in 1980 ROA was 19 percent, but it declined steadily to 8.4 percent by 1983.

What had gone wrong? What had brought a high-flying, successful company so close to extinction? By 1992 it had nearly recovered all that lost ground. What enabled it to do so?

XEROX'S GLOBAL ADVANTAGE

Xerox avoided going belly-up because it was able to make corrections in time by using characteristic global learning organization techniques. It had seen the whole scenario in advance in Japan—and learned. Following its founding in 1962, Xerox's subsidiary in Japan, Fuji Xerox, experienced a period of extraordinary growth. Also like Xerox, it had the emerging copier industry almost to itself. In 1975 the big changes occurred. Japan's economy was jolted by the worldwide oil crisis. Both

FIGURE 25–2
Xerox Return on Assets from 1980 to 1983

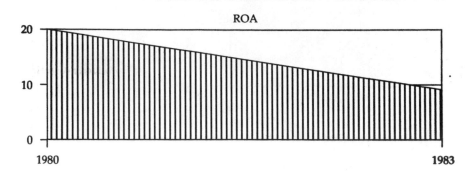

Ricoh and Canon became serious competitors, and Fuji Xerox did not have adequate new products to respond.

Fuji Xerox woke with a jolt from the sweet dream of success to the shocking reality of a competitive marketplace. Sales began to slip. Something bold had to be done, and quickly. The very survival of the company was at stake.

In 1976 Fuji Xerox launched a new total quality process. Called the "new Xerox movement," its short-term objectives were to develop new products to satisfy market requirements, strengthen the marketing organization, bring costs under control throughout the company, and introduce new basic technologies.

The four basic responsibilities of the new Xerox movement were as follows:

- Harnessing the power of each employee and each department through clear management objectives.

- Establishing and communicating companywide philosophy rooted in an absolute dedication to continuous quality improvement.

- Promoting the use of scientific and statistical tools and techniques.

- Seeking the coveted Deming prize—Japan's prestigious award for a companywide total quality process.

Fuji Xerox employees responded with both enthusiasm and commitment. Absolute dedication to quality improvement and cost reduction became the accepted way of doing business. Quality circles grew and the use of statistical tools became the norm. Management fostered and rewarded teamwork. Not only Fuji Xerox, but also the entire family of

Xerox at a Glance

	Organizational learning	Global learning
	✔ Appropriate structures	Acculturization
	Corporate learning culture	Borders
	✔ Empowerment	✔ Globalization
	✔ Environmental scanning	✔ Language
	Knowledge creation and transfer	✔ Leadership
	Learning technology	✔ Workforce diversity
	✔ Quality	
	✔ Strategy	
	Supportive atmosphere	
	Teamwork and networking	
	✔ Vision	

© Michael Marquardt and Angus Reynolds, 1992

Headquarters:	Stamford, Connecticut
Founded:	1906
Main business:	Document processing products and systems and financial services.
Chief executive officer:	Paul A. Allaire
Number of countries where located:	130 .
Total employees worldwide:	99,000

operating companies, subsidiaries, and suppliers, were brought into the new Xerox movement. A participative management style was encouraged.

Fuji Xerox's turnaround bordered on the supernatural. In 1978 Fuji launched the highly successful Xerox 3500 copier. Four years after the crisis, the Deming award was bestowed on Fuji Xerox. Revenues and profits increased.

This was the birth of Xerox's extraordinary dedication to quality. It learned firsthand that quality does work. Out of that realization, leadership through quality was born.

Xerox, warned by its Fuji Xerox experience, read the signals in time. Major changes were put in place to blunt the competitive threat and to improve Xerox. Xerox applied these solutions by changing its approach to product development and delivery, the way it approached its customers, and its cost base.

COMPETITIVE BENCHMARKING

Other changes were also occurring at Xerox. For instance, in 1979 the company established competitive benchmarking. This is Xerox's process of measuring products, services, and practices against its toughest competitors. Benchmarking's goal is to strive for superiority in quality, product reliability, and cost. By 1981 benchmarking was implemented corporatewide. Xerox continues to be recognized as a leader in the utilization of benchmarking for learning and application.

EMPLOYEE INVOLVEMENT

Starting in the manufacturing section in 1979, Xerox people at all levels now participate in employee involvement, thereby influencing their work and work life. The objective of employee involvement is to ensure that the minds and talents of Xerox people are applied fully and creatively to the problems and opportunities the company faces.

Despite the improvements made by the early 1980s, it became clear that still other changes were needed. Xerox needed to fundamentally change the way it managed its business while making still better use of the energies, talents, and ideas of its people. Xerox also needed to bring more discipline and precision to its business functions.

ENTER LEADERSHIP THROUGH QUALITY

Then-chairman David T. Kearns and the corporate management committee concluded in September 1982 that Xerox needed to implement a total quality process if the company was to remain competitive in the global market. The committee reasoned that quality is a very powerful vehicle for change. Proof of this was evident in its own Fuji Xerox experience as well as the experience of other Japanese companies.

Since the early 1950s, the Japanese have been applying the tools and principles of quality and with results that are the envy of the industrialized world. In modern times they have become a dominant force in automobiles and motorcycles, televisions and stereo equipment, calculators and copiers.

Once the decision was made to adopt quality as the basic business principle for Xerox, it became clear that no existing total quality process could be transplanted to the Xerox environment. As is the case with any large institution, Xerox is unique. It has its own culture, values, and philosophy. It has its own opportunities and challenges. And it has its own products and businesses. It was necessary to create ownership of a quality process by developing a Xerox approach based on the best teachings of the gurus and the benchmarking of total quality companies.

It became equally apparent that for a quality strategy to succeed at

FIGURE 25–3
Leadership through Quality

	Conventional	*Xerox*
Definition	"Goodness"	"Conformance to customer requirements"
Performance standard	Acceptable level of defects	"Products and services that fully satisfy the requirements of our customers"
System of achieving	Detect and correct	"Prevention of errors"
Measurement	Indices	"Costs we incur when we do not satisfy customer requirements"

Xerox, the highest levels of management would have to lead the implementation and act as examples for the rest of the corporation. In 1983, 25 senior operating executives from around the world, working as a team, designed leadership through quality. They hammered out a Xerox quality policy and the broad outlines of a quality strategy and implementation plan. The policy says simply, but powerfully,

> Xerox is a quality company. Quality is the basic business principle for Xerox. Quality means providing our external and internal customers with innovative products and services that fully satisfy their requirements. Quality improvement is the job of every Xerox employee.

The management team took great pains to define precisely what it meant by quality. As shown in Figure 25–3, quality as referred to in leadership through quality differs from the conventional view of quality in at least four respects.

The management team realized that implanting this view of quality into the Xerox culture would require massive change. It was equally aware that change of this magnitude required that Xerox develop new principles, new behaviors, and new tools for Xerox people to work with. Finally, the senior management team articulated some very precise objectives for what it wanted to accomplish by embarking on leadership through quality:

- To instill quality as the basic business principle in Xerox and to ensure that quality improvement becomes the job of every Xerox person.
- To ensure that Xerox people, individually and collectively, provide external and internal customers with innovative products and services that fully satisfy their existing and latent requirements.

- To establish as a way of life management and work processes that enable all Xerox people to continuously pursue quality improvement in meeting customer requirements.

Such massive cultural change and ambitious objectives required careful planning. After senior management developed its broad plan to help the company achieve its quality objectives, a quality implementation team (QIT) was formed with representatives from each operating unit and corporate headquarters. The QIT assisted in implementing the strategy and managing the transition.

The QIT, with the support of senior management and a quality training task force, used the broad plan to develop the detailed strategy for leadership through quality. The strategy required a transition team and four other mechanisms for change that are still used today at Xerox. The four mechanisms are as follows:

- Standards and measurements
- Recognition and reward
- Communications
- Training

Standards and measurements. These provide all Xerox people with new ways of assessing and performing their work, solving problems, and improving quality. Tools to do this include a six-step problem solving process; a nine-step quality improvement process; competitive benchmarking; an emphasis on error prevention and doing things right the first time; and techniques for determining the cost of quality.

Recognition and reward. These ensure that Xerox people are encouraged and motivated to practice the behaviors of leadership through quality. Both individuals and groups are recognized for their quality improvements, whether this recognition takes the form of a simple thank-you or a cash bonus.

Communications. This ensures that all Xerox people are kept informed of the objectives and priorities of the corporation in general and their work group in particular and their progress toward meeting these priorities. Communication includes both formal media, such as magazines, films, and communications events, and informal means, such as staff meetings.

Training. This provides every Xerox person worldwide with an understanding of leadership through quality and a working knowledge of the tools and techniques for quality improvement. Training is delivered in "family groups" consisting of a manager and his or her direct reports. The manager, assisted by a professional trainer, conducts the week-long problem-solving and quality-improvement training.

During the course of the week, the group selects a problem or project for application of the quality process and tools. After training, the manager guides the family group in the use of the quality process. Once the project is underway, members of the family group work with a professional trainer to deliver the week-long training to their own subordinates, who then choose their own application project.

This method of training top managers first and having them participate in the training of their subordinates is called a training cascade. It is designed to ensure that managers are trained in and understand the quality process and to actively involve them in the training of their family groups. This enables the management chain to practice Xerox's "learn, use, leader inspired" sequence to reinforce the quality improvement objectives of the training.

EXTERNAL RECOGNITION

Xerox's good work was recognized and rewarded by others. After winning the Deming award in Japan in 1980, other Xerox divisions won quality awards in France in 1987, England in 1983 and 1985, and the Netherlands in 1984.

In late 1988 the company decided that the business products and systems organization in the United States should apply for the Malcolm Baldrige National Quality Award. Company officials thought Xerox had an outside chance of winning, but more importantly they wanted an objective appraisal of the company's quality efforts.

In forming an application team and putting together its application, Xerox learned more about its products and services as seen through the eyes of the customer. Xerox also learned that it could improve on its quality efforts, a finding that served as the basis for an intensification of the company's quality efforts.

In November 1989 Xerox was named a Malcolm Baldrige award winner. Later that year, Xerox Canada Ltd. won the Canadian national quality award.

Because of the lessons learned, Xerox is now committed to competing for quality awards in every country in which it does business. And in countries that don't have quality awards, Xerox seeks to work with those governments to establish award programs.

The bottom line is that Xerox firmly believes that the competition for these quality awards provides management with an external focus that not only is essential to judging how well the company is doing, but also is vital in setting future goals.

LEARNING FROM WARTS

The company's goals in the 1990s are to intensify its quality efforts in the United States and abroad. In competing for the Baldrige award, members of the Xerox application committee turned up more than 500 "warts," or problems, in the business products and systems operation that need to be corrected. The warts have been re-focused into six principles on which the intensification effort is based:

- A customer defines our business.
- Our success depends on the involvement and empowerment of trained and highly motivated people.
- Line management must lead quality improvement.
- Management develops, articulates, and deploys clear direction and objectives.
- Quality challenges are met and satisfied.
- The business is managed and improved by using facts.

In looking at where Xerox has been and where it's going, CEO Paul Allaire says that there are five "lessons" that should be kept in mind when implementing a quality strategy.

1. Senior management must be committed to change. Without a genuine, hands-on commitment, a quality process will not succeed in quality improvement and employee involvement.

2. The support of union leadership is essential. The quality process at Xerox could not work without the support of its principal union, the Amalgamated Clothing and Textile Workers Union, which has understood the important role union workers have played in the success of Xerox.

3. A company making a commitment to quality must realize it will require some initial investments. Xerox provides every employee six full days of training in problem solving, quality improvement, and team building. When that's added up for 100,000 employees worldwide, the investment totals 2,500 labor years. That's a significant investment in both financial and

human resources. But Xerox believes it is one of the best investments it's ever made and further believes that it has resulted in far greater savings.

4. Leaders of an organization implementing a quality process must be patient and disciplined. Xerox has learned that results don't come quickly. Some groups, employees, and managers are more reluctant than others to adopt new procedures. The successful implementation of a quality process requires continuous self-examination and review of people and processes to prevent errors and improve results.

5. Senior executives, managers, and all employees must realize that quality improvement is a continuous process. Xerox has learned that every time it improves, so does the competition. Xerox also has discovered that every time it improves, customer expectations increase. The result is a never-ending spiral of increased competition and customer expectations. At Xerox, the quality process has become the way Xerox people around the world think and work.

This culture of quality, this commitment to continuous improvement, this determination to learn from mistakes, and this dedication to employee development has made Xerox the envy of global organizations, a trait that is a challenge for anyone to copy.

IV

THE LEARNING HORIZON

Chapter Twenty-Six

The Future of the Global Learning Organization

A s we look to the beginning of the 21st century, many events will occur that will be totally unexpected. Two things we can predict with some confidence, however, are that the world will be ever more a global village, and that learning will be ever more important for organizations and individuals. What global learning organizations will look like will also be even more interesting, exciting, and of course, strange to us relatively slow organizational learners of the 20th century.

There are many new and exciting events beginning to take place in global learning organizations. 3M has established an organizational learning services group to provide learning guidance for its activities in 57 countries. The International Labor Office with the American Society for Training and Development and Cornell University recently conducted a highly successful participative workplace systems laboratory in Turin. This learning technology is laying the foundation for future global organizational learning methodologies. Harrison Owen has experimented for the past few years with open space technology, a process that may have significant implications for global group learning.

What do these and other events tell us about the future scope, structure, and power of global learning organizations? Four different but complementary visions have been developed to describe the global learning organization of the future. These comprise: the emerging new organizational paradigm of Michael Ray; the streamlined, project-focused organization envisioned by Tom Peters; the transfigured organization of Jones and Hendry; and the interactive organization of Harrison Owen. Let's explore their visions of the future.

THE EMERGING NEW PARADIGM FOR ORGANIZATIONAL LIFE

Michael Ray, professor of creativity and innovation at Stanford University, believes that corporations in the future will adopt an ''emerg-

FIGURE 26–1
New Organizational Paradigm

Present Paradigm	New Paradigm
Short-term goals	Corporate and individual vision
Rigid culture	Flexible culture
Product orientation	Market orientation
Internal focus	External focus
Regional emphasis	Global emphasis
Management direction	Employee empowerment
Procedure bias	Risk bias
Analysis only	Creativity, analysis, intuition
Competition only	Cooperation

ing new paradigm" for organizational life. The new paradigm, described in Figure 26–1, will be different from the present paradigm in nine key dimensions.

This new paradigm appears to be a wonderful fit for global learning organizations. It is a place that global learners can call home.

THE PROJECT-FOCUSED, STREAMLINED ORGANIZATION

The organizations that will survive the 1990s, according to Tom Peters, will contain the following structures and elements:

1. Organizations, no matter the overall size—whether 200,000 or 20—will be broken down in fast, learning-efficient units of 2- to 50-member teams.
2. The key work, in whatever form or kind, will be head work (knowledge work).
3. Every business process will be erased, and then revived. Horizontal business processes, which will weld all former functional activities into seamless wholes, will be the main way of doing business.
4. Middle management levels will be eliminated because they only obstruct learning and speed.
5. Most of tomorrow's work will be done in project teams. The life span of a project team can be indeterminate or just a few hours. Dynamic, short-lived project configurations will be commonplace. It will not be unusual to work on four or five project teams in a year—but you might never work twice with the same configuration of colleagues.

6. The average project team will include "outsiders," for example, a vendor, customer, or distributor.

7. Who reports to whom will change over time, and you will routinely report to a person for one task who reports to you for another.

8. The goal for business will be more than winning "this game." Developing a world-class team with world-class members will be more important than any single victory.

9. Feedback loops will become ever shorter.

10. Peer evaluation will be more important than boss evaluation. The employee will be evaluated on the following criteria:
    - Team play.
    - External relationship management.
    - The ability to encourage new experiences and ideas.
    - Commitment to learning and improving expertise.
    - Becoming a teacher.
    - Passing lessons learned on to teammates and the broader network.

11. There will be constant reorganization, in the sense of endless reconfiguration of project team and network structures.

12. Much of the value-added of the organization will come from special learning and communication resources responsible for guiding the organizational knowledge development process.

13. Organizational learning will be highly regarded, as will contributing to the knowledge development process of the organization. It will be one of the main ways in which performance and compensation will be judged.

14. Information technology will be everything, especially if applied to newly structured organizations.

15. Real-time access to all information, including information from outside, will be a must for everyone in the organization.

16. The project manager and network manager will be the star players for tomorrow's company.

17. Super subcontractors will be used to handle everything that is not a core competency of the organization. Working with a shifting array of supersubs will enable the organization to

stay lean, agile, and ready to respond with a new assortment of partners for any foreseen or unforeseen opportunity.

18. Organizations will be of three principal forms:

- Systems integrators, which chiefly construct and manage networks.

- Specialists (supersubs), which have unique competencies that they feed into various networks.

- Independent talents, who may act alone or be part of a talent bank.

19. Marketplace power will be a result of the array of networks and the learning power you have created.

20. As an organization's units become more loosely coupled to each other, they will be more tightly coupled to customers and suppliers.

What would Peters think to be an excellent example of the future learning organization? A favorite is Oticon, a Danish world-leading hearing aid manufacturer. Everything about the firm is making it a company for tomorrow. The difference begins with its offices' physical layout. The traditional physical structure of separate offices and long corridors has been eliminated. Walls have been taken down. Those barriers limit communications, the flow of information, and the expansion of learning. The staff can gather wherever and with whomever they wish to work on the projects they are involved in.

The "mobile office" allows staff to cross functional lines and to understand how things work in other groups. Each workstation in the large undivided space is identical. No workstations are assigned. Instead, people roll their personal and professional items to the spot where they will work during the day. Thus, Oticon has already become a company for tomorrow, being more creative, and learning things faster and better.

Oticon also shapes jobs to fit the person instead of the other way around. Each person has a portfolio of functions, so that the engineer learns how to do sales as well as handle the phones (customer and marketing skills). Functional departments are gone and a project-based free-for-all occurs. Anyone can be a project leader, and project leadership tends to shift over time. Project leaders are financially responsible for their jobs.

Communication flows with greater openness, and opportunities for growth and learning are almost infinite. According to Peters, excitement and enthusiasm have already made Oticon a success story for the future.

THE TRANSFIGURED ORGANIZATION

Jones and Hendry believe there is an additional stage of organizational learning besides the four stages mentioned in Chapter 7—foundation, formation, continuation and independence, and transformation. A fifth-level stage in the development of learning organizations is possible. They call it the *transfiguration stage.* The transfiguration stage represents a fully developed learning organization, having the capacity to cope with any change. At this level of development the global learning organization does not simply deal with events as they arise or are foreseen. The organization "elevates" activities to their purest form, proceeding with superior products and services combined with superior personal ability. Multiple levels of management become a thing of the past. Leaders and envisioners who act as facilitators for learning become "the all-important managers and organizers." Different people and different groups take responsibility in an adaptive way depending on the task to be performed. These leaders act as catalysts to speed up the learning. The emphasis of this type of global learning organization is on teams exploring and envisioning new approaches. They seek to find out how the organization can develop its capabilities, not only for competitive advantages, but also for the well-being of the employees. Whatever learning happens can be shared throughout the organization. Teams and groups will produce extensive, innovative work. The transfigured organization will be able to step outside its existing frameworks and patterns of thinking—able to replace existing operating styles. There will be a concern for spirituality in the organization. It will be like an amoeba, able to change shape to suit its environment and to react to the pressures of external demands. Learning will flow naturally, inside the organization and throughout the global environment in which the organization interacts.

THE INTERACTIVE ORGANIZATION

With some similarities and some marked differences, Harrison Owen sees a stage yet to be achieved by learning organizations. He calls this the interactive learning phase.

Interactive learning organization. The key element of the InterActive Organization is that there is learning, not some of the time, but every instant, not in spite of itself, but with clear intention. The learning is whole and organic. The totality is infinitely more than the sum of the parts. Owen compares learning in organizations to the evolution of human consciousness, and the role of the organization is to facilitate that process.

In the interactive organization, there cannot be a tight set of specifications to be implemented or a structure to follow. There are however, five key characteristics:

- High learning
- High play
- Appropriate structure
- Appropriate control
- Authentic community

High learning. Owen defines *high learning* as learning that happens when there is a genuine shift in consciousness. One quite literally sees the world with new eyes, permitting oneself to see some truly significant and meaningful differences. By comparison, *normal learning* is what happens as one gets used to the new way of seeing things. It is about bodies of knowledge and specific skills. Although high learning is not unique to the InterActive Organization, in such an organization it becomes a way of life. High learning is not only a natural and automatic response to the environment, but it is also an intentional act, a perfectible skill, and an improvable way of life. Content (what is learned) must take a back seat to process (how it's learned).

"High learning, as an intentional way of life, begins, with embracing chaos. Every chaotic event is seen as pure gold," says Owen, "creating the open space in which innovation can be manifested. Chaos represents the growth point of any system. The InterActive Organization actively seeks out those moments as new opportunities for learning. To avoid chaos is to avoid life itself. The intentional, ongoing interaction with the external environment enables the organization to grow. The only risk 'is not to risk' " (p. 130).

The InterActive Learning Organization not only embraces chaos; it creates some of its own. Mistakes are moved from the "cost of doing business" category over to the asset side of "corporate knowledge balance sheet."

High play. In interactive learning organizations, play is not the opposite of work, nor is it trivial. It is high play that creates open space or, alternatively, uses the open space created by some random event. For every time the game is changed, all the structures and procedures of the preceding game are wiped away. Suddenly, it is all new with new possibilities. People are freed from the tyranny of the past.

In play employees are enabled to do in pretend time what is impossible, unthinkable, or dangerous to do in real time. Much innovation and creativity can occur when the line between pretend and real has been removed.

Play can be very powerful—note the effectiveness of business games, war games, and so forth. Play is also important and may be the critical factor during those moments "of superb intellectual adventure when the walls of the possible are shattered."

Without play in learning organizations, things get too serious and people may be deluded into the belief that they already possess *the Truth* or that there is one right way. Then growth stops and creativity dies.

High play is needed to operate effectively in the world of chaos, where there is opportunity for total despair or wonderful creation.

Appropriate structure.   Structure and control are both characteristics of the emerging organization, but the key word, for Owen, is *appropriate*. It may generally be round, flat, decentralized, networked, and marked by high levels of participatory decision making. It may sometimes be hierarchical or autocratic. The important thing is that it works.

In interactive learning organizations, there are usually multiple structures operating simultaneously, with new ones emerging constantly and old ones passing away as appropriate. When the organization and people are clear about purpose, as Owen says, structure "just happens." Structure is a natural expression of the purpose. Large numbers of people from different parts of the organization or even different organizations can self-organize a multiday meeting in less than an hour with a structure that integrates time, place, topics, and leadership. The prime and necessary condition is that everybody knows what he or she wants to do, and all are in agreement that it should be done.

Appropriate control.   Appropriate structure creates the conditions for appropriate control, but control in interactive learning organizations is different from control in other organizations. Control "becomes a sometime thing, assumed and released as structures come and go. It pertains only to a particular structure for a particular time and task. Control is no longer the center of the activity. It is merely an occurrence that happens.'' Because no one is permanently in charge, the natural questions are as follows:

- How do you keep everything together?
- Where is the center of gravity that can keep the organization whole and functional.
- Who's in charge?

For Owen, the answer is obvious—nobody—but maybe that also means *everybody*. Giving up control and authority is obviously very difficult for most leaders and is the reason why interactive learning organizations will be so hard to create and maintain.

Authentic community. The final characteristic of the interactive learning organization is the presence of a real, genuine community of people. Because everyone is in charge and bears responsibility for others in the organization, all have no choice but to be a community. We have been dreaming about the ideal of community since the dawn of history, but only at this stage will organizations have reached the needed level of maturation.

HUMAN LEARNING AND DEVELOPMENT AS WORKPLACE'S PURPOSE

Willis Harman and John Hormann have suggested that, when it no longer makes sense for an economically successful society to have economic production and consumption as its central focus, learning and development can become the society's central project. Society's real purpose may become self-development. Learning organizations will, therefore, be important because they provide meaning to work and reflect the beginnings of a fundamental restructuring of the purpose of business and of society. As Linda Morris says, ''This concept of the learning organization is so attractive because it affords us the potential to address problems affecting us in all the contexts in which we act, whether as individuals, in teams, in organizations, and in communities of interests, professions, and nations'' (p. 8). The global community will be the concern and joy of us all.

FUTURE RESEARCH AND EXPLORATION FOR GLOBAL LEARNING ORGANIZATIONS

The crucial importance and the rapidly evolving nature of global learning organizations obliges us to continue to explore and expand the

FIGURE 26–2
Issues that Need Answers

---

1. What are the best ways to create a global learning organization—is the entry point from within or from the top down?
2. How do we handle the distribution of power and authority within global learning organizations?
3. How will the issues of rewards, commitment, and ownership be resolved?
4. What about the responsibility to one's country versus one's global company?
5. How can we reduce the tension between time spent on production and time spent on learning?
6. How can managers best create an environment that enables autonomous learning?
7. Are certain cultural values or practices more conducive to establishment of learning organizations? (Remember that Nonaka suggests the Japanese culture is.)
8. How can we best help values and practices cross cultures?
9. How can we help organizations learn better from chaos and global surprises?
10. How can we better blend technologies to support organizational thinking and learning?
11. How can we use global communications to better connect those with the problem or challenge with those who have the answers and resources?

---

subject of global learning organizations. Figure 26–2 lists the issues that we believe are among those that each would-be global learning organization should consider first.

The exploration and explication of these and other questions will be extremely important to all of us, especially those in global organizations who are continually transforming their companies to become ever better places for learning, where the world itself can become a community of learners.

A VIEW FROM THE TOP

Top executives are responsible for looking at the horizon. Cray Research's CEO, John Rollwagen, says, ''I'm like a periscope for the rest of the company. Nobody else gets to see the company and the world from exactly my vantage point. So I try to spread that view around.'' In a way, that makes people in those positions ''professional'' futurists— they have a stake in the future. Organizational leaders must contribute to the creation of a corporate learning culture and mindset. These qualities promote global cooperation and a vital flow of information throughout the organization on a worldwide basis. They must devote their efforts to creating an environment in which organizational learning can flourish. It must be one where the continual search for improvement and competitive advantage involves the worldwide organization. We think the ideas that leaders have about the future have more force than those of amateurs. We could not do better than to end this book with the reflections of top executives about the challenges of the future for global learning organizations.

Harold McInnes, chairman and CEO of AMP, says, "The leaders of the future will be those prepared to shift from specific quality and productivity programs to corporatewide 'excellence programs' that seek to involve all employees in a continuous process of improvement, cycle time reduction, and waste elimination.

"It will not be enough to be a six-sigma, low-cost producer meeting prevailing standards. There will be an evolution away from designing to a price, rapid obsolescence, short useful life, and a throwaway mentality.

"There will instead be a sophisticated process of understanding customers' needs, extracting the maximum contribution from partners, using flexible manufacturing approaches to offer variety at reasonable cost, and providing more advanced marketing that educates and informs on longer-term benefits and costs."

Ray Stata, CEO of Analog Devices, strikes a sobering note about learning when he says, "Now we are on the right track, and we are seeing real progress across a broad front. But the question remains, are we learning fast enough? Or will one of our competitors, either here or abroad, learn even faster in the future? That unsettling question concerns me most of all."

PPG's CEO, Vincent Sarni, states, "PPG established a blueprint for the decade, from 1985 to 1994. Currently, we continue to be guided by commitment to the principles, goals, and strategies of the blueprint. In addition to achieving profitable growth and the related numerical goals, the document calls for the company to lead in all areas of our business, to be cost-effective in the use of all resources, to meet customer requirements and expectations for quality products, and to operate so as to preserve safety, health and a sound environment. In the interest of our customers, shareholders and employees, we intend to pursue our blueprint goals not only through 1994 but into the next century."

David Kearns (former Xerox CEO), writing with David Nadler in *Prophets in the Dark: How Xerox Reinvented Itself and Beat Back the Japanese*, said, "Xerox can't beat Canon on quality alone. Quality is a big step. In many industries, it may indeed be required to survive, but it ultimately may not be sufficient to succeed."

ABB's CEO Percy Barnevik has widely predicted that two-thirds of the giant European companies will fail following European economic integration. He is quick to point out that ABB will not be among them.

GE's Jack Welch sees a strikingly different future emerging. He often says, "We've got to take out the boss element." He thinks that future managers will have to forgo the traditional roles—to plan, organize, supervise, direct, control—for a new set of duties. These roles include counseling groups, and providing the resources they need. A big item is helping the groups to think for themselves. As he told *Fortune*, "We're going to win on our ideas, not by whips and chains."

Apple's CEO, John Scully, echoed much of what we have covered in this book at Bill Clinton's December 1992 economic summit. He said that the critical needs for corporations are as follows:

- High skills (or low wages)
- Empowered workers
- Ideas
- Information
- Lifelong learning

Medtronic's CEO, Bill George, sets a daunting task for himself and his company. He says, "To solve intractable medical diseases will take creativity, bold action, and tenacity. We must reward our champions who will lead the Medtronic teams which will tackle those challenges. Equally important, we cannot become bureaucratic, overly control oriented, or too heavily staffed. We must allocate our limited funds wisely, investing as though the money were our own. We must stay focused, yet flexible, in our strategies. In a phrase, we must continually 'reinvent Medtronic.' To grow at 15 percent per year, we must create a whole new Medtronic every five years. At our current size, that means creating another $1.2 billion corporation by 1997. And two more Medtronics by the year 2002. A daunting task. We believe it can be done."

Samsung chairman Lee Kun-Hee says, "The 1990s represent a decade of significant change. As the world prepares to meet the challenges of the 21st century, integrating people and technology with the environment represents major issues and opportunities, a mission we at Samsung continue to pursue.

"These strategic priorities, designed to address rapidly changing world environments, have facilitated more effective business unit restructuring, and improved competitiveness and instituted more responsive human resource management.

"As we approach the 21st century, Samsung reaffirms its commitment to the active and innovative partnership and participation required to lead the charge in changing global markets . . . both at home and abroad."

John Rollwagen, CEO of Cray Research, takes a philosophical view. He told Pat Galagan, "Most important, I believe, is to have a very clear vision of where you think the future is and to live in that future, not in the present. If you look back five years you can usually wind back through the mountains to where you were and it makes some sense. You can understand how it happened. Yet if you go back five years from the present and try to guess from that spot how you would have visualized the future, it probably doesn't look much like where you really are. But time is just a dimension. You can follow it the other way. If you look ahead five years it's very hard to see what's going to happen. If on the other hand, through a leap of faith, you can visualize what five years from now feels like, then you can look back to now and see a path or a first step that might work.

"Here's another thing I learned from Seymour (Cray). I used to take people to see him during the early days of the company. When they were finished talking business with him they'd want his view of the world, like he was an oracle or something. That used to tickle me because he's just a guy. And he'd always have a wonderful description of the next 5 or 10 years. It made a lot of sense. It was consistent with our past and our present. And I'd go away thinking, 'Gosh, now I know! I don't have to think about that any more.' But more and more people started coming, and sometimes I'd go two days in a row. Seymour would describe the same future just as consistently as before, except that every day it was just a tiny bit different from the day before. Now I know that looking at the future and looking back again is an ongoing process. You have to plan all the time, and you have to change it every day" (1992, pp. 33–34).

The future is not only about global competition or collaboration—it is also about global learning. Managing across borders means learning across borders. Organizations need a much wider perspective than they did in the past. Organizations must think of learning for the whole organization instead of for individuals. The successful organizations will build the global learning culture needed for worldwide business. Whatever the future brings, we believe that it will be exciting for people in global learning organizations.

Good luck!

Appendix A

Global Learning Organizations' Strength Chart

T he charts on the following pages list the strengths of the organizations mentioned in this book. The strengths recognized in this chart are those that we believe are most notable from the global learning organization viewpoint and are described in this book.

We screened and surveyed from an original list of over 200 organizations that seemed potential candidates as global learning organizations. There are 39 organizations that are mentioned in the various chapters of this book to provide an example of a good practice. Finally, we narrowed the list to the 16 organization that appear in Part III, Exemplary Global Learning Organizations. We decided to tell their stories in greater detail for two reasons:

- Their strength in several components of the Global Learning Organization Model.
- Their representation of variety in industry, geographic location, or size.

Many organizations were discarded based on initial inquiries with people inside the organization. When a person you know who is an employee tells you emphatically that his or her organization is *not* a learning organization, it isn't. There were many surprises:

- The most frequent disqualifier occurred when an employee of a U.S. division of a company based elsewhere in the world told us, "They don't talk to us. We don't talk to them." This was much more common than we would like to have assumed.
- One company had a successful global sharing history. It was based primarily on bringing its people from around the world

for sharing. The company cut the program to save money—
without finding another way to share.

- In another case our learning organization contact sort of dried
  up. When we talked with another person in the same company,
  that person said something to the effect of, ''It's a shame. Joe
  (name changed) ran the only real global learning organization
  I've ever seen. It was great! People there were really energized
  and doing great stuff. The last reorganization wiped out learning organizations. Joe is really down. He probably doesn't
  know how to explain it to you.'' Obviously a learning organization that can be abolished in a simple structural reorganization
  was a faux learning organization at best. This story also reinforces our point from early chapters that the global learning organization concept must be supported from the top. Joe was
  apparently running a guerrilla learning organization that never
  captured the power to survive.

The following chart lists 39 organizations, noting the elements of the
Global Learning Organization Model in which each is particularly noteworthy. We would like to emphasize that the strengths listed here are
not the only strengths of these organizations. In fact, they may have
many others. Nor is it intended to point out weaknesses. The categories
in which a check is not placed for an organization do not point to a weak-
ness. They are areas in which the organization is not among the strong-
est. On close inspection some may rate checks in every block. Certainly,
some divisions of organizations do. Being noteworthy in every element
of the model is the goal of every organization listed here.

Finally, use the last row of cells to rate your own organization. We
welcome news of other organizations that are attempting to become
global learners or that are succeeding in one or more elements of the
model.

To facilitate a more formal assessment, we have developed the
Global Learning Organization Assessment Instrument. The instrument is
designed for self-administration. To facilitate organizations that desire
a more in-depth approach, we have also developed the Global Learning Organization Training Program (Michael Marquardt and Augus
Reynolds, © 1993). For news about the efforts of your organization, or
to obtain more information about the instrument or program, contact
us at the following address or fax number:

Global Learning Organizations Unlimited
1688 Moorings Drive
Reston, VA 22090 USA
Fax (703)437-3725

	Organizational learning											Global learning					
	Appropriate structures	Corporate learning culture	Empowerment	Environmental scanning	Learning technology	Knowledge creation and transfer	Quality	Strategy	Supportive atmosphere	Teamwork and networking	Vision	Acculturization	Borders	Globalization	Language	Leadership	Workforce diversity
ABB	✓		✓			✓				✓			✓			✓	✓
AMP				✓			✓			✓		✓		✓		✓	
Anderson Consulting	✓	✓						✓	✓				✓				✓
Analog Devices	✓	✓				✓	✓	✓		✓				✓		✓	✓
Armstrong World Ind.						✓				✓		✓		✓	✓	✓	
AutoMind	✓			✓	✓		✓	✓				✓	✓				
Blanchard T&D			✓					✓		✓		✓					
Carvajal			✓				✓		✓			✓	✓	✓		✓	✓
Caterair International		✓	✓		✓	✓		✓			✓		✓		✓	✓	
Coca-Cola	✓	✓				✓	✓	✓		✓		✓	✓	✓		✓	
Colgate Palmolive		✓		✓					✓		✓	✓		✓	✓		✓
Corning		✓	✓		✓		✓			✓			✓			✓	
Cray	✓		✓						✓				✓				
Digital			✓			✓		✓	✓					✓			✓
DHL		✓		✓				✓				✓		✓			✓
Electrolux	✓						✓					✓	✓	✓			✓
Ernst & Young		✓			✓	✓			✓	✓	✓						✓
Federal Express			✓		✓	✓	✓			✓		✓					✓
General Electric	✓		✓			✓	✓			✓		✓		✓	✓	✓	
Honeywell	✓					✓			✓	✓	✓	✓	✓	✓		✓	✓
Hewlett-Packard	✓				✓			✓	✓					✓			✓

	Organizational learning											Global learning					
	Appropriate structures	Corporate learning culture	Empowerment	Environmental scanning	Learning technology	Knowledge creation and transfer	Quality	Strategy	Supportive atmosphere	Teamwork and networking	Vision	Acculturization	Borders	Globalization	Language	Leadership	Workforce diversity
Honda		✔	✔				✔	✔		✔			✔	✔			✔
MCI	✔		✔	✔	✔								✔				
McKinsey	✔		✔	✔	✔	✔		✔		✔					✔		
Medtronic	✔			✔	✔	✔						✔	✔				✔
Motorola		✔	✔	✔	✔	✔	✔	✔	✔	✔		✔	✔		✔		✔
NEC		✔				✔			✔			✔	✔			✔	
PPG		✔	✔	✔			✔	✔			✔	✔				✔	
Proctor & Gamble			✔	✔		✔	✔					✔	✔			✔	
Rover		✔	✔	✔	✔			✔			✔						✔
Royal Bank of Canada		✔		✔	✔	✔	✔	✔	✔	✔	✔	✔			✔		
Royal Dutch/Shell			✔							✔		✔					
Samsung	✔			✔			✔		✔	✔	✔	✔	✔		✔		✔
Saudia Airlines	✔				✔								✔				
Singapore Airlines	✔	✔				✔	✔		✔		✔					✔	✔
Tatung		✔	✔		✔		✔	✔	✔	✔		✔	✔				
3M	✔	✔	✔			✔		✔	✔	✔			✔	✔	✔		✔
Unilever	✔			✔		✔								✔		✔	
Whirlpool		✔				✔		✔		✔	✔	✔	✔	✔	✔		
Xerox	✔		✔	✔		✔	✔	✔	✔		✔		✔	✔	✔	✔	✔
Rate your own organization here																	

Appendix B
Bibliography

Adler, Nancy. *International Dimensions of Organization Behavior.* Boston: Kent Publishing Co., 1986.

Argyris, Chris. "Teaching Smart People How to Learn," *Harvard Business Review.* May–June 1991, pp.99–109.

Argyris, Chris and Donald Schon. *Organization Learning: A Theory of Action Perspective.* Reading, MA: Addison-Wesley, 1978.

Barham, Kevin and Marion Devine. *The Quest for the International Manager: Survey of Global Human Resource Strategies.* London: Business International Press, 1991.

Bartlett, Christopher and Sumantra Ghoshal. "What Is a Global Manager?" *Harvard Business Review,* September–October 1992, pp.124–132.

Beck, Michael. "Learning Organizations—How to Create Them." *Industrial & Commercial Training* 21 no.3 (Spring 1992), pp. 21–28.

Byrd, Mary. *Learning Organizations—A Model for the Future.* Unpublished paper, 1992.

Byrne, John. "Management's New Gurus." *BusinessWeek,* August 31, 1992, pp. 44–52.

Dixon, Nancy. "Organizational Learning: A Review of the Literature with Implications for HRD Professionals." *Human Resource Development Quarterly* 3, no.1 (Spring 1992), pp. 29–49.

Drucker, Peter. "The New Society of Organizations." *Harvard Business Review,* September–October, 1992 pp.95–104.

Economic Change and the American Workforce. U.S. Department of Labor. Washington, DC: U.S. Government Printing Office, March 1993.

Galagan, Patricia. "Focus on Results at Motorola." *Training and Development Journal* 40, no.10 (May 1986), pp. 43–46.

Galagan, Patricia. "On Being a Beginner: An Interview with John Rollwagen." *Training and Development* 46, no.11 (November 1992), pp. 30–38.

Galagan, Patricia. "The Learning Organization Made Plain." *Training and Development Journal* 45, no.10 (October 1991), pp. 37–44.

Handy, Charles. *The Age of Unreason.* London: Basic, 1989.

Harman, Willis and John Hormann. *Creative Work: The Constructive Role of Business in a Transforming Society.* An Institute of Noetic Science publication. Indianapolis: Knowledge Systems, Inc., 1990.

Hofstede, Geert. *Cultures and Organizations.* London: McGraw-Hill, 1991.

Honold, Linda. "The Power of Learning at Johnsonville Foods." *Training* 28, no.4 (April, 1991), pp. 54–58.

Imai, Masaaki. "Adapting a Japanese HRD Idea for Use in Another Country" in *The Global HRD Consultant's and Practitioner's Handbook.* eds. Angus Reynolds and Leonard Nadler. Amherst, MA: HRD Press, 1993.

Jaccaci, August. "The Social Architecture of a Learning Organization," *Training and Development Journal* 43, no. 11 (November 1989), pp. 49–51.

Johnston, William. "Global Workforce 2000: The New World Labor Market." *Harvard Business Review*, March–April 1991, pp. 115–127.

Jones, Alan and Chris Hendry. *The Learning Organization.* Coventry, UK: HRD Partnership, 1992.

Kearns, David and David Nadler. *Prophets in the Dark: How Xerox Reinvented Itself and Beat Back the Japanese.* New York: Harper Business, 1992.

Kiechel, Walter. "The Organization That Learns." *Fortune* 121, no. 6 March 12, 1990, pp.133–136.

Kohls, L. Robert. "Preparing Yourself for Work Overseas." In *The Global HRD Consultant's and Practitioner's Handbook.* eds. Angus Reynolds and Leonard Nadler. Amherst, MA: HRD Press, 1993.

Laabs, Jennifer. "Whirlpool Managers Become Global Architects." *Personnel Journal*, December 1991, p. 39.

Laurant, Andre. "The Cultural Diversity of Western Conceptions of Management." *International Studies of Management and Organization*, Spring–Summer 1983, pp. 75–96.

"Learning from the Competition—How Companies Use Benchmarking." *BusinessWeek*, November 30, 1992, pp. 74–75.

Marquardt, Michael. ed. *Corporate Culture: International HRD Prespectives.* Alexandria, VA: ASTD Press, 1988.

Marquardt, Michael and Dean Engel. *Global Human Resource Development.* Englewood Cliffs, NJ: Prentice Hall, 1993.

McInnes, Harold. "Quality Isn't the Goal." *Electronic Buyer's News*, September 16, 1991, p. 21.

Mellander, Klas. *The Power of Learning.* Homewood, IL: Business One Irwin, 1993.

Mann, Jim. *Beijing Jeep: The Short, Unhappy Romance of American Business in China.* New York: Simon and Schuster, 1989.

Michael, Donald. *On Learning to Plan—and Planning to Learn*. San Francisco: Jossey-Bass, 1989.

Moran, Robert and William Stripp. *International Negotiation*. Houston: Gulf Publishing, 1991.

Morris, Linda. "Learning Organizations: Settings for Developing Adults." In *Development in the Workplace*., eds. Jack Demick and Patrice Miller. Hillsdale, NJ: Lawrence Earlbaum Associates, Inc., 1993.

Morton, Michael. *The Corporation of the 1990s*. New York: Oxford University Press, 1991.

Noel, James, and Ram Charan. "GE Brings Global Thinking to Light." *Training and Development*, July 1992, pp. 29–33.

Nonaka, Ikujiro. "The Knowledge-Creating Company." *Harvard Business Review* 69, no.6 (November–December), pp. 96–104.

Owen, Harrison. *Riding the Tiger: Doing Business in a Transforming World*. Potomac, MD: Abbott Publishing, 1991.

Owen, Harrison. *The Business of Learning*. Potomac Mills, MD: Abbot Publishing, 1991.

Odenwald, Sylvia. *Global Training: How to Design a Training Program for the Multinational Corporation*. Homewood, IL: Business One Irwin, 1993.

Pascale, Richard. *Managing on the Edge*. New York: Simon and Schuster, 1990.

Pedler, Mike; John Burgoyne; and Tom Boydell. *The Learning Company: A Strategy for Sustainable Development*. London: McGraw-Hill, 1991.

Peters, Tom. *Liberation Management*. New York: Alfred A. Knopf, 1992.

Por, George. *What Is a Corporate Learning Expedition?* Paper presented at Collaboration in Social Architecture, June 20–21, Cambridge, MA, 1991.

Porter, Michael. *The Competitive Advantage of Nations*. New York: Free Press, 1990.

Quinn, Brian. *The Intelligent Organization*. New York: Free Press, 1992.

Rapaport, Richard. "To Build a Winning Team: An Interview with Head Coach Bill Walsh." *Harvard Business Review*. January–February 1993, pp. 110–20.

Ray, Michael. "The Emerging New Paradigm in Business." In *New Traditions in Business Spirit & Leadership in the 21st Century*. ed. John Renesch. San Francisco: New Leaders Publications, 1991.

Reich, Robert. *The Work of Nations*. New York: Random House, 1991.

Revans, Reginald. "The Enterprise as a Learning System." In *The Origins and Growth of Action Learning*. ed. R. W. Revans. London: Chartwell-Bratt, 1982.

Reynolds, Angus. "SUCCESS in International HRD." In *Technology Transfer*. ed. Angus Reynolds. Boston: International Human Resource Development Corp., 1984.

Reynolds, Angus and Leonard Nadler. *The Global HRD Consultant's and Practitioner's Handbook.* Amherst, MA: HRD Press, 1993.

Rhinesmith, Stephen. *A Manager's Guide to Globalization.* Homewood, IL: Business One Irwin, 1993.

Savage, Charles. *Fifth-Generation Management.* Burlington, MA: Digital Press, 1990.

Schein, Edgar. *Career Dynamics—Matching Individual and Organizational Needs.* Reading, MA: Addison-Wesley, 1978.

Schein, Edgar. *How Can Organizations Learn Faster?* Address to World Economics Forum, 1992.

Schwandt, David. *Thoughts on Organization Learning Theory,* Unpublished paper.

Senge, Peter. *The Fifth Discipline.* New York: Doubleday, 1990.

Senge, Peter. "The Leader's New Work: Building Learning Organizations." *Sloan Management Review* 32, no.1 (Fall 1990), pp. 7–23.

Shrivastava, Paul. "Learning Structures for Top Management." *Human Systems Management* 6, no.1 (1986), pp. 35–44.

Stata, Ray. "Organizational Learning—The Key to Management Innovation." *Sloan Management Review* 30 no.3 (Spring 1989), pp. 63–74.

Sterniczuk, Henry and Krzysztof Lis. "Rules for Consulting in a Communist Economy." *Organization Development Journal* Spring 1990, pp. 58–65.

Stewart, Thomas. "Brainpower." *Fortune,* June 3, 1991, pp. 44–60).

Sueiby, Karl and Tom Lloyd. *Managing Knowhow.* London: Bloombury, 1987.

Taylor, Sally. "Managing a Learning Environment." *Personnel Management,* October 1992, pp. 54–57.

"The Virtual Organization." *BusinessWeek* February 8, 1993, p. 100.

Toffler, Alvin. *Power Shift.* New York: Bantam, 1990.

Vogt, Judith and Kenneth Murrell. *Empowerment in Organizations.* San Diego: Pfeiffer & Company, 1993.

Waterman, Robert. *The Renewal Factor: How the Best Get and Keep the Competitive Edge.* New York: Bantam Books, 1987.

Watkins, Karen and Victoria Marsik. *Sculpting the Learning Organization.* San Francisco: Jossey-Bass, 1993.

Watkins, Karen and Victoria Marsik. *The Learning Organization.* Unpublished paper, 1991.

Webber, Alan. "What's So New about the New Economy?" *Harvard Business Review,* January–February 1993, pp. 24–42.

White, Bren, Michael Marquardt, and Quentin Englerth. *Globalization Basics.* Bethesda, MD: The World Group, 1992.

Wick, Calhoun and Lu Stanton Leon. The *Learning Edge.* San Diego: Pfeiffer & Company, 1993.

Willis, V. J. "The New Learning Organization: Should There Be a Chief Learning Officer in the House?" *Human Resource Development Quarterly* 2 no.2, pp. 181–187.

Wriston, Walter. *The Twilight of Sovereignty: How the Information Revolution Is Transforming the World.* New York: Charles Scribner & Sons, 1992.

Yip, George. *Total Global Strategy.* Englewood Cliffs, NJ: Prentice Hall, 1992.

Zuboff, Shoshana. *In the Age of the Smart Machine: The Future of Work and Power.* New York: Basic Books, 1988.

Glossary

Many special terms are used in learning organizations, and more so in global ones. The terms here are among those heard frequently that may not be familiar. Some of these terms are taken with permission from *The Trainer's Dictionary* (Amherst, MA: HRD Press, 1993).

acculturization the conversion of operations, people, and materials across cultures in a culturally sensitive, effective, and synergetic manner.

action learning deliberate, conscious effort to review and reflect on an action of the organization.

adaptive learning an individual's or organization's learning from experience and reflection.

anergy a concept in which the whole is less than the sum of its parts (for example, 2+2=3). Anergy is the opposite of synergy.

anticipatory learning an individual's or organization's learning in order to meet needs that are projected for the future. The anticipatory learning sequence is vision-reflection-action.

client the person responsible for the result of the consultation. This may be a different person from the person who served as the initial contact, go-between, or sponsor in securing a particular consultant.

client system the organizational unit most directly affected by the consultation. It is generally led by the client.

consultant a person who provides needed information, help, and perspective. Consultants may be employees of an organization (internal) or under contract with the organization (external) because of competence, status, reputation, or experience. Strictly, this term should not be used to describe a person from outside the organization who only provides instruction. Also called a *resource person*.

continuous learning culture the milieu or environment in which people are encouraged and enabled to learn on an ongoing, continuous basis.

core competencies focus of organizations that structure themselves according to competencies rather than according to products or markets.

cross-cultural incorporating information and values of a second culture on an equal basis with the original culture.

culture a way of life shared by members in a group. Culture includes values and practices that guide the thinking, doing, and living of people.

culture shock an adverse reaction experienced by people who travel or work in an unfamiliar place.

deutero learning an organization's or individual's learning from critical reflection on taken-for-granted assumptions.

development learning activities that are not job focused. Development prepares an employee for future, often higher-level, responsibilities in the organization.

domestic an organization with operations in only one country.

double loop learning in-depth organizational learning that looks at organizational norms and structures that cause the organization to function the way it does. Double loop learning, developed by Chris Argyris, questions the system itself and reasons why errors or successes occurred in the first place.

education HRD activities designed to improve the performance of an employee in a specific direction beyond the current job. Education emphasizes future learning objectives and gives employees the broad knowledge and understanding needed to excel across a range of jobs. HRD use of the term does not try to account for the widespread use of the term in other contexts in public and higher formal education.

expatriate An employee who works for an extended time in a country other than the one in which citizenship is held.

explicit knowledge formal, systematic, and easily shared knowledge (in contrast to tacit knowledge).

federalism an organizational structure type, typified by a core center with tremendous flexibility and power decentralized to autonomous units and projects.

foreign from anywhere outside the country in question.

generative organizational learning the learning that an organization generates or creates itself from its reflection, analysis, or creativity.

global learning audit a comprehensive analysis of how effective an organization is relative to the learning capability of its various functions (finance, marketing, manufacturing, and so on) and its organizationwide systems.

global learning curve a scale to determine to what stage an organization has advanced relative to corporate globalization.

global learning organization any organization that is global and that is implementing, or has implemented, activities that qualify it as a learning organization. *See also* globalization.

globalization the converging of economic and social forces generated by increased sharing of social and economic values and opportunities. Includes the globalization of businesses and values that have been caused primarily by trade, travel, and television.

home country any country where the person or organization involved in the international HRD activity or project originates.

host country any country where the international HRD activity or project will be carried out.

human resource development (HRD) a concept developed by Leonard Nadler and published in *Developing Human Resources.* Nadler defines human resource development as organized learning experiences provided by employers within a specified period of time to bring about the possibility of performance improvement or personal growth. HRD activities comprise training, education, and development. HRD is differentiated from adult education in that it is focused on learning activities provided by organizations to their employees.

indigenous of local or native origin, endemic; opposite of foreign.

informate the use of computer-generated data collected during implementation for planing and decision making. For example, the supermarket checkout data scan provides information—what foods were bought, who buys what, when were they bought, and so forth—that enables the owner to plan advertising, hiring, purchasing, and inventory control.

intercultural in this book the term is synonymous with cross-cultural.

international a person or organization with origin in one country, with intent on personal and business success in at least one other country.

know-how value-added information.

know-how company an organization that produces and sells information, ideas, and complex problem solving to others. Key features include non-standardization, creativity, and high dependence on knowledge of individuals.

know-how workers skilled and creative employees primarily involved in problem-solving, problem identifying, and strategic-brokering activities for outside customers. Know-how workers may include programmers, consultants, physicians, accountants, engineers, and others. (Also called gold-collar employees.)

knowledge architecture the repository for shared knowledge and collective intelligence that is organized for easy access by any staff member at, any time, from anywhere. Examples include a database that collects key learning of individuals and an on-line newsletter that systematically gathers, organizes, and disseminates the collective knowledge of the organizations members.

mentofacturing the production of products and services through the efforts of the mind (through brainpower). Mentofacturing stands in contrast to manufacturing, which is derived from the Latin *manus*, meaning hand.

multinational business term describing an organization with origin in one country, incorporating intent on success, focus on realities, and adaptation to conditions in several other nations.

national (1) a person who retains his or her original citizenship despite the country in which work is carried out, or time involved; (2) an organization with the origin, focus, and behavior of one country.

native a person with origin in the country in which he or she currently lives. This is not a derogatory term. It has nothing to do with "natives in grass huts." An American in downtown New York City is a native. Your experience might suggest to you that, aside from being a native of a country, there are probably regional differences.

open space technology an innovative approach, developed by Harrison Owen, to enhance individual and group performance in which up to 400 people self-organize and self-manage multiday meetings and conferences around complex issues.

organizational architecture structural form of organizations that revolves around autonomous work teams and strategic alliances.

parent company company with ownership and control of the investment.

patterns of organizational learning learning patterns that are based on tacit and explicit knowledge and their interaction. Ikujiro Nonaka identifies four patterns: tacit to tacit, explicit to explicit, tacit to explicit, and explicit to tacit.

reengineering restructuring of organizations around outcomes, rather than tasks or functions.

reentry return to the home country by an employee after service in a foreign country.

single loop learning gaining information to stabilize and maintain the existing operational systems.

social architecture the cultural, symbolic relationship orientation of the organization that enhances learning by encouraging teams, self management, empowerment, and sharing. Social architecture is the opposite of a closed, rigid, bureaucratic architecture.

synergy a concept in which the sum is greater than the parts (for example, $2+2=5$).

tacit knowledge knowledge that is held inside and is difficult to express (in contrast to explicit knowledge).

technological architecture the supporting, integrated set of technical processes, systems, and structure for collaboration, coaching, coordination, and other knowledge skills. Technological architecture may include such electronic tools and advanced methods for learning as computer conferencing, simulation software, and computer-supported collaboration, all of which work to create knowledge freeways.

tecknowledgy process awareness held by true technical experts (termed coined by Bill Whitmore of Corning).

third-country national (TCN) a person with citizenship in a country other than the host country or the country of origin of the organization involved.

trainer one who helps individuals improve performance on their present jobs by providing organized learning experiences. Loosely, the person in charge of a class, or anyone responsible for providing the instructional process. A generic term used to describe a range of instructional personnel in business, industry, and government.

training instruction that emphasizes job-specific, near-transfer learning objectives; traditionally skills-based instruction, as opposed to education. In HRD, instructional experiences provided primarily by employers for employees, designed to develop new skills, knowledge, and attitudes that are expected to be applied immediately on (or within a short time after) arrival on or return to the job.

transnational that which is above or beyond any nation or border. Many global organizations would be considered transnational.

virtual organization a temporary network of independent companies, suppliers, and customers linked by information technology to share skills, costs, and access to one another's markets.

world-class superb, high-quality, cost-effective, and customer-focused products and services.

Index